OXFORD EARLY CHRISTIAN STUDIES

General Editors
Gillian Clark   Andrew Louth

THE OXFORD EARLY CHRISTIAN STUDIES series in-
cludes scholarly volumes on the thought and history of the early
Christian centuries. Covering a wide range of Greek, Latin, and
Oriental sources, the books are of interest to theologians, ancient
historians, and specialists in the classical and Jewish worlds.

Asceticism and Anthropology in Irenaeus and Clement

JOHN BEHR

OXFORD
UNIVERSITY PRESS

OXFORD

UNIVERSITY PRESS

Great Clarendon Street, Oxford OX3 6DP

Oxford University Press is a department of the University of Oxford.
It furthers the University's objective of excellence in research, scholarship,
and education by publishing worldwide in

Oxford New York

Athens Auckland Bangkok Bogotá Bombay Buenos Aires Calcutta
Cape Town Chennai Dar es Salaam Delhi Florence Hong Kong Istanbul
Karachi Kuala Lumpur Madrid Melbourne Mexico City Mumbai
Nairobi Paris São Paulo Singapore Taipei Tokyo Toronto Warsaw

with associated companies in Berlin Ibadan

Oxford is a registered trade mark of Oxford University Press
in the UK and in certain other countries

Published in the United States
by Oxford University Press Inc., New York

© John Behr 2000

British Library Cataloguing in Publication Data

Data available

Library of Congress Cataloging in Publication Data
Behr, John.
Asceticism and anthropology in Irenaeus and Clement / John Behr.
p. cm.—(Oxford early Christian studies)
Includes bibliographical references and indexes.
1. Asceticism—History—Early church, ca. 30–600. 2. Man (Theology)—History of
doctrines—Early church, ca. 30–600. 3. Irenaeus, Saint, Bishop of Lyon. 4. Clement, of
Alexandria, Saint, ca. 150–ca. 215. I. Title. II. Series.
BV5023.B442000
233'.092'2–dc21   99-056664
ISBN 0-19-827000-3

1 3 5 7 9 10 8 6 4 2

Typeset in Imprint
by Joshua Associates Ltd., Oxford
Printed in Great Britain
on acid-free paper by
T.J. International Ltd., Padstow, Cornwall

For Tatisha

PREFACE

This work explores the ways in which Irenaeus and Clement, the two earliest Christian writers with a substantial body of extant work, reflected on the related topics of asceticism and anthropology, that is, how they understood what it is to be human. Writing before monasticism became the dominant paradigm for Christian asceticism, these two figures offer us fascinating glimpses of alternative approaches. Their reflections, however, are embedded within writings concerned with larger theological issues, and can therefore only be comprehended fully from the theological perspective of each corpus. It has thus been necessary to examine in detail the theological visions, different as they are, of each author. While these studies can stand by themselves, they also substantiate a theological critique, examined in the introduction and the conclusion, of those approaches to the asceticism of late antiquity which overlook the theological perspective of the texts being used, treating them instead as raw, uninterpreted material for their own concerns—in the cases of M. Foucault and P. Brown, tracing the genealogy of the modern (sexual) subject. The works of these two authors might appear to be far more sensitive and sympathetic than the vitriolic pages of Gibbon and his epigones, and the characters which populate their pages more plausible than the emaciated fanatics who haunted earlier studies—and indeed, their works do have much to offer—but unless the texts upon which these histories are built are first examined as what they are, the resulting mirages will be no less our own projections. Clearly this also entails that the analyses in the present study, which examine how two writers engaged in their own polemics reflected upon the nature and place of human beings within God's larger scheme, can be no more than episodes in the history of thought. The works of these writers say little, if anything, about the actual lives of real people in the second or third century. For this, other types of evidence—economic, legal, or artistic—are needed, each requiring its own proper hermeneutic. But this is not a limitation; such reflections are capable of inspiring real people and transforming history.

This work is a revised version of a thesis submitted to the University of Oxford in 1995. I would like to express my gratitude to Bishop Kallistos of Diokleia for gently guiding my research and reading my work and for his constant inspiration, and to all the others from whom I benefited so greatly while in Oxford, and to the British Academy for making those years possible. I would also like to thank Bishop Rowan Williams and Andrew Louth, my examiners, for their insightful suggestions about how the work might be revised, and the readers appointed by the editors of Oxford Early Christian Studies for their comments. I have been fortunate in being able to explore some of the material contained here while teaching at St Vladimir's Orthodox Theological Seminary, New York; for this opportunity, and for their comments, I thank both my colleagues and my students. Finally, the publication of this work is the result of the diligent labours of the staff at Oxford University Press, to whom my thanks.

I would like to point out that, without wishing to minimize the problems involved, I have used the word 'man' throughout this work to refer to all human beings, male and female, and the human race considered generically.

JOHN BEHR

March 1999

CONTENTS

ABBREVIATIONS

The following abbreviations are used in the course of this work. The numeration of the editions cited in the Bibliography is followed, except where stated otherwise. For the works of Philo, I have used the abbreviations as given after the title in the Bibliography.

AH	Irenaeus, *Against the Heresies* (in the numeration of Massuet)
Dem.	Irenaeus, *Demonstration of the Apostolic Preaching*
EH	Eusebius, *Ecclesiastical History*
Exc. Th.	Clement of Alexandria, *Excerpta ex Theodoto*
Paed.	Clement of Alexandria, *Paedagogus*
Prot.	Clement of Alexandria, *Protrepticus*
QDS	Clement of Alexandria, *Quis Dives Salvetur*
Strom.	Clement of Alexandria, *Stromata*
SVF	*Stoicorum Veterum Fragmenta*, ed. J. Von Arnim

JOURNALS AND SERIES

ACW	Ancient Christian Writers
ANF	Ante-Nicene Fathers
BKV	Bibliothek der Kirchenvater
CSCO	Corpus Scriptorum Christianorum Orientalium
CSEL	Corpus Scriptorum Ecclesiasticorum Latinorum
ECR	*Eastern Churches Review*
ETL	*Ephemerides Theologicae Lovanienses*
FC	Fathers of the Church
GCS	Die griechischen christlichen Schriftsteller der ersten drei Jahrhunderte
GOTR	*Greek Orthodox Theological Review*
Greg.	Gregorianum
HJ	*Heythrop Journal*

HTR	*Harvard Theological Review*
JAAR	*Journal of the American Academy of Religion*
JBL	*Journal of Biblical Literature*
JECS	*Journal of Early Christian Studies*
JEH	*Journal of Ecclesiastical History*
JRS	*Journal of Roman Studies*
JTS	*Journal of Theological Studies*
LCL	Loeb Classical Library
LV	*Lumière et Vie*
NAWG	*Nachrichten von der Akademie der Wissenschaften in Göttingen*
NPNF	Nicene and Post-Nicene Fathers
NRT	*Nouvelle Revue Théologique*
OCP	*Orientalia Christiana Periodica*
OECT	Oxford Early Christian Texts
PG	Patrologia Graeca
PO	Patrologia Orientalis
PTS	Patristische Texte und Studien
RAM	*Revue d'Ascétique et Mystique*
RB	*Revue Bénédictine*
REA	*Revue des Études Anciennes*
REG	*Revue des Études Grecques*
RSPhTh	*Revue des Sciences Philosophiques et Théologiques*
RSR	*Recherches de Science Religieuse*
SC	Sources Chrétiennes
SJT	*Scottish Journal of Theology*
SM	*Studia Moralia*
St. Patr.	*Studia Patristica*
SVTQ	*Saint Vladimir's Theological Quarterly*
TS	*Theological Studies*
TSK	*Theologische Studien und Kritiken*
TU	Texte und Untersuchungen zur Geschichte der altchristlichen Literatur
TZ	*Theologische Zeitschrift*
VC	*Vigiliae Christianae*
ZKG	*Zeitschrift für Kirchengeschichte*
ZKT	*Zeitschrift für katholische Theologie*
ZNTW	*Zeitschrift für die neutestamentliche Wissenschaft und die Kunde der Urchristentums*
ZTK	*Zeitschrift für Theologie und Kirche*

Introduction

Although the term 'asceticism' tends to evoke images of emaciated fanatics populating long gone and far removed deserts, a wide range of contemporary popular culture and scholarship exhibits an intense attraction to, and interest in, asceticism; it is perhaps no surprise that a culture whose catchword is 'Just say no'[1] should have occasioned the first multi-disciplinary conference devoted to this subject.[2] The phenomenon of asceticism is indeed a subject of perennial and universal interest. It brings into prominence fundamental questions concerning what, as human beings, we think we are and, intrinsically related to this, questions pertaining to what is the appropriate way, or ways, of realizing this in our lives.

Within this broad phenomenon of asceticism, the history of Christian asceticism is of particular interest, if only because it is a significant part, whether accepted or rejected, of the background of modern Western civilization. But, to be able to speak in this way, of 'Christian asceticism', demands a prior consideration of the specificity of this asceticism: is Christian asceticism, as some have alleged, a corruption of true Christianity, or is it intrinsic to Christian existence, and if so, how does it differ from other forms of asceticism?

It has long been popularly supposed that the ideals of virginity, abstinence, and continence were unique to Christianity,

---

[1] As G. Harpham points out, this injunction extends beyond drugs to include dietary intake (non-fat, non-dairy, etc.), relationship to the self (on the psychiatrist's couch), and also, though Harpham does not mention this, sexual relationships, all in the search for a particular culture and life-style ('Old Water in New Bottles', *Semeia*, 58 (1992), 137). He was drawing upon M. O'Neill, 'Party's Over: Self-Denial is Hot', *The Times-Picayune*, 27 May 1990, A-16, who encapsulates this modern attitude neatly: '"Non" is more than a prefix—it has become a lifestyle.'

[2] V. L. Wimbush and R. Valantasis (eds.), *Asceticism* (Oxford, 1995).

and stood in stark contrast to a sensual and licentious antiquity;
or, alternatively, that Christianity introduced a repressive sense
of guilt and shame into an ancient world that otherwise had a
more healthy attitude towards sexuality.[3] However, neither of
these two representations accurately reflects the way that early
Christians and their pagan contemporaries themselves reflected
on the distinctiveness which marked Christians out as a 'third
race', neither Jew nor Gentile but children of the one God.
Justin Martyr, for instance, writing in the middle of the second
century, certainly knew of various practices of virginity and
continence. One of his anecdotes concerns a Christian youth
who was so enthusiastic that he went to the governor of
Alexandria to request permission for the surgeons to castrate
him (Justin, interestingly, shows no signs of disapproval for
this act).[4] Justin also insists that sexual intercourse be engaged
in only for the sake of procreation, and that one could find
many men and women in the Christian communities who had
chosen to remain virgin.[5] However, Justin never supposed that
such practices were the distinguishing features of Christian
life. Similarly, Athenagoras, a little later, describes procreation
as the limit set for our lust, and states, as if it were an accepted
commonplace, that virginity and abstention from sexual intercourse bring us closer to God.[6] But, as with Justin, in the

---

[3] P. Veyne: 'If any aspect of ancient life has been distorted by legend, this is
it. It is widely but mistakenly believed that antiquity was a Garden of Eden
from which repression was banished, Christianity having yet to insinuate the
worm of sin into the forbidden fruit' ('The Roman Empire', in P. Ariès and
G. Duby (eds.), *A History of Private Life*, 1: *From Pagan Rome to Byzantium*,
ed. P. Veyne, trans. A. Goldhammer (Cambridge, Mass., 1987), 202). The
first contrast is typically drawn by theologians: e.g. W. Rordorf, 'Marriage in
the New Testament and in the Early Church', *JEH* 20 (1969), 208, and H. I.
Marrou, 'Virginity as an Ideal, and the Position of Women in Ancient
Civilization', in L. C. Sheppard (trans.), *Chastity*, Religious Life, 5
(London, 1955), 28–38. The latter contrast is one generally favoured by
historians: it was standardized by Gibbon in *The Decline and Fall of the
Roman Empire*, and was still being drawn two centuries later, e.g. by E. R.
Dodds, *Pagan and Christian in an Age of Anxiety* (Cambridge, 1965), 32–6,
who nevertheless argues that Christian asceticism was an extreme represen-
tative of a more 'endemic disease' in the later Empire; see also R. L. Fox,
Pagans and Christians (New York, 1987), 336–74.

[4] Justin, *First Apology*, 29.

[5] Ibid. 15, 29.

[6] Athenagoras, *Legatio*, 33. 1–3.

context of an apologetic text these assertions were intended to defend devout Christians from the charge that promiscuous intercourse formed part of their mysteries, and to assimilate them to the cultivated ideals of the time. The clearest text which demonstrates that Christians saw themselves as a 'third race', yet did not differ from the rest of the population as regards the outward expression of their lives, is found in the *Epistle to Diognetus*:

For the distinction between Christians and other humans is neither in country nor language nor customs. For they do not dwell in cities in some place of their own, nor do they use any strange variety of dialect, nor practice (ἀσκοῦν) an extraordinary kind of life. . . . Yet while living in Greek and barbarian cities, according as each obtained their lot, and following the local customs, both in clothing and food and in the rest of life, they show forth the wonderful and confessedly strange constitution of their own citizenship (τὴν κατάστασιν τῆς ἑαυτῶν πολιτείας). (5. 1–4)

The specificity and distinctiveness of Christian existence, that which makes them a 'third race', is not to be found in the outward forms and practices of their lives, but in 'the constitution of their citizenship'.

Contemporary pagan evidence leads to the same conclusion. For example, in a commentary on Plato, preserved in Arabic, Galen writes of Christians:

Just as now we see the people called Christians drawing their faith from parables [and miracles], and yet sometimes acting in the same way [as those who philosophize]. For their contempt of death [and of its sequel] is patent to us every day, and likewise their restraint in cohabitation. For they include not only men but also women who refrain from cohabiting all through their lives; and they also number individuals who, in self-discipline and self-control in matters of food and drink, and in their keen pursuit of justice, have attained a pitch not inferior to that of genuine philosophers.[7]

Galen praises the Christians for possessing three important virtues: courage, temperance, and justice. Rather than being

---

[7] From Galen's lost commentary on Plato's *Republic*, in *Galeni compendium Timaei Platonis aliorumque dialogorum synopsis quae extant fragmenta*, ed. P. Kraus and R. Walzer, Plato Arabus, 1, ed. R. Walzer (London, 1951), 99; trans. in R. Walzer, *Galen on Jews and Christians* (Oxford, 1949), 15; cf. 56–74.

struck by the practice of temperance displayed by the Christians in matters of food and sexual relations, Galen takes it as a sign of their cultivation: by demonstrating these virtues, Christians are 'not inferior to genuine philosophers'.[8] The supposed harmfulness of sexual activity was a problem that continually vexed ancient doctors from the time of Hippocrates. Some, including Galen, suggested that, if practised under a strict regime, sexual intercourse need not necessarily be harmful. Others, such as Soranus, argued that, despite the natural necessity of procreation, 'permanent virginity is healthful in males and females alike' as 'intercourse is harmful in itself'.[9] More importantly, such thought did not develop in a vacuum. According to A. Rousselle, self-imposed restraint in sexual relations and the desire for a life of continence had become such a common phenomenon in late antique society that research was dedicated to the problems that such abstention might cause, whilst reassurance had to be given to those who were unable to abstain completely from sexual activity.[10]

The popular, hackneyed contrast between the pleasure-loving, licentious (or healthy) pagans and the virtuous, chaste (or repressed) Christians does not stand up to close scrutiny. As Foucault comments, regarding different moralities:

one notices that they ultimately revolve around a rather small number of rather simple principles: perhaps men are not much more inventive when it comes to interdictions than they are when it comes to pleasures.[11]

---

[8] Marrou cites the first half of the third sentence as a demonstration that the idea of virginity or chastity was practically foreign to the pagan mentality of the Graeco-Roman world ('Virginity as an Ideal', 28). Galen's charge that Christians rely upon faith drawn from parables, rather than a reasoned basis, is significant; as J. A. Francis points out, 'Though the results may be admirable, they are vitiated by a method that appeals to emotion and faith rather than reason' (*Subversive Virtue: Asceticism and Authority in the Second-Century Pagan World* (University Park, Pa.: Pennslyvania State University Press, 1995), 34 n. 35).

[9] Soranus, *Gynaecia*, 1. 7. 32.

[10] A. Rousselle, *Porneia* (Paris, 1983), 32; trans. F. Pheasant (Oxford, 1988), 20. Fox (*Pagans and Christians*, 349–50), reminds us, however, that such writings were addressed to a small section of the population.

[11] M. Foucault, *Histoire de la sexualité*, 2: *L'Usage des plaisirs* (Paris, 1984), 39; trans. R. Hurley (Harmondsworth, 1987), 32.

The similarities between the philosophical moralities of late antiquity, especially Stoicism, and early Christian morality, at least in their external codification, are striking. However, simply to affirm a continuity between the precepts and prohibitions of pagan and Christian morality is to miss the specificity of each. The debate concerning the relationship of Epictetus to Christianity, for instance, has added little to our knowledge of either.[12] To achieve a fuller appreciation of their particular characteristics, it is necessary to analyse the internal dynamics at work within each morality—that is, their particular style of asceticism.[13]

CONTEMPORARY SCHOLARSHIP: THE SEARCH FOR THE SUBJECT

The gradual erosion of the traditional boundaries between academic disciplines that has occurred during the second half of this century has resulted in a move away from the traditional accounts of the development of Christian dogma or philosophical thought, written in and for themselves, to a broader horizon which takes into account insights from other disciplines affecting our understanding of late antiquity as a whole, such as investigations into social relations, marriage and the family, and the changing patterns of morality.[14] This phenomenon has prompted a more considered investigation of the question of the continuity or lack of continuity between pagan and Christian morality, and their understanding of sexuality entailed by each, by concentrating on the internal mechanisms of morality or the particular style of asceticism advocated.

Amongst the many works written on this subject in recent years, there have been two outstanding contributions to our comprehension of the internal dynamics of the morality, the asceticism, displayed in the ancient, late antique, and early

---

[12] Cf. M. Foucault, *Histoire de la sexualité*, 3: *Le Souci de soi* (Paris, 1984), 269–71; trans. R. Hurley (Harmondsworth, 1990), 235–7.

[13] Cf. Veyne, 'Roman Empire', 49.

[14] Cf. E. A. Clark, 'The State and Future of Historical Theology: Patristic Studies', *Union Papers*, 2 (New York, 1982), 46–56; repr. in Clark, *Ascetic Piety and Women's Faith: Essays on Late Ancient Christianity*, Studies in Women and Religion, 20 (Lewiston, NY, 1986), 3–19.

Christian worlds. The first comprises the second and third volumes of Michel Foucault's *Histoire de la sexualité*, *L'Usage des plaisirs* and *Le Souci de soi* respectively. Although the projected fourth volume of the *Histoire*, in which Foucault intended to study early Christian asceticism, never appeared, it is pre-eminently his work that has stimulated and informed a more considered investigation of Christian asceticism.[15] This is in fact fitting, as it was this phenomenon, rather than the Greeks themselves, which was crucial for Foucault in his attempt to trace the genealogy of the modern self.[16] It is moreover possible, from occasional comments in the second and third volumes together with various articles and interviews published in the last years of his life, to see the general lines along which his thought might, perhaps, have developed.[17] The second important work is Peter Brown's *Body and Society: Men, Women and Sexual Renunciation in Early Christianity*.[18]

[15] This is not to say that his work is without (major) problems, especially for classicists, in particular with regard to the status of the work—Is it history or, as Foucault claimed, only philosophy? See the reviews by M. Nussbaum, *New York Times Review Book Review*, 10 Nov. 1985, 13–14, and G. E. R. Lloyd, 'The Mind on Sex', review of Foucault, *The Use of Pleasure*, *New York Review of Books*, 33. 4 (13 Mar. 1986), 24–8. For an evaluation of his contribution to the study of Christian asceticism, see A. Cameron, 'Redrawing the Map: Early Christian Territory after Foucault', *JRS* 76 (1986), 266–71; E. A. Clark, 'Foucault, the Fathers, and Sex', *JAAR* 56. 4 (1988), 619–41; and the various articles in V. L. Wimbush (ed.), *Discursive Formations: Ascetic Piety and the Interpretation of Early Christian Literature*, *Semeia*, 57–8 (1992).

[16] As Harpham points out, 'Old Water in New Bottles', 139–40.

[17] The main sources are: 'Le Combat de la chasteté', *Communications*, 35 (1982), 15–25, first trans. in P. Ariès and A. Béjin (eds.), *Western Sexuality* (Oxford, 1985), 14–25 (Foucault prefaced this essay by stating that it belonged to the third volume of his *Histoire*, although it seems to have been intended for a projected fourth volume, *Les Aveux de la chair*); 'Technologies of the Self', in L. H. Martin, H. Gutman, and P. H. Hutton (eds.), *Technologies of the Self: A Seminar with Michel Foucault* (London, 1988), 16–49; 'The Ethic of Care for the Self as a Practice of Freedom, an Interview with Foucault on Jan. 20, 1984', in J. Bernauer and D. Rasmussen (eds.), *The Final Foucault* (Cambridge, Mass., 1988), 1–20; 'Sexuality and Solitude', in P. Rabinow (ed.), *Michel Foucault: Ethics, Subjectivity and Truth* (New York, 1997), 175–84; 'Self Writing', ibid. 207–22; 'On the Genealogy of Ethics: An Overview of Work in Progress', ibid. 253–80.

[18] P. Brown, *The Body and Society: Men, Women and Sexual Renunciation in Early Christianity* (New York, 1988; London, 1989).

If Foucault's work acted as a catalyst, it is Brown's opus which has become 'the standard historical-interpretive work on early Christianity'.[19] Both of these works, in different ways, direct our attention away from the outward forms or codes of morality, to focus, instead, on how and why they were framed, what mechanisms were at work within them, and what the implications were either for the individuals whose lives took shape within this asceticism, or, more generally, for the relationship between the individual and society. By this reorientation, both works also avoid the common attempt to trace the principles of sexual restraint back to the Greek dualism of body and mind, and its consequent discomfort with the body, which, it is argued, had festered since the days of Plato and plagued the early years of Christianity.[20] Because of the importance of their respective works, it will be useful to consider their projects in some detail.[21]

Foucault argued that the medical and philosophical thought of antiquity offered a set of techniques for the formation and shaping of the self, of the ethical subject in particular. For Foucault, this formation of the individual as an ethical subject was not simply a matter of the individual's self-awareness. Rather, Foucault expressly broke with the common assumption of Western thought that there is a universal form of the subject which is the foundational ground of all experience.[22]

[19] V. L. Wimbush and R. Valantasis, introduction to their *Asceticism*, p. xxi.

[20] For such an explanation see Dodds, *Pagan and Christian*, 1–36.

[21] For a more detailed analysis of the positions of Foucault and Brown, and their problems, see my article 'Shifting Sands: Foucault, Brown and the Framework of Christian Asceticism', *HJ* 34. 1 (1993), 1–21. Mention must also be made of A. Rousselle's *Porneia*; but as her work focuses primarily on the historical study of behaviour, the various practices of abstention and their effects, rather than the whole framework within which such behaviour is located, whilst being very useful, it remains outside the concerns of this work. Other important works concerned with asceticism in terms of a 'spiritual exercise' are P. Rabbow, *Seelenführung: Methodik der Exerzitien in der Antike* (Munich, 1954) and P. Hadot, *Exercices spirituels et philosophie antique*, 3rd rev. edn. (Paris, 1993).

[22] 'In the first place, I do indeed believe that there is no sovereign founding subject, a universal form of subject to be found everywhere. . . . I believe, on the contrary, that the subject is constituted through practices of subjection, or, in a more autonomous way, through practices of liberation, of liberty, as in Antiquity, on the basis, of course, of a number of rules, styles, inventions to be found in the cultural environment' ('An Aesthetics of Existence', *Le*

Instead, he investigated how, through differing styles of life and various processes of subjectivization, a subject, or rather a mode of subjectivity, is formed, a subjectivity which is only one of the possible forms of the organization of self-consciousness.[23] Foucault explained what he meant by this process of subject formation by appealing to the practices referred to as the 'arts of existence', an idea he derived from Burkhardt's studies on the Renaissance. By these 'arts of existence' or, in his terminology, these 'technologies of the self', Foucault understood:

> those intentional and voluntary actions by which men not only set themselves rules of conduct, but also seek to transform themselves, to change themselves in their singular being, and to make their life into an *œuvre* that carries certain aesthetic values and meets certain stylistic criteria.[24]

So instead of a history of behaviours, or a history of their codification in moral systems, Foucault's intention was to write a history of the technologies of the self, a history of the various ways in which individuals constitute themselves as subjects of their experience. This would be a history of 'ethics' or 'ascetics', in which the study of the experience and problematization of sexuality in antiquity was but an initial chapter.

The formation of individuals as ethical subjects, according to Foucault, involves a fourfold process: (a) of delimiting and defining that part of themselves and their experience which is to be the object of their moral practice, the ethical substance; (b) of determining a relationship to the precept codifying or expressing such behaviour, the mode of subjection; (c) thereby establishing a relationship to themselves; and (d) deciding upon a manner of being that is to be the goal of the moral activity, the final *œuvre* of the arts or technologies of the self. Whilst any number of forms of subjectivity can be constructed through this process, there are basically only two directions which can be taken. Either the relationship between our action

---

Monde, 15–16 July 1984; trans. A. Sheridan in L. D. Kritzman (ed.), *Michel Foucault: Politics, Philosophy, Culture* (London, 1988), 50–1).

[23] Cf. M. Foucault, 'The Return to Morality', *Les Nouvelles*, 28 June 1984; trans. T. Levin and I. Lorentz in Kritzman (ed.), *Michel Foucault*, 253.

[24] Foucault, *L'Usage des plaisirs*, 16–17; trans. 10–11.

and its codification is paramount, in which case the resulting morality will be concerned primarily with the codification of behaviour, stipulating, for instance, what is permissible or according to nature and what is not. In such a system the relationship between the subject and the codes will be one of obedience, to a divine law, perhaps, or to a utilitarian principle. Alternatively, the greatest weight can be asigned to the relationship with the self. This will result in an ethics or 'ascetics' which is primarily concerned with the practices of the self, the formation of the self as a work of art or through whatever other criterion one takes as the standard or goal.

With regard to early Christianity specifically, it was Foucault's contention that despite the fairly constant character of the problematization of sexual activity throughout history (similar themes and principles recurring in various moralities, albeit with a difference of degree and emphasis), the ethical subject and the construction of human 'sexuality' in early Christianity were markedly different from those of earlier epochs in all four of the dimensions involved in the formation of the ethical subject.

According to Foucault, in Classical Greece, (a) the ethical subject was elaborated by delimiting the *aphrodisia*, sexual activity itself, as the substance of moral concern; (b) the style of subjectivity was developed through a concern for the way in which these pleasures were used, rather than by codifying the legitimate forms of sexual activity; (c) this demanded virile moderation, an agonistic form of self-mastery or *enkrateia*, in the use of pleasure; and (d) the goal of this asceticism was *sōphrosynē*, a freedom from the potential enslavement to the *aphrodisia* that one risked in their use. This 'heautocratic' structure of subjectivity, nevertheless, needed to buttress itself by advising austerity in the domain of sexual activity. The Imperial epoch retained the same basic 'heautocratic' structure, but increasingly brought it under a preoccupation with the self, and by this attention strengthened and intensified the themes of austerity. Foucault claims that both these technologies of the self were centred upon the acceptance of death: that their reputations, the *œuvres* which they made of their lives, would be the only memorial left for posterity, freed the individuals for a care for the self based entirely upon the self.

According to Foucault, Christianity upset this balance by introducing the idea of a salvation beyond this life, connected with a certain transformation of the self in this life.[25] Foucault suggests that the specificity of the Christian technology of the self and its style of subjectivity are characterized, quite differently, by (a) the stigmatization of the ethical substance, desires, rather than the *aphrodisia*, as evil in themselves rather than in their effects; (b) a mode of subjection which took the form of obedience towards divine precepts and the confessor; (c) a relationship to oneself elaborated in terms of a hermeneutics of the self, probing ever deeper into the realm of desires that lurk within the heart and that need to be deciphered; and (d) the ideal of self-renunciation as the goal and fulfilment of this asceticism. It is this necessity for verbalization, developed within the Christian confessional, but refined within the context of the 'human sciences' on the psychoanalyst's couch, without, however, a corresponding demand for renunciation, that Foucault considers to be the process at work in the formation of the modern subject.[26]

The work of Peter Brown presents Christian asceticism and its experience of sexuality from a different perspective to that of Foucault. Rather than analysing different styles of subjectivity, Brown attempts to explain what the ideals of chastity and renunciation meant for the early Christians in their understanding of sexuality, by reconstructing, in a series of vivid sketches situated throughout the lands of the Mediterranean, the experiences of individuals and their communities. His analysis is developed through three major 'tectonic plates', structural axes or tendencies which were operative in shaping Christian asceticism: first, the tendency to treat sexuality as an indication of the most irreducible aspects of the human will; second, the idea that sexual renunciation was constitutive and descriptive of true human freedom; and, third, the defiant struggle, through the body itself, for freedom from the demand for procreation placed upon the body by the needs of society.[27]

---

[25] Cf. Foucault, 'Ethic of Care for the Self', 9.

[26] Cf. Foucault, 'Technologies of the Self', 48–9.

[27] In addition to his numerous earlier articles and his magnum opus, *Body and Society*, P. Brown's later essay, 'Bodies and Minds: Sexuality and

The first tendency is a result of the sexualization of the hidden impulses of the heart. The heart was the place where Christians expected to meet God; but it was also the domain in which desires and thoughts remained unspoken and even unknown to the subjects themselves. To meet God face to face in the heart, therefore, required the transparency gained through simplicity. With the sexualization of the hidden desires,[28] the attempt to avoid the duplicity of a soul trusting in God but still caught up in the affairs of the world became, somewhat exclusively, the pursuit of chastity. The connection between freedom and sexual renunciation developed through the attempt to realize the victory achieved by Christ over the 'present age'. Since sexuality was a result of the Fall—if indeed it had not caused the Fall—sexual renunciation was understood as a means of reversing the momentum of the 'present age', while continence and virginity were emblems of this victory, anticipating the angelic state of those worthy of the resurrection.[29] Finally, the connection between sexuality and the 'present age' meant that the struggle for freedom through sexual renunciation became a social battle. This resulted in a new 'horizontal' dualism, that of the individual against society, rather than the older 'vertical' relation of the individual to the cosmos; and it was through this horizontal dualism that

Renunciation in Early Christianity', in D. M. Halperin, J. J. Winkler, and F. I. Zeitlin (eds.), *Before Sexuality: The Construction of Erotic Experience in the Ancient Greek World* (Princeton, 1990), 479–93, is especially important; in this essay he attempts to summarize his early work in terms of the interplay between three 'tectonic plates'. The reference is to 'Bodies and Minds', 480.

[28] While Brown ascribes this 'sexualization' to Paul, who thus stands apart from his pagan and Jewish contemporaries (cf. *Body and Society*, 55), D. Boyarin argues that a pessimistic attitude towards sexuality was more prevalent in contemporary Judaism than has previously been thought ('Body Politic among the Brides of Christ: Paul and the Origins of Christian Sexual Renunciation', in Wimbush and Valantasis (eds.), *Asceticism*, 459–78).

[29] The protological and eschatological dimensions of sexual renunciation have been the subject of many recent studies. For general surveys, see. T. H. J. van Eijk, 'Marriage and Virginity, Death and Immortality', in J. Fontaine and C. Kannengiesser (eds.), *EPEKTASIS* (Paris, 1972), 209–35, and G. Sfameni Gasparro, *Enkrateia e Antropologia: Le motivazioni protologiche della continenza e della verginità nel cristianesimo dei primi secoli e nello gnosticismo* (Rome, 1984).

sexuality and its renunciation acquired both intensity and new significance.[30]

It is via the interplay of these three tendencies that Brown guides us through the first five centuries of the history of Christian asceticism. The three forces were not always of equal importance; insistence on the resurrection of the body balanced pretensions to an angelic life, although the imagery was to remain, while the Christianization of the Empire and the development of monasticism necessarily redirected the battle against society. For Brown, the most important and the most influential aspect of Christian asceticism was the tendency first delineated: that sexuality was used as a 'seismograph' of the hidden recesses of the heart meant, conversely, that sexuality became the most personal aspect of the individual. Body and mind were connected in and through sexuality, resulting in a new form of the unity of the self, a unity based upon our own sexuality.[31]

Although various individual details of their analyses are debatable, the work of Foucault and Brown has the great merit of drawing our attention away from the outward forms and codes of morality and directing it instead to the inner mechanics, the style of asceticism and the mode of subjectivity, operating within different moralities. However, this undoubted merit cannot be allowed to obscure the issue of the adequacy of their work to the early Christian texts themselves. Given that a stated concern of both writers is to help elucidate the movements that led to the formation of the modern subject and the modern experience of sexuality, careful attention must be given to whether this desire has in fact unduly shaped their reading of early Christian texts.

With regard to the first tendency Brown delineates, duplicity of soul (δυψυχία) was certainly a problem for early Christians, but it is doubtful whether hidden thoughts were ever sexualized as exclusively as Brown's argument suggests; monastic literature in particular remained sensitive to all types of known or unknown thoughts which might shut us off from God. The interplay between protology and eschatology as a motivation for asceticism certainly entered Christian theology in the third

[30] Cf. Brown, 'Bodies and Minds', 485.
[31] Cf. ibid. 492.

century, finding its apogee, perhaps, in the works of Gregory of Nyssa, but it does not form part of the matrix of the thought of Justin and Athenagoras, referred to earlier; neither, as we will see, does it significantly influence the theologies of Irenaeus and Clement. Indeed, in the second century, this perspective seems to have been the exclusive concern of those outside the 'Catholic' Church, various 'Gnostics' and the Encratites. This is not to suggest that such arguments may not thereafter have been adopted by writers of the 'Catholic' Church, but great care needs to be taken in determining to what extent such arguments are intrinsic to the broader context of Christian theology, or whether they were used as an *ad hoc* or *post factum* justification of a style of asceticism already practised by Christians, such as that proposed by Justin, Athenagoras, or Clement. It is, finally, doubtful whether the 'horizontal' or social dimension of sexual renunciation contains anything that is intrinsic to the Christian revelation: one does not need to be 'born again' to act defiantly towards society.

Brown's socio-historical analysis certainly provides an insight into some of the roles that Christianity was made to play and the battles that were being fought through it, aspects which were no doubt important both for the early Christians and for us as we try to understand their concerns. But it is questionable whether Brown's own interpretative framework, in his reconstruction of early Christian asceticism, is sufficiently open and sensitive to those of his subjects as they themselves attempted to explain and interpret their own experience.[32] We do not possess their experiences as raw data for our own historical reconstructions; rather, we gain access to their thought through their texts, their experience as they themselves interpreted and understood it. And for the early Christian writers, their interpretative frameworks and the resulting texts were primarily theological, concerned with Christian revelation. Brown notes the importance of this fact when discussing the martyrdom of Blandina.[33] After citing the

---

[32] Cf. A. Louth's review of *The Body and Society*, *JTS* ns 41 (1990), 231–5; and, on Foucault and Brown, G. G. Stroumsa, '*Caro salutis cardo*: Shaping the Person in Early Christian Thought', *History of Religion*, 30. 1 (1990), 25–50.

[33] I owe this observation to M. Burch.

description of her martyrdom, which recalls how her companions 'in their agony saw with their outward eyes in the person of their sister the One who was crucified for them',[34] Brown then comments:

For Irenaeus, such a person stood for nothing less than human nature at its highest. . . . Only a very trivial man, indeed, would have asked, at such a time, whether Blandina had prepared herself for the presence of the Spirit by practising sexual abstinence. Irenaeus was not such a man.[35]

Yet, despite this recognition, it is this very question which Brown asks of Perpetua and the Montanists in the pages that follow and which recurs throughout his work! This question clearly did trouble early Christian writers, but it nevertheless forms part of a larger matrix. Brown's work is full of references to theological thematics, but these are always subordinated to his overall project. It would surely be more appropriate to enquire into the relationship between this highest manifestation of human nature and co-crucifixion with Christ, and to understand their asceticism from this perspective. W. Treadgold's not unjust description of the later work of Brown and Cameron on rhetoric, as being 'a map redrawn without regard for the real topography', is perhaps equally appropriate here.[36]

As the early Christians themselves felt that they were a 'third race', Foucault's analysis of Christian asceticism in terms of a new style of subjectivity might perhaps be more promising. However, his analysis of the Christian style of subjectivity as the interplay between obedience, the hermeneutics of the self in the realm of desires, and renunciation suggests that he also 'bracketed' too many of the concerns expressed by the early Christians themselves, as a result of his self-confessed interest

[34] *EH* 5. 1. 41; an account perhaps written by Irenaeus himself, as argued by P. Nautin, *Lettres et écrivains chrétiens des IIe et IIIe siècles* (Paris, 1961), 54–61.

[35] Brown, *The Body*, 73.

[36] W. Treadgold, 'Imaginary Early Christianity', *International History Review*, 15. 3 (1993), 545. If there is an allusion in this quotation to the title of the article by Cameron mentioned earlier (n. 15), 'Redrawing the Map: Early Christian Territory after Foucault', then his complaint falls equally upon Foucault.

in the relationship between, and deployment of, power and knowledge. More importantly, we cannot assume, in comparing the theories of asceticism elaborated by Christians and their pagan contemporaries, that we are dealing with parallel or commensurate modalities of subjectivity. For, beyond the horizontal plane of the differing technologies of the self offered by the philosophical schools of late antiquity, the Christian style of subjectivity is elaborated in a vertical and eschatological perspective. Consequent upon the incarnation, crucifixion, and resurrection of Christ, Christians claimed to be born again as children of God, a 'third race' with a 'confessedly strange constitution of their own citizenship' (*Diognetus* 5. 4). Granted a personal immortality in Christ, Christians did not need to stylize their lives into an *œuvre*, which could only ever gain them a relative immortality. It is on the foundation of the evangelical proclamation that early Christian texts were written, and it is only within this perspective that we can begin to appreciate what was distinctive in their style of subjectivity, their asceticism. We might wish to suspend our belief in these claims, but it would be hermeneutically unsound to do so on behalf of those whom we are studying, and so fail to take account of the perspective described by the early Christian texts themselves.[37] The temptation to do so is, perhaps, the shadow side of the erosion of the boundaries between academic disciplines, a phenomenon which has otherwise offered so much and has revitalized our interest in the late antique world.

IRENAEUS AND CLEMENT: THE SUBJECTS FOR STUDY

If, then, a history of Christian asceticism written from the theological perspective of the writers under study has yet to be undertaken, or at least has been neglected by contemporary scholarship, so too has one which is not dominated by the classical form of Christian asceticism: that is, monasticism.

[37] This, of course, entails the reverse demand that we consciously acknowledge our own presuppositions, with all the inevitable problems that this entails, as analysed especially by H. G. Gadamer, *Wahrheit und Methode*, 5th edn. (Tübingen, 1986), trans. J. Weinsheimer and D. G. Marshall (New York, 1997).

Alongside the stimulating 'turn to the subject' of contemporary scholarship, historical theology has, at least since Harnack, consciously attempted to work without the conventional categories, such as orthodox/heretical or normative writings/other writings, which it claims were only drawn up through processes of conflict and exclusion, demarcating the victorious position. It is generally held that such categories are applicable only (if at all) retrospectively, and should not influence unbiased research into the earlier periods during which the boundary lines are still being erected. S. Elm, in her recent investigation into fourth-century female asceticism, has suggested that a similar dyad is that of asceticism/monasticism:

Historiography, in focusing on the eventual results of these gradual processes, and often anachronistically presupposing them for the earlier period, thus allowed the later results to be seen as being original, as if the ways of ascetic perfection which became the norm were indeed the only ones ever conceived as possible.[38]

With regard to Christian asceticism, this tendency has effectively meant that its classical form, monasticism, has assumed a hegemony by virtue of which studies into the history of Christian asceticism have taken the form of tracing the roots of monasticism;[39] similarly, reflection on non-monastic asceticism has proceeded by assimilation to monasticism: to be a Christian ascetic means to be a monk or a nun, at least inwardly; and, taken to its ultimate conclusion, to be a real, 'perfect' Christian necessitates the withdrawal into the desert.[40]

---

[38] S. Elm, *'Virgins of God': The Making of Asceticism in Late Antiquity* (Oxford, 1994), 385; cf. 1–18.

[39] The contention of J. C. O'Neill, 'The Origins of Monasticism', in R. Williams (ed.), *The Making of Orthodoxy* (Cambridge, 1989), 270–87, that Christian monasticism dates back to apostolic times, originating in Jewish ascetic communities which converted to Christianity and continued perhaps in Gnostic communities, does not weaken the point being made here: it is the appearance of one particular form of asceticism 'with startling suddenness in great power', together with 'the prejudice that God requires the same obedience from all' (ibid. 285–6), that occasioned the belief that monasticism began with Antony and Pachomius and obscured from view other possible forms of asceticism.

[40] K. Ware has pointed out that the various stories which relate how a desert monk is led into the city to be shown married Christians who excel him in virtue (such as acts of mercy and charity) invariably include an affirmation

The two subjects chosen for study here, the near contemporaries Irenaeus of Lyons (*c*.130–*c*.200) and Clement of
Alexandria (*c*.150–*c*.215), were writing almost a century
before Antony retreated into the desert. For them, asceticism
was not a detachable dimension of Christian life, a specialized
technique within the more general life of the Christian, or the
domain of ascetic specialists, the monastics. Rather, asceticism
was the realization, the putting into practice, of the new
eschatological life granted in baptism within the confines of
the present life. They are, moreover, two of the earliest
Christian writers from whom a sizeable body of work remains.
Tertullian would have been an obvious companion, but the
problems which arise from a study of his writings, from the
different periods of his life, are too numerous to be adequately
dealt with here. Nevertheless, the styles of asceticism proposed
by Irenaeus and Clement, together with their understanding of
the human person, are sufficiently different to invite comparison.

A further aspect common to both Irenaeus and Clement is
that the positions which they articulate, as different as they may
be, are developed in response to common opponents. While
these opponents are now usually grouped together under the
umbrella title of 'Gnostics', Irenaeus and Clement, and also
Hippolytus, perhaps conforming to their opponents' own
usage, do not employ this term for the more familiar figures
such as Basilides and Valentinus, but reserve it for various
obscure yet related sects.[41] Nevertheless, in so far as the

___

of their celibacy, and often conclude with an exhortation to the married
person not to neglect their salvation, at which point they forsake everything
and follow the monk back to the desert, where they also become monks ('The
Monk and the Married Christian: Some Comparisons in Early Monastic
Sources', *ECR* 6. 1 (1974), 72–83).

[41] Cf. M. J. Edwards, 'Gnostics and Valentinians in the Church Fathers',
JTS ns 40. 1 (1989), 26–47. The body of scholarship on Gnosticism is vast,
but very uneven. Standard works, such as H. Jonas, *The Gnostic Religion*, 2nd
rev. edn. (London, 1992 [1958]) and K. Rudolph, *Gnosis*, trans. R. McL.
Wilson 1977; Edinburgh, 1983), are still useful; of more recent works,
S. Pétrement, *Le Dieu séparé: Les origines du gnosticisme* (Paris, 1984; trans.
C. Harrison, San Francisco, 1990), and M. A. Williams, *Rethinking "Gnosticism": An Argument for Dismantling a Dubious Category* (Princeton, 1996), are
the most important and challenging.

systems of these diverse thinkers exhibit certain similar characteristics, the title 'Gnostic' is a convenient one to use here.[42]
However, this must not be taken to imply that the acquisition
of *gnōsis* is outside the purview of our writers, or that *gnōsis*
itself is necessarily other than faith even for the Gnostics, at
least the earliest of them. For both, the *gnōsis* concerned, albeit
variously understood, is the saving knowledge delivered
uniquely by the Saviour and accepted by faith.[43] If Valentinus
came to differentiate between the faith of those in the Church,
who have remained at the 'psychical' level, and the deeper
gnōsis, as above all a knowledge of the self, possessed by those
like himself who were truly 'spiritual', it is perhaps in recognition of the distance which separated him from the larger body
of the Church in Rome.[44] Moreover, although Clement, in a
manner alien to Irenaeus, consistently describes his ideal
mature Christian as a 'Gnostic', not even Irenaeus disparages
gnōsis itself or its acquisition; it is the abuse of this term, by
those who lay claim to it, that leads to his polemic against
'*gnōsis* falsely so-called'.

As the studies which follow are primarily concerned to
investigate the asceticism and anthropology of Irenaeus and
Clement, rather than their polemic against the Gnostics, it will
be useful to consider briefly some of the characteristic features
of 'Gnosticism' and the different responses of Irenaeus and
Clement. The first and most important criticism that Irenaeus
levels against the Gnostics concerns the radical distinction that
they introduced between the Creator God, the Demiurge, and
the true God, the Father of Jesus Christ. Perhaps carrying to
an extreme the characteristic Johannine assertion that the Jews
do not know the true God (cf. John 5: 37–8, 8: 19, etc.) rather

---

[42] M. Williams argues very convincingly against the continued use of the
typological categories of 'gnostic' and 'gnosticism' as misleading over-general-
izations, and proposes instead 'biblical demiurgical traditions' (*Rethinking
"Gnosticism"*, 51 and *passim*). But, as most of the points I raise here
concerning 'gnosticism' are ones which Williams himself acknowledges are
common traits of these 'biblical demiurgical traditions', and as I raise them
only to illustrate the context in which Irenaeus and Clement developed their
work, rather than to make genealogical claims about their opponents, I have
retained the terms 'gnostic' and 'gnosticism' for the sake of simplicity.

[43] Cf. Pétrement, *Le Dieu séparé*, 185–99; trans. 129–39.

[44] Cf. ibid. 190–1, 273, 505–17; trans. 133, 192, 370–8.

than modifying some pre-Christian dualism,[45] it was a fundamental belief of the Gnostics that the Demiurge was other than
the true God.[46] Consequent upon this was the Gnostic division
of Scripture into two discontinuous sections, the Jewish
Scriptures and the apostolic writings, relating to the Demiurge
and the true God respectively, and the introduction of various
narratives describing the origin of the Demiurge and his
activity, narratives which assume a higher, because explanat-
ory, status than Scripture.[47] Paul was perhaps aware of such
teaching when, in his Second Letter to the Corinthians, he
emphasized the identity of the Creator, the God who said 'Let
light shine out of darkness', and the God whose glory has given
the light of knowledge (*gnōsis*) in the face of Christ (2 Cor.
4: 6).[48] This Pauline conviction forms the basic determinant of
Irenaeus's theology, the ground-plan or plot (ὑπόθεσις) of
Scripture and of the truth itself: that there is one God who
has acted continuously in one economy, unfolded in Scripture,
to bring his creation to share in his own life. While this
presupposition is shared by Clement, his understanding of
the history of salvation is somewhat different from that of
Irenaeus: not without important implications, as we will see,
Clement is prepared to look upon philosophy as a pedagogue
leading the Greeks to Christ, parallel to, though not necessarily
independent of, the Jewish Law.

To distinguish between the Creator and the true God,
Irenaeus repeatedly insists, is to despise God himself and to
disparage his creation. The Gnostics were not dualists, in the
sense of postulating two eternal principles, for the Demiurge
and the matter he uses are derived ultimately from the
Pleroma; but their understanding of the salvific call from the
true God, who is other than the Demiurge, leads to a
transcendental dualism together with a marked devaluation of
the world.[49] That which is ultimately saved is not so much the

---

[45] As argued by Pétrement, ibid. 49–77; trans. 29–50.

[46] Cf. Williams, *Rethinking "Gnosticism"*, 26–8, 51, 265.

[47] Cf. ibid. 87 on Ptolemy's 'metamyth'.

[48] Cf. G. W. MacRae, 'Why the Church Rejected Gnosticism', in E. P.
Sanders (ed.), *Jewish and Christian Self-Definition*, i: *The Shaping of Christianity in the Second and Third Centuries* (Philadelphia, 1980), 130–1.

[49] Williams argues that the Gnostics in fact had a much higher estimation of
the body than has previously been acknowledged (cf. *Rethinking "Gnosticism"*,

body and soul resurrected in Christ, but only that which Christ awakens in the Gnostic, that which is itself of Christ rather than of the Demiurge. Thus a shared theme in Irenaeus and Clement is the insistence on the resurrection of the body, and the possibility that the flesh itself may be sanctified, along with the appropriate attitude of gratitude towards God for his munificent creation. The emphasis, more so in Irenaeus than in the Alexandrian Clement, upon flesh illustrates the way in which key terms were transformed through the course of the controversy. Used predominantly in a negative sense by Paul, the term 'flesh' begins to be used as a Christological shibboleth by John (1 John 4: 2) and culminates in Irenaeus's exegetical *tour de force* of 1 Cor. 15: 50: flesh and blood do not inherit the Kingdom, but they certainly are inherited (*AH* 5. 9)![50] By insisting upon the radical otherness of the Creator and creation, his absolute transcendence rather than what is ultimately only a relative transcendence of the Gnostic's God, who remains connected with the world through a kind of chain of being, Irenaeus can paradoxically maintain the presence of God to his creation and his salvific activity within it and for it.[51]

One further charge raised against the Gnostics by Irenaeus and Clement is that they either demand an excessively rigorous asceticism or offer a hedonistic libertinism, opposite sides of the same coin of their mythologies.[52] Such allegations are frequent in polemical literature, and there is no evidence, apart from the Christian writings of this genre, that the Gnostics did adopt an antinomian attitude. However, if, as MacIntyre has argued, the narrative structure in which the subject is embedded and which provides a framework for his ethical thought is a central element in (at least) ancient morality,[53] then the narratives which the Gnostics elaborated

esp. 116–38). Yet he cannot extend this re-evaluation to material reality itself; as he comments regarding the body in Gnostic thought: 'Its substance was doomed. Yet its form was a mirror on the divine. Somehow, even the physical human form recalled the divinity, in spite of the imperfect and defiled material medium in which the shape had been cast' (ibid. 130).

[50] Cf. R. Noormann, *Irenäus als Paulusinterpret* (Tübingen, 1994), 508–12.

[51] Cf. D. Minns, *Irenaeus* (London, 1994), 30–4.

[52] On this whole polemic, cf. Williams, *Rethinking "Gnosticism"*, 139–88.

[53] A. MacIntyre, *After Virtue*, 2nd edn. (Notre Dame, Ind., 1984), esp. 174–6.

to explain themselves and their situation would inevitably be taken to include an anti-cosmic moral dimension.[54] The relationship between the narrative in which the subject is located and the morality or asceticism proposed for that subject is also evident in the positions elaborated by Irenaeus and Clement: while Irenaeus places the subject firmly within the economy of God as unfolded in Scripture, which entails an asceticism understood as living the life of God as exemplified in the crucified and risen Christ, Clement, by recasting this economy to a form which includes Greek philosophy, relates a different narrative, one of a cultivated *paideia*, and proposes instead what *he* considers to be a godly life.

This relationship between asceticism and anthropology, as understood by Irenaeus and Clement, is the subject of this study. In so far as Clement's works are already concerned, to a large extent, with elaborating Christian asceticism from anthropological and cosmological considerations, the section on Clement can be much more straightforward than that on Irenaeus. However, as I stressed earlier, it is necessary to attempt to understand any early Christian text within its own terms of reference. As such, in both cases my analyses will necessarily be much broader than investigations of asceticism and anthropology usually are, considering these themes as they fall within a wider context, one which is properly theological. I will need to tackle the full spectrum of theological issues concerning the nature and existence of human beings, from our creation in the image and likeness of God to the resurrection and eschatology. However, whilst addressing many different issues, I will not necessarily proceed along traditional lines. It is important, for an adequate interpretation of both authors, that we do not approach their works with unacknowledged, preconceived ideas or paradigms (for instance, concerning the Fall or the question of the presence of the Spirit in the human person) derived from later theological developments. As my readings of the texts of Irenaeus, and to a lesser degree those of Clement, differ significantly from standard interpretations,

---

[54] Williams, *Rethinking "Gnosticism"*, 118, speaks of a '*mythological* devaluation of the human body', what the gnostics *said* about their bodies rather than what they *did*. Plotinus's criticisms, according to Williams, were also based on 'rhetorical logic rather than direct observation' (ibid. 178).

especially in the complex question of the relationship between the soul, the breath of life, and the Holy Spirit in Irenaeus's theology, my analyses may appear to be both more intensive and extensive than at first seems necessary. It has at times been a question of the correct interpretation of a single sentence of Irenaeus, referring to both the Latin and the Armenian versions, but it has also been necessary to establish such particulars within a more comprehensive reading.

PART I

Irenaeus of Lyons:
From Breath to Spirit

'No early Christian writer has deserved better of the whole Church than Irenaeus.'[1] This assessment by H. B. Swete, writing early in this century, is unfortunately borne out both by the transmission of Irenaeus's writings themselves and by much modern scholarship, at least until the middle of this century. Of Irenaeus's writings, only two have survived to the present day: the *Refutation and Overthrow of Knowledge falsely so-called* or, more simply, *Against the Heresies*,[2] and the *Demonstration of the Apostolic Preaching*.[3] *Against the Heresies* initially found a receptive audience; a copy of the Greek text was even circulating in Egypt within a few decades of its composition, while in Carthage Tertullian referred to 'Irenaeus, that very exact inquirer into all doctrines' in his own work against the Valentinians.[4] However, the last

---

[1] Foreword in F. R. M. Hitchcock, *Irenaeus of Lugdunum: A Study of his Teaching* (Cambridge, 1914).

[2] The first title is given by Irenaeus himself, in *AH* 4. pref. 1; it is mentioned by Eusebius, *EH* 5. 7. 1, who also uses the abbreviated 'title', *EH* 3. 23. 3. I have used the Source Chrétiennes edition prepared by A. Rousseau *et al.*, *Irénée de Lyon*, *Contre les hérésies*, SC 100, 152–3, 210–11, 263–4, 293–4 (Paris, 1965–82), and the Armenian version edited by K. Ter-Mekerttschian and E. Ter-Minassiantz, *Irenäus, Gegen Die Häretiker*, Ἔλεγχος καὶ ἀνατροπὴ τῆς ψευδωνύμου γνώσεως, *Buch IV u. V in armenischer Version*, TU 35. 2 (Leipzig, 1910). I have also consulted the various available translations. For a history of the various versions and manuscript traditions see the chapters by B. Hemmerdinger, L. Doutreleau, C. Mercier and A. Rousseau, in SC 100, 15–191.

[3] This is the title given by Eusebius, *EH* 5. 26. I have used my own translation (*The Apostolic Preaching* (New York, 1997)), based upon the edition of K. Ter-Mekerttschian and S. G. Wilson, Εἰς ἐπίδειξιν τοῦ ἀποστολικοῦ κηρύγματος. *The Proof of the Apostolic Preaching, with Seven Fragments*, PO 12. 5 (Paris, 1917; repr. Turnhout, 1989), the emendations suggested by C. Mercier in A. Rousseau (ed.), *Démonstration de la prédication apostolique*, SC 406 (Paris, 1995), 389–92, and a microfilm of the sole extant manuscript (E 3710).

[4] Cf. C. H. Roberts, *Manuscript, Society and Belief in Early Christian Egypt* (London, 1979), 23, 53; Tertullian, *Against the Valentinians*, 5.

recorded sighting of the complete Greek text was by Photius in Baghdad in the ninth century.[5] The complete text (apart from an important paragraph in *AH* 5. 36. 3) survives only in a Latin version, originating from a translation made sometime before 421–2, when it is cited by Augustine.[6] The extant Latin manuscripts demonstrate that *Against the Heresies* continued to be read during the Middle Ages. But it was really only after Erasmus published the first printed edition in 1526, referring to the author as 'my Irenaeus',[7] that the work was read with renewed vigour, though now in the context of the religious controversies of the sixteenth century, as polemicists mined his work for support and ammunition in a confessional reading that has persisted to this century.[8] Numerous Greek, Syriac, and Armenian fragments of *Against the Heresies* have also been located, preserved in the works of other authors. Most important, however, is a thirteenth-century manuscript discovered at Erevan in 1904, which contains an Armenian version of *AH* 4 and 5, probably translated in Constantinople in the sixth century.[9] This discovery also brought to light an Armenian

[5] B. Hemmerdinger, 'Les "Notices et extraits" des bibliothèques grecques de Bagdad par Photius', *REG* 69 (1956), 101–3, suggests that the manuscript consulted by Photius was lost in the sacking of the city in 1258.

[6] Augustine, *Answer to Julian*, 1. 3. 5.

[7] D. Erasmus (ed.), *Opus eruditissimum divi Irenaei episcopi Lugdunensis in quinque libros digestum . . .* (Basel, 1526), a2.

[8] Cf. O. Reimherr, 'Irenaeus Lugdunensis', in V. Brown (ed.), *Catalogus translationum et commentariorum: Mediaeval and Renaissance Latin Translations and Commentaries, Annotated Lists and Guide*, 7 (Washington, 1992), 21–5; and for the later period, J. Friesen, 'A Study of the Influence of Confessional Bias on the Interpretations in the Modern Era of Irenaeus of Lyons' (Ph.D. Diss., Northwestern University, Evanston, Ill., 1977).

[9] The discovery of an Armenian version made from the Greek, independently of the Latin version, has enabled an assessment of both versions, and persuaded Rousseau to undertake a Greek retroversion. Both versions show a high degree of literalism; but while the Latin translator had a tendency to rethink (and occasionally to modify deliberately) what he was translating, the Armenian translator kept more slavishly to the original (cf. Rousseau, SC 100, 107–57). As the variant readings of the Armenian version are presented in the Sources Chrétiennes edition in a Latin translation (which, due to the idiosyncrasies of the languages, is necessarily an interpretation), it is still necessary, despite the remarkable achievement of Rousseau *et al.*, to refer to the Armenian text, noting the emendations suggested by Mercier at the end of SC 100, pt. 1, and 152. I refer to the Greek where it exists, otherwise to the Latin and Armenian as necessary.

version of the *Demonstration*, which was otherwise known only from the mention of its title by Eusebius and a few Armenian fragments. The surviving Greek fragments of *Against the Heresies* suggest that in the Greek-speaking world Irenaeus's works were used mainly as source material by later heresiologists.[10] It is ironic that Irenaeus's work, which, in von Balthasar's words, marks the 'birth of Christian theology' and which was produced in conscious opposition to the real threat of Gnosticism, would later be used systematically only by those cataloguers of heresies for whom Gnosticism was no longer a living force or by those of a later era engaged in their own confessional polemics.[11]

With regard to modern scholarship, Swete could not have foreseen the massive assault that would be launched two decades later as the methodology of 'Quellenforschung' was pushed to its limits. Building on the work of Harnack[12] and Bousset,[13] Loofs autoptically dissected *Against the Heresies* into its various supposed sources (even if these 'sources' are no longer extant), and, by discounting any traces of their influence, delimited what he claimed was 'Irenaeus selbst'; not surprisingly, he concluded that 'Irenaeus ist als theologischer Schriftsteller viel kleiner gewesen, als man bisher annahm. . . . Noch kleiner wird Irenaeus als Theologe.'[14] As Benoît notes in

---

[10] Apart from the fragments preserved in the papyrii (Oxyrhynchus 405 and Iena), there are occasional fragments in the Catenae on the Scriptures and the *Sacra Parallela*, and, less frequently, citations in patristic works: e.g. Basil of Caesarea cites Irenaeus twice in *On the Holy Spirit*, 29, amongst the many fathers who testify to the divinity of the Spirit. In contrast, about 80 per cent of book 1 of *Against the Heresies* is preserved in the works of Hippolytus, Epiphanius, and Theodoret of Cyrhus. Cf. J. Fantino, *L'Homme, image de Dieu chez saint Irénée de Lyon* (Paris, 1984), 188–90. Reimherr is more optimistic regarding the influence of Irenaeus on later Greek and Latin theology (cf. 'Irenaeus', 16–21).

[11] H. U. von Balthasar, *The Glory of the Lord: A Theological Aesthetics*, 2 (Edinburgh, 1984), 31–2. Cf. F. M. M. Sagnard, *La Gnose valentinienne et le témoignage de saint Irénée* (Paris, 1947), 82.

[12] A. Harnack, 'De Presbyter-Prediger des Irenäus (IV, 27, 1–32, 1): Bruchstücke und Nachklänger der ältesten exegetisch-polemischen Homilien', in *Philotesia: Paul Kleinerts zum LXX Geburtstag* (Berlin, 1907), 1–37.

[13] W. Bousset, *Jüdisch-christlicher Schulbetrieb in Alexandria und Rom: Literarische Untersuchungen zu Philo und Clemens von Alexandria, Justin und Irenäus* (Göttingen, 1915), 272–82.

[See p. 28 for n. 14]

28 *Irenaeus of Lyons*

his study of Irenaeus, the imposing character of Loofs's work was such that it effectively halted work on Irenaeus for the following decades.[15] However, Benoît himself, despite setting his 'literary analysis' in conscious opposition to *Quellen-forschung*, in an attempt to break free from the work of Loofs, did not successfully manage to escape the divisive tendencies of earlier German research.[16] He concluded—and this was the general consensus—that, whilst displaying the unity one would expect from the work of a single author, Irenaeus's work was nevertheless composed from several sources put together somewhat thoughtlessly and clumsily.[17]

Beginning with G. Wingren's book *Man and the Incarnation*,[18] the last forty years have seen a new appreciation of Irenaeus's writings and theology.[19] Simply learning how to read Irenaeus on his own terms has been a long process. For instance, with regard to the literary form of *AH* 4, the primary focus of the source critics' attention, Bacq has magisterially established that its unity and coherence is located not, as we tend to expect from a work, in a systematic, linear, logical development of ideas, but in Irenaeus's use of the 'words of the Lord', joined together by means of a series of *mots crochets* or other scriptural quotations.[20]

As regards his theology, it has often been stated, with insufficient analysis, that Irenaeus is a Biblical theologian, and that the unity of his theology is grounded upon that of Scripture.[21] Such unity, however, would have been as prob-

[14] F. Loofs, *Theophilus von Antiochien Adversus Marcionem und die anderen theologischen Quellen bei Irenaeus*, TU 46. 2 (Leipzig, 1930), 432.

[15] A. Benoît, *Saint Irénée: Introduction à l'étude de sa théologie* (Paris, 1960), 33–4.

[16] Ibid. 40–1. Cf. H. I. Marrou's Review of Benoît's book, *REA* 65 (1963), 453.

[17] Benoît, *Saint Irénée*, 199. Such was also the assessment of J. Quasten, *Patrology*, 1 (Utrecht, 1950), 289.

[18] G. Wingren, *Man and the Incarnation*, first published in Swedish (Lund, 1947) and then in an English translation (London, 1959).

[19] For works published between 1970 and 1984, see M. A. Donovan, 'Irenaeus in Recent Scholarship', *Second Century*, 4. 4 (1984), 219–41.

[20] P. Bacq, *De l'ancienne à la nouvelle alliance selon S. Irénée: Unité du livre IV de l'Adversus Haereses* (Paris, 1978).

[21] Cf. R. Seeberg's oft repeated dictum: 'Irenäus ist Biblizist und er ist der erste große Vertreter des Biblizismus' (*Lehrbuch der Dogmengeschichte*, 3rd

lematic then as it is now albeit in different, even reverse, ways. While we have inherited the idea of the unity of Scripture, but undermine this recognition by seeing conflicting theologies and traditions in Scripture, Irenaeus stands at the decisive historical moment, 'le tournant irénéen', in which the apostolic writings are recognized as Scripture, the unity of which he has to substantiate.[22] It is, in fact, his understanding of the apostolic preaching, its particular texture and authority, that enables him to embrace in one comprehensive and consistent vision the whole history of salvation as it is unfolded in the one body of Scripture.[23]

It is this unity of Scripture and its narrative that Irenaeus expounds, with deceptive simplicity, in the *Demonstration of the Apostolic Preaching*. What is especially striking about this work is that, while it is clear that Irenaeus knows the apostolic writings, and regards them as Scripture, they are not explicitly used as the foundation for his exposition.[24] So, for instance, that Christ was born of a virgin and worked miracles is shown by Isaiah (*Dem.* 53), and, while the names of Pontius Pilate and Herod are known from the Gospels, that Jesus was bound and brought to them is shown by Hosea (*Dem.* 77).

The work itself falls into two distinct parts (*Dem.* 3b–42a, 42b–97), each of which is a 'demonstration' (ἐπίδειξις) in a different sense. First, Irenaeus demonstrates, or unfolds, the content of Scripture, the Old Testament, as it pertains to the

---

rev. edn. (Leipzig, 1920), 1. 365). For a negative assessment, see the works of the nineteenth-century German theologians, who saw in Irenaeus an unresolved juxtaposition of a mystical realism and an apologetic rationalism: e.g. J. Werner, *Der Paulinismus des Irenaeus* (Leipzig, 1889), and A. Harnack, *History of Dogma*, trans. of 3rd German edn. (London, 1896), 2. 231–79.

[22] Cf. Y. M. Blanchard, *Aux Sources du Canon: Le témoignage d'Irénée* (Paris, 1993); for the cited phrase, cf. 281–3.

[23] Cf. the introduction to my translation of *The Apostolic Preaching*.

[24] He cites Paul three times (*Dem.* 5, 8, 87) and John twice (*Dem.* 43, 94), refers to the apostles (*Dem.* 3, 41, 46, 86, 98, 99), and occasionally cites an Old Testament text, giving it in the form used by the New Testament, yet attributing it to its Old Testament source (e.g. the passage attributed to Jeremiah in *Dem.* 81). It is this relative paucity of New Testament texts cited as Scripture, compared with *Against the Heresies*, that leads Blanchard, in *Aux Sources du Canon*, to suggest that the *Demonstration* is in fact earlier (and that *Dem.* 99–100 is a later addition), so that *Against the Heresies* marks the decisive turning-point.

revelation of Jesus Christ as preached by the apostles, after the manner of the great speeches in Acts. Second, he demonstrates, or proves, that what the apostles proclaimed as having been fulfilled in Christ was indeed so foretold, and so, as their preaching is itself shaped by Scripture, it thus is of Scripture, and possesses its unique authority as the word of God. This latter task in particular—gathering the passages in the Old Testament which refer to Christ—clearly follows the tradition of Christocentric exegesis of the Old Testament as practised by the apologists, the apostolic fathers, and the New Testament itself (cf. Luke 24: 27). Ignatius of Antioch, for instance, who clearly knew some of the apostolic writings (cf. *Ephesians*, 12. 2) but never cites them, states, in a discussion concerning the relationship between the Gospel and what is written, that 'For me, the archives [i.e. the Old Testament] are Jesus Christ' (*Philippians*, 8. 2). Justin Martyr, from whom Irenaeus derived much of his material, and who begins to appeal to the apostolic testimony in a written form (described as 'memoirs'), claims more specifically that all the events of the revelation of Christ, as preached by the apostles, from his birth to the Passion and the inclusion of the Gentiles, are to be found in the books of the Prophets.[25] But it is Irenaeus who first combined this Christocentric exegesis with the recounting, in an orderly fashion, of all the great deeds of God, from the creation and fall of man onwards, culminating in the exaltation of his crucified Son, the bestowal of his Holy Spirit, and the gift of a new heart of flesh.

The apostolic preaching, therefore, announcing that what the prophets have foretold, Christ has realized, is the key to Scripture, constituting it as the definitive word of God. It is because of this particular scriptural texture of the apostolic preaching that Irenaeus can maintain that Scripture is indeed one, without himself imposing an extraneous unity upon it. It is the way in which he understands the texture of these sources of our knowledge of God and his salvific work that shapes the unity and coherence of his own theology. Moreover, it is because of its scriptural texture that the apostolic preaching is uniquely authoritative. After having presented various Gnostic systems and demonstrated their inconsistencies in the first two books of *Against the Heresies*, Irenaeus begins

[25] Cf. Justin, esp. *First Apology*, 31. 7.

the exposition of his own theology, in book 3, by emphatically stating that in matters of theology the apostolic word is absolute: 'We have learned from none others the economy of our salvation, than from those through whom the Gospel has come down to us' (*AH* 3. 1. 1). It is they who have declared to us that there is one God, the Creator, spoken of by the Law and the Prophets, and one Christ, his Son; to scorn them is to despise the Father and Son and to reject our salvation.[26]

As this Gospel was first proclaimed aloud, and then handed down in the Scriptures as 'the foundation and pillar of our faith',[27] it is preserved, on the one hand, in 'the tradition which originates from the apostles'—that is, the continued proclamation of the same Gospel by successive generations of presbyters in the Church[28]—and, on the other hand, in the apostolic writings themselves; yet it is the same apostolic word in both.[29] As such, when the Gnostics appealed to a tradition which contained information not in Scripture, or principles which would legitimize their interpretation of Scripture, Irenaeus, on the basis of the identity between Scripture and tradition, could accuse them of not having understood either.[30] However, after formally acknowledging and demonstrating, in *AH* 3. 2–5, that the tradition delivered by the apostles is maintained by the Church, preserving and preaching the same Gospel, Irenaeus himself turns exclusively to Scripture for his exposition of theology.[31]

---

[26] *AH* 3. 1. 2.

[27] *AH* 3. 1. 1, alluding to 1 Tim. 3: 15; while Paul had spoken of the Church as the 'ground and pillar of truth', for Irenaeus, in his polemical context, it is Scripture which supports our faith. [28] Cf. *AH* 3. 3.

[29] Hence Irenaeus can hypothetically consider how it would be if the apostles had not written anything: Christians would be as the barbarians, preserving 'the ancient tradition of the apostles', with salvation written on their hearts (*AH* 3. 4. 1–2).

[30] *AH* 3. 2.

[31] Cf. *AH* 3. 5. 1. Although Irenaeus occasionally cites various witnesses of the tradition (Ignatius, Polycarp, Hermas, and the presbyters/elders who were the disciples of the apostles), this clear-cut distinction between tradition (used sixteen times here) and Scripture is limited to *AH* 3. 2–5, and as such is perhaps occasioned by its particular polemic; he uses the term six other times in *Against the Heresies*, usually to denote the message delivered by the apostles and preached by the Church. Cf. E. Flesseman-van Leer, *Tradition and Scripture in the Early Church* (Assen, 1954), 100–6.

To designate this unity of Scripture, Irenaeus occasionally employs the term 'hypothesis'. This term had been used by Greek writers, especially the rhetoricians, to refer to the 'argument' or the 'plot' of a speech or drama.[32] It is precisely for having ignored the real hypothesis of Scripture that Irenaeus criticizes the Gnostic interpretation of Scripture. After describing some of their narratives, Irenaeus claims:

Such is their hypothesis which neither the prophets preached, nor the Lord taught, nor the apostles handed down. They boast rather loudly of knowing more about it than others do, citing it from unwritten sources,[33] and, venturing to weave the proverbial ropes of sand, they try to adapt to their statements in a manner worthy of credence either the Lord's parables, or the prophets' sayings, or the apostles' words, so that their fabrication might not appear to be without witness. They disregard the order and the connection (τὴν τάξιν καὶ τὸν εἱρμὸν) of the Scriptures and, as much as in them lies, they disjoint the members of the Truth. (*AH* 1. 8. 1)

Irenaeus likens the Gnostics' handling of Scripture to the activity of those who take a jewelled mosaic of a king and rearrange the stones to form a picture of a dog or a fox, or to those who take diverse lines from Homer and place them in a different order. Just as those who are well versed in Homer will not be deceived by such centos, so also, Irenaeus continues,

anyone who keeps unchanged within himself the rule of truth received through baptism[34] will recognize the names and sayings and parables from the Scripture, but not their blasphemous hypothesis. If he recognizes the jewels, he will not accept the fox for the royal image.

---

[32] For the rhetorical background of Irenaeus's use of the terms 'hypothesis', 'economy', and 'recapitulation', see R. M. Grant's introduction to his translation, *Irenaeus of Lyons* (London, 1997), 46–53.

[33] ἐξ ἀγράφων ἀναγινώσκοντες. Rousseau maintains that the term ἄγραφον refers to apocryphal written works. However, as ἀναγινώσκω can indicate 'to acknowledge', 'to own', as well as 'to read' (cf H. G. Liddell and R. Scott (eds.), *Greek–English Lexicon*, 9th edn. rev. H. S. Jones and R. Mackenzie (Oxford, 1996), s.v.), this phrase could equally refer to unwritten oral traditions, as *AH* 3. 2–5 would suggest.

[34] Besides any pre-baptismal instruction, that the rule of truth is received through baptism would seem to refer to the fact that baptism is performed in the three names which constitute the articles of the rule of truth (cf. *Dem.* 6–7).

Replacing each word to its proper context, and, harmonizing it to the body of the truth, he will lay bare their fabrication and show that it is without support. (*AH* 1. 9. 4)

This 'rule of truth' is, as it were, the formal expression of the hypothesis of Scripture, but can no more be detached from this context, to become an abstract system of doctrine, than can 'the order and connection of Scripture' be detached from 'the body of truth'. It is only within the context of this hypothesis that the elements deployed within its narrative acquire their meaning, and as such it is only within its perspective that we will be able to analyse Irenaeus's anthropology and asceticism.

Irenaeus employs the term 'economy' to express the 'arrangement' of the hypothesis of Scripture or particular details within its overall structure.[35] While earlier writers, both Christian and Gnostic, as well as Irenaeus, had used the term 'economy' or 'economies' to describe particular salvific acts of God, such as the Incarnation or the Passion,[36] it seems probable that it was Irenaeus who first used the term in a singular, universal sense, bringing together all the various aspects of this relationship into one all-embracing divine plan or economy.[37] If, as Widmen suggested, this universal sense of 'economy' originated in his polemic against the Gnostics, it nevertheless enabled Irenaeus to achieve a unified understanding of the purposeful arrangement of the narrative unfolded in Scripture, the singleness of God's purpose in his dealings with the human race throughout history, in the various covenants and epochs, instructing and guiding his creatures in the vision of God, to the point where created human eyes can rest upon the uncreated God.[38]

[35] For the term 'economy' in Irenaeus and the Gnostics, see J. Fantino, *La Théologie d'Irénée: Lecture des Écritures en réponse à l'exégèse gnostique: Une approche trinitaire* (Paris, 1994), chs. 2–4.

[36] e.g. Eph. 1: 10; 3: 9; Ignatius, *Ephesians*, 18. 2, 20. 1; Justin, *Dialogue with Trypho*, 30. 3, 31. 1, 45. 4, 87. 5, 103. 3, 120. 1; Basilides, *AH* 1. 24. 4; Markus, *AH* 1. 14. 6, 15. 3.

[37] e.g. *AH* 3. 16. 6, 24. 1; 4. 1. 1; 5. 2. 2. Cf. M. Widmen, 'Irenäus und seine theologischen Väter', *ZTK* 54 (1957), 159.

[38] *AH* 4. 20. 5; R. A. Markus, 'Pleroma and Fulfillment: The Significance of History in St Irenaeus' Opposition to Gnosticism', *VC* 8 (1954), 193–224. It must, however, be recognized that some Gnostics did grant a certain value to history: for instance, according to Ptolemy, historical time enables the development of the pneumatic seed deposited in the Gnostic elect to the point where it is ready to be liberated from this world and its history (cf. *AH* 1. 5. 6).

Chapter 1

The Economy of God

In *AH* 1. 10. 3 Irenaeus specifies that it is only within the overall economy of the true hypothesis of Scripture that theologians are to pursue their theological reflections.[1] After giving his fullest exposition of the rule of truth in *AH* 1. 10. 1 and claiming that this faith is held equally by all churches throughout the world who hold to one and the same tradition, for eloquent leaders can add nothing to its fullness any more than poor speakers can detract from it, Irenaeus turns to consider how it is that some, by virtue of their intelligence (κατά σύνεσιν, *AH* 1. 10. 3), nevertheless know more than others. He excludes the acquisition of more knowledge by the alteration of the 'hypothesis' itself, by positing, for instance, another God besides the Creator or another Christ,[2] but offers instead a series of theological topics, all pertaining to the economy, for further investigation: bringing out more fully what is contained in the parables by adapting them to 'the hypothesis of truth'; explaining the economy of God, which is for the sake of man; why God was patient in regard to the apostasy; why some things were made temporal and others eternal; the different characters of the various covenants; the consignment of all to disobedience, so that God can have mercy on all (cf. Rom. 11: 32); the Incarnation and the appearance of

---

[1] On *AH* 1. 10. 3, see A. Bengsch, *Heilsgeschichte und Heilswissen: Eine Untersuchung zur Struktur und Entfaltung des theologischen Denkens im Werk "Adversus Haereses" des hl. Irenäus von Lyon* (Leipzig, 1957), 51–6, and W. C. van Unnik, 'An Interesting Document of Second Century Theological Discussion (Irenaeus, Adv. Haer. 1. 10. 3)', *VC* 31 (1977), 196–228.

[2] Elsewhere Irenaeus excludes speculation about what God was doing before the creation of the world (*AH* 2. 28. 3) and the use of human analogies to explain the indescribable generation of the Word by the Father (*AH* 2. 28. 4–6), subjects which fall outside of what is revealed in Scripture.

the Beginning, Christ at the end; the inheritance of incorruptibility and the extension of the promise to the Gentiles.
Although *Against the Heresies* does not rehearse all the events
of the economy in as straightforward a fashion as the *Demonstration*, Irenaeus does offer considered reflection on most of
these topics throughout *Against the Heresies*. It will therefore
be useful, first, to follow these reflections, the economy and its
unfolding, together with the way in which man is inscribed
within it, before turning to Irenaeus's anthropology and
asceticism proper.

I THE HANDIWORK OF GOD

The first and most obvious characteristic of this economy is
that the economy itself and all its various stages relate to the
human race, to what God has done for man: Irenaeus gives the
theologian the task of explaining 'the arrangement and economy of God which is for the sake of man' (*AH* 1. 10. 3).
Although, as a consequence of his insistence on the creative
activity of the one God, Irenaeus does develop a fairly
sophisticated theology of creation *ex nihilo*,[3] the question of
the origin of matter in an original act of creation is not central
for him. Rather, his attention is captivated by the continual
divine activity of the Hands of God, the Son and the Spirit,
fashioning the creature formed from mud into the image and
likeness of God.[4] It is in the human race, in each generation,
that the 'economies' of the Father and Son are performed or
enacted by the Holy Spirit according to the will of the Father.[5]

[3] Cf. G. May, *Creation* Ex Nihilo: *The Doctrine of 'Creation out of Nothing'
in Early Christian Thought*, trans. A. S. Worrall (Edinburgh, 1994), 164–78;
A. Orbe, 'San Ireneo y la creación de la materia', *Greg.* 59. 1 (1978), 71–127;
J. Fantino, 'La Création *ex nihilo* chez saint Irénée: Étude historique et
théologique', *RSPhTh* 76. 3 (1992), 421–42.

[4] Cf. Noormann: 'Irenäus versteht die Schöpfung als Inauguration einer
creatio continua, welche gesamte Heilsgeschichte umfaßt und erst im Reich
des Vaters zu ihrem Ziel kommt' (*Irenäus*, 468; cf. 468–77).

[5] *AH* 4. 33. 7: [τὸ πνεῦμα τοῦ θεοῦ . . .] τὸ τὰς οἰκονομίας πατρός τε καὶ υἱοῦ
σκηνοβατοῦν καθ᾽ ἑκάστην γενεὰν ἐν τοῖς ἀνθρώποις καθὼς βούλεται ὁ πατήρ.
Following the text of the *Sacra Parallela*, as edited by Holl, TU 20. 2
(Leipzig, 1899), rather than the variant preferred by Rousseau (εἰς τοὺς
ἀνθρώπους, 'publie en vue des hommes'), to preserve the immediacy of
God's activity in and on the human race, in accord with Irenaeus's

Likewise, it is in the one human race that 'the mysteries of God, which the angels desire to see, are wrought',[6] and the workings of God, and his power and wisdom, are deployed.[7]

In *AH* 4. 14. 1 Irenaeus examines why God initiated the whole economy. It is within the vision of the trinitarian life of glory, evoked by Christ in the sacerdotal prayer recorded in the Gospel of John, that Irenaeus inscribes this economy, beginning with the creation of man. Having described, in the previous chapter, how God accepted the friendship of Abraham, not because he was in need of it, but so that he might bestow eternal life upon Abraham, for friendship with God imparts immortality to those who embrace it,[8] Irenaeus continues:

Neither in the beginning was it because God had need of man that he formed Adam, but that he might have someone on whom he might confer his benefits. For not only before Adam, but also before all creation, the Word glorified his Father, remaining in him, and was himself glorified by the Father, as he did himself declare, 'Father, glorify thou me with the glory which I had with thee before the world was' [John 17: 5]. (*AH* 4. 14. 1)[9]

Irenaeus continues by explaining how, just as to follow the light is to be enlightened, so also to follow the Saviour is to be a partaker in salvation; similarly, those who serve and follow God give nothing to God, but God bestows on those who follow him 'life, incorruption and eternal glory'.[10] That is, if man orientates himself towards God, if he follows him, he is able to receive life and share in his incorruptibility and glory. Man does not possess life in himself, or even a spark or seed of divinity; he does not live from himself. As a created being, man needs God. So Irenaeus continues: 'For as much as God is in

---

fundamental axiom: 'Et hoc Deus ab homine differt, quoniam Deus quidem facit, homo autem fit' (*AH* 4. 11. 2).

[6] *AH* 5. 36. 3.

[7] *AH* 3. 20. 2.

[8] *AH* 4. 13. 4.

[9] Cf. Rousseau's note, SC 100, 233–4.

[10] *AH* 4. 14. 1. Irenaeus uses these terms almost as synonyms, always referring them to God himself; cf. *AH* 2. 13. 9. For a synopsis of the function of these terms in Irenaeus, see Y. de Andia, *Homo vivens: Incorruptibilité et divinisation de l'homme selon Irénée de Lyon* (Paris, 1986), 16–31.

want of nothing, by so much does man stand in need of communion with God. For this is the glory of man, to continue and remain permanently in God's service' (*AH* 4. 14. 1). A few lines later, Irenaeus again picks up the theme of glory evoked by the prayer of Christ: 'I will, that where I am, there they may also be, that they may behold my glory' (John 17: 24); not that Christ vainly boasted of his glory, but that in beholding his glory, the disciples may also participate in it.[11] Irenaeus then concludes this section, as he began it, by emphasizing man's participation in the glory of God as the inspiration for creation. In typical fashion, demonstrating the unity between the Old and the New Testaments, Irenaeus cites a passage from Isaiah, regarding the gathering of the posterity from the four corners of the earth, of 'everyone who is called by my name, whom I created for glory, whom I formed and made' (Isa. 43: 6–7), and links this to the words of Christ:

Inasmuch, then, as 'wheresoever the carcase is, there shall also the eagles be gathered together' [Matt. 24: 28], participating in the glory of the Lord, who has both formed us and prepared us for this, that when we are with him, we may partake of his glory. (*AH* 4. 14. 1)

The divine economy thus begins in the glory which the Word had with the Father before the creation of the world, and culminates in the glorification of the Incarnate Son by the Father, a glory in which the disciples, by beholding it, participate.

The relationship between God and man is based on the unalterable fact of creation: it is God who has skilfully created man, while man has been made by God. And, being made, man must also have a beginning and receive growth and increase:

And indeed in this respect God differs from man, that God indeed makes, but man is made. And he who makes is always the same, while he who is made must receive a beginning, a middle, addition and increase.[12] And God indeed makes well, while man is well made. (*AH* 4. 11. 2)

---

[11] *AH* 4. 14. 1.

[12] Rousseau, referring to the last lines of *AH* 4. 11. 1, argues that *adjectionem et augmentum* should be translated by 'une maturité' (ἀκμήν), as, having received a beginning and a middle, one would 'a priori' expect 'le point culminant ou maturité' (SC 100, 228). The parallel text in *AH* 4. 11. 1 (in both the Latin and the Armenian) would in fact seem to support the Latin

Irenaeus frequently uses the word *plasma*, 'handiwork', to denote man, particularly Adam.[13] This word has the advantage of emphasizing the immediacy of the fashioning of man by God: it is, quite literally, a 'hands-on affair'. It also emphasizes the materiality of man, the fact that man is made from the earth, from mud. Human beings are, for Irenaeus, essentially and profoundly fleshy or earthy: they are skilfully fashioned mud.[14] Furthermore, the term *plasma* indicates the solidarity of the whole human race 'in Adam', a prominent and important principle for Irenaeus.[15]

There are two aspects of the divine fashioning of man that should be noted. First, that in this activity each Person of the Trinity has a particular role: the Father plans and orders, the Son executes these orders and performs the work of creating, and the Spirit nourishes and increases, while man makes continual progress.[16] The Father is the origin of all creation, expressed by the prepositions ἐκ and ἀπό, but he created everything through (διά) the Son and in (ἐν) the Spirit, making the creation of man into a trinitarian activity of the one God.[17] The second important point is the continuity of the creative activity of God, the ordering of the Son, and the nourishing of the Spirit: 'For never at any time did Adam

---

version of *AH* 4. 11. 2. The sense of both *AH* 4. 11. 1 and *AH* 4. 11. 2 must, ultimately, reflect the quotation from Genesis given in 11. 1: 'Increase and multiply.' The context is no less clear: a few lines later, Irenaeus specifically states that man's perfection is to continue indefinitely progressing towards God, 'homo in Deo inventus semper proficiet ad Deum', for while God is uncreated, and so eternally the same, it belongs to the very nature and existence of man to draw ever closer to his Creator. Cf. Bacq, *De l'ancienne à la nouvelle alliance*, 96 n. 2.

[13] Basing himself, perhaps, on Paul's use of Isaiah, Rom. 9: 20 citing Isa. 45: 9. For Irenaeus's use of the word *plasma* and its cognates, see G. Joppich, *Salus Carnis: Eine Untersuchung in der Theologie des hl. Irenäus von Lyon* (Münsterschwarzach, 1965), 49–55.

[14] Cf. Orbe, who characterizes the anthropology of the Gnostics (true man = seed of the divine *pneuma*) as pneumatology, that of Origen (true man = human *nous*) as psychology, and that of Irenaeus as sarcology (*Antropología de San Ireneo* (Madrid, 1969), 527–8).

[15] e.g. *AH* 1. 9. 3; 3. 21. 10; 5. 1. 3.

[16] Cf. *AH*, esp. 4. 38. 3; 2. 30. 9; 3. 24. 2; 4. 20. 1; *Dem.* 5; Andia, *Homo vivens*, 65–7; Fantino, 'La Création *ex nihilo*', 428–38.

[17] Cf. Fantino, 'La Création *ex nihilo*', 429.

escape the Hands of God, to whom the Father speaking said
"Let us make man in our image, after our likeness." '[18] As there
is one God, so there is but one Word and one Spirit, who are
always present with the one human race throughout the various
events which constitute the one economy of God. Yet, as it is
only recently that the Word was made manifest, and 'in the last
times' that the Spirit was poured out in a new manner, all our
knowledge of God is thus bound to his manifestation in the
Incarnation of Christ and his bestowal of the Spirit: that the
Word and the Spirit were no less present in the Old Testament
economies indicates their prophetic or proleptic, and preparatory, but no less real, presence in that period of history.[19]

Whereas God is perfect in all things, man receives advancement and growth towards God; and whereas God, as uncreated, is always the same, so man, as created, will always
advance towards God, his Creator.[20] God never ceases bestowing gifts upon man; nor does man ever cease from receiving
these benefits and being enriched. It is for each human being to
choose how to respond to God's bounteousness, thankfully or
ungratefully, and everything depends on this reaction:

For the vessel of his goodness and the instrument of his glorification is
the man who is thankful towards him that made him; and again, the

---

[18] *AH* 5. 1. 3; cf. *AH* 5. 16. 1, 28. 4.

[19] This is stated in a formula that has the characteristic of a rule of truth in
AH 4. 33. 15. For the continuing presence of the Word, cf. e.g. *AH* 3. 16. 6,
18. 1, and of the Holy Spirit, *AH* 4. 33. 1, 7. As it is through Jesus Christ that
God has chosen to make himself manifest, the Old Testament theophanies are
proleptic, prophetic events, referring to the Incarnate Word; cf. *Dem.* 44–5
and *AH* 4. 5. 2–8. 1. A. Orbe (*Estudios Valentinianos*, 1: *Hacia la primera
teología de la procesión del Verbo* (Rome, 1958), 407, 655–9), and J. Ochagavía
(*Visibile Patris Filius: A Study of Irenaeus's Teaching on Revelation and
Tradition* (Rome, 1964), 69, 89–92), have argued that, prior to the Incarnation, the Word was visible to the mind, an essential visibility or cognoscibility,
fundamentally different from his visibility to the eyes of flesh: two types of
visibility corresponding to his two generations, *ex Patre Deo* and *ex Matre
Virgine*. Such an interpretation, however, undermines the unity and uniqueness of the revelation of God in the incarnate Christ, and, furthermore,
ignores the realism of Irenaeus's understanding of 'seeing', while misunderstanding the nature of prophecy and biblical typology. Cf. A. Houssiau, *La
Christologie de saint Irénée* (Louvain, 1955), 87–93, and R. Tremblay, *La
Manifestation et la vision de Dieu selon saint Irénée de Lyon* (Münster, 1978),
67–76, 91–103.   [20] *AH* 4. 11. 2.

vessel of his just judgement is the ungrateful man, who despises his Maker and is not subject to his Word. (*AH* 4. 11. 2)

Corresponding to the basic principle of the relationship between God and man, that God makes and man is made, is the necessary attitude of thankfulness with which man must respond in order to be able to receive and benefit from the goodness of God: man must *allow* himself to be made, to be fashioned in the image and likeness of God.

II THE TEMPORALITY OF THE ECONOMY

The second important feature of this divine economy is that it is historical: it unfolds in time.[21] Irenaeus states the connection between the divine economy and temporality more explicitly in a shorter rule of truth given in *AH* 1. 22. 1: 'Now, it is the Father who made all things through him [the Word], whether visible or invisible, whether sensible or intelligible, whether temporal, for the sake of some economy, or eternal.' God himself has created all things in the same manner: that is, through the Word. Some things were created invisible and intelligible, the spiritual beings who are eternal and thereby neither subject nor able to change, at least within the course of human temporality. It is not that they themselves are eternal, sustained indefinitely by their own nature, independently of God; for, like all created things, they exist as long as God wills.[22] Rather, their indefinite existence is itself a gift from God and depends on him to maintain it.[23] Others, however, were created visible and sensible, and they are also temporal, and are thus subject to change. It is, therefore, God himself who is responsible for the temporal nature of the sensible universe, and hence its mutability.[24]

More specifically, God created the sensible world and the things in it to be of a temporal or transitory nature in view of an

---

[21] Cf. J. Daniélou, 'S. Irénée et les origines de la théologie de l'histoire', *RSR* 34 (1947), 227–31; Markus, 'Pleroma and Fulfilment'; J. Fantino, 'La Création *ex nihilo*', 438–42.

[22] *AH* 2. 34. 3.

[23] Cf. Fantino, 'La Création *ex nihilo*', 438–9.

[24] Cf. *AH* 2. 3. 1–2.

economy. In *AH* 4. 4. 1–5. 1 Irenaeus provides an important analysis of the rationale for this. The Gnostics argued that if the author of the Law was indeed the true God, then Jerusalem, 'the city of the great King' (Matt. 5: 35), should not have been deserted. Irenaeus suggests that this is similar to maintaining that if straw or vine twigs were a creation of God, they would never be separated from the wheat or grapes. The truth is, rather, that they were created for the sake of the fruit that they produce. All things created in time necessarily have an end in time, so the passing away of the things of the world is a natural occurrence.[25] Thus the law of bondage, which originated with Moses, finished with John the Baptist, when Christ came to fulfil the law and produced the fruit of liberty. Similarly, Jerusalem, which began with David, fulfilling its own time of legislation, came to an end when the New Covenant was revealed. This does not apply only to Jerusalem, for 'the fashion of the whole world must also pass away when the time of its disappearance has come', so that the fruit may be gathered into the granary and the chaff be consumed by the fire.[26] In *AH* 5. 36. 1, referring to a 'preceding book' in which he has explained as far as possible 'the cause of the creation of this world of temporal things', Irenaeus specifies that it is the 'fashion' (*figura*, σχῆμα) of this world that will pass away—that is, that in which the transgression occurred and man has grown old—while the nature or substance (ὑπόστασις, οὐσία) will remain, as its Creator is true and faithful.[27] The beginning and end of all these things is with God, 'who does all things by measure and in order',

[25] Cf. *AH* 4. 4. 1: 'Quaecumque enim temporale initium habent, necesse est ea et finem habere temporalem.'

[26] *AH* 4. 4. 3. Irenaeus is referring to 1 Cor. 7: 31 and to *AH* 4. 3, where he demonstrated, from Paul, David (Ps. 101: 26–9 LXX), and Isaiah (51: 6), that though 'the fashion of the world passes away', God and his servants will remain. In *AH* 2. 34. 2 Irenaeus criticizes those who extend the scope of this principle beyond those things created for the sake of their fruit, as in *AH* 4. 4, to deny the perpetuity of the soul itself. For Irenaeus's position on the soul, cf. Ch. 2.

[27] This ageing of man in the world in which the transgression occurred is to be distinguished from the growth and maturing which brings him, as a creature, ever closer to his Creator. The ageing described in *AH* 5. 36. 1 is thus contrasted with the renewing of man in a new heaven and a new earth, where he continually holds new converse with God.

for they have been realized by the Son who is himself the measure of the immeasurable Father.[28]

In the midst of all these changeable things is man, who, being created, is also changeable, but who has nevertheless been created for immortality. Unlike the wheat and the chaff, where the One who creates them is also the One who separates them, man has been created like God, endowed with reason and free will, and so is himself the cause of his becoming either wheat or chaff.[29] Man belongs to the world of changeable things, yet differs from the rest of the world, in that the world was created to enable the growth of man into the immortality of God.[30] So Irenaeus concludes this section in *AH* 4. 5. 1 thus:

God, therefore, is one and the same, who rolls up the heaven like a book and renews the face of the earth; who made the temporal things for man, so that, maturing in them, he may bear as fruit immortality, and who, through his kindness, also confers eternal things, 'that in the ages to come he may show the exceeding riches of his grace' [Eph. 2: 7]. (*AH* 4. 5. 1)[31]

Thus the various temporal economies have as their goal the growth of man into the immortality of God. Just as the present fashion (σχῆμα) of the world will pass away, so too, when man participates in his immortality, God will transfigure (μετασχη-ματίσει) the initial fashion of man, conforming the corruptible body to the body of his glory.[32] Although he will remain a created being, man has the possibility of sharing in the eternal life of God, and thus of receiving the power of the Uncreated.[33] Only things which are subject to time can grow, and have the possibility of changing their mode of existence while remaining

---

[28] *AH* 4. 4. 2, 19. 2; cf. Bacq, *De l'ancienne à la nouvelle alliance*, 58 n. 2.

[29] *AH* 4. 4. 3. Irenaeus is here countering the Valentinian position, in which, as he reports it, some humans are good by nature and others bad; cf. *AH* 1. 7. 5. For more recent comparisons of the anthropology of Irenaeus and the Gnostics, see R. Berthouzoz, *Liberté et grâce suivant la théologie d'Irénée de Lyon* (Fribourg en Suisse and Paris, 1980); Andia, *Homo vivens*; and the numerous studies by Orbe.

[30] *AH* 5. 29. 1.

[31] For the first section of *AH* 4, finishing with 5. 1, cf. Bacq, *De l'ancienne à la nouvelle alliance*, 60.

[32] *AH* 5. 13. 3, commenting on 1 Cor. 15: 53–5 and Phil. 3: 20–1.

[33] *AH* 4. 38. 3.

what they are by nature. Thus, the temporality of sensible creation is a pre-condition for the possibility of the created sharing in the life of the Uncreated, and this is precisely the outcome of the economy, the reason for which sensible creation was created as temporal.

A further point of interest is that man, although made to be the lord of the earth, was, according to Irenaeus, but newly created, and so appeared as a child in a world specially prepared for his nourishment and growth. The angels were also appointed to be the servants of man. But as they are eternal, and thus not subject to change or growth within the temporal unfolding of sensible creation, they were already fully developed. The infant man was thus 'secretly' established as their lord.[34] Neither in protology nor in eschatology does Irenaeus ever characterize or assimilate man or human life to the angelic: it is man, and the becoming fully human in communion with God in Christ, that is the centre of the divine economy and of Irenaeus's theology.[35]

III THE SIGN OF JONAH

If the aim of God in creating man was to create beings who could partake of his glory and incorruptibility, why then did he not create man as a 'god' from the outset, rather than 'be patient ($\epsilon\mu\alpha\kappa\rho o\theta\acute{\nu}\mu\eta\sigma\epsilon\nu$) in regard to the apostasy of the angels who transgressed and in regard to the disobedience of man', and 'consign all to disobedience that he may have mercy on all' [Rom. 11: 32] (*AH* 1. 10. 3)? Irenaeus provides a sustained analysis of this question in *AH* 4. 37–9 and 3. 20. 1–2. *AH*

---

[34] *Dem.* 12. In *Dem.* 16 Irenaeus explains that the angel 'became jealous and looked on him [the man] with envy, and [so] ruined himself and made the man a sinner, persuading him to disobey the commandment of God'. Cf. Orbe, *Antropología*, 134–5.

[35] For eschatology, cf. *AH* 5. 36. 3. Cf. Orbe, *Antropología*, 206–7; *idem*, 'Supergrediens angelos: AH V. 36. 1', *Greg.* 54 (1973), 5–69; *idem*, *Teología de San Ireneo: Comentario al libro V del Adversus Haereses*, 3 (Madrid, 1988), 659–64. The idea of becoming equal to, or like, the angels played a great role in some strands of contemporary Gnosticism and later Christianity; for the latter, cf. [K.] S. Frank, *ΑΓΓΕΛΙΚΟΣ ΒΙΟΣ: Begriffsanalytische und begriffsgeschichtliche Untersuchung zum 'engelgleichen Leben' im frühen Mönchtum* (Münster, 1964).

4. 37–9 is an exposition, from Scripture, of 'the ancient law of human liberty', the fact that 'God created man free, having, from the beginning, power over himself'.[36] Only such creatures are capable of initiative and response, and this is of fundamental importance, for only such creatures are capable of changing their mode of existence, of growing into the immortality of God. Irenaeus draws out the presuppositions in his opponents' question, by rephrasing it rather bluntly:

'But', they say, 'he should not have created angels such that they were able to transgress, nor men such that they immediately [*statim*] became ungrateful towards him, because they were created rational and capable of examining and judging, and not like irrational or inanimate creatures which are not able to do anything of their own will but are drawn by necessity and force towards the good, with one inclination and one bearing, unable to deviate and without the power of judging, and unable to be anything other than what they were created.' (*AH* 4. 37. 6)

Irenaeus points out that it would not have benefited either God or man for this to have been the case: communion with God would have been something neither desired nor sought after; it would be by nature and not by choice.[37] Freedom, therefore, along with temporality, is a pre-condition for creatures to be capable of becoming 'other' than what they were created: for creatures to enter into communion with God, and so be transfigured.

Irenaeus continues, in *AH* 4. 37. 7, by citing Matt. 11: 12 and 1 Cor. 9: 24–7, to emphasize the need for struggle, on the grounds that endeavour heightens the appreciation of the gift. He further points out that just as sight is desired more by those who know blindness and health is prized more by those who know disease, so life is treasured more by those acquainted with death. In *AH* 4. 39. 1 Irenaeus develops this analysis by contrasting two types of knowledge: that gained through experience and that arrived at by opinion. As the tongue

[36] *AH* 4. 37. 1. On the place of *AH* 4. 37–9, the so-called Treatise on Free Will, in *Against the Heresies*, see Bacq, *De l'ancienne à la nouvelle alliance*, 363–88. For a more comprehensive analysis of this section, see Berthouzoz, *Liberté et grâce*, 189–243. For Irenaeus's understanding of 'free will', see Orbe, *Antropología*, 165–95, and Berthouzoz, *Liberté et grâce*, 195–8.

[37] *AH* 4. 37. 6.

learns of bitterness and sweetness only through experience, so
the mind receives knowledge (*disciplina*) of the good—obedience to God, which is life for man—through the experience of
both good and evil—the latter being disobedience, which is
death for man. In this way, through experience of both, and
casting away disobedience through repentance, man becomes
ever more tenacious in his obedience to God. But if he tries to
avoid the knowledge of both of these, and the twofold faculty of
knowledge, he will forget himself and kill his humanity.[38] So,
Irenaeus continues in *AH* 4. 37. 7, the heavenly kingdom is
more precious to those who have known the earthly kingdom,
and, if they prize it more, so will they love it more; and loving it
more, they will be more glorified by God. Irenaeus thus
concludes:

God therefore has borne[39] all these things for our sake, in order that,
having been instructed through all things, henceforth we may be
scrupulous in all things and, having been taught how to love God in
accordance with reason, remain in his love: God exhibiting patience
[*magnanimitatem*] in regard to the apostasy of man, and man being
taught by it, as the prophet says: 'Your own apostasy shall heal you'
[Jer. 2: 19]. (*AH* 4. 37. 7)

Irenaeus continues immediately by placing this particular
action of God within the economy as a whole:

God, thus, determining all things beforehand for the perfection of
man, and towards the realization and manifestation of his economies,
that goodness may be displayed and righteousness accomplished, and
that the Church may be 'conformed to the image of his Son' [Rom.

---

[38] *AH* 4. 39. 1: 'Si autem utrorumque eorum cognitionem et duplices
sensus cogitationis quis defugiat, latenter semetipsum occidit hominem.' On
this passage, see Berthouzoz, *Liberté et grâce*, 234–8.

[39] Rousseau translates 'sustinuit' by 'a permis'; however, as Berthouzoz
observes, such a translation reflects a later theological perspective, so he
proposes instead 'a supporté' (*Liberté et grâce*, 216 n. 79). *AH* 5. 2. 3 employs
ἀνέχω in a similar context, a verb which in its NT usage (the background for
much of Irenaeus's vocabulary) always appears in the middle voice, generally
with the sense of 'to bear, to endure'—e.g. Matt. 17: 17, etc. The Armenian of
AH 4. 37. 7 seems to be an attempt to explain the middle voice, 'He took to
himself' (TU 35. 2, 137. 23, for *AH* 5. 2. 3, 157. 5). The idea mentioned in
AH 5. 2. 3, that God has borne our death that we might not be ignorant either
of God or of ourselves, echoes Irenaeus's startling words at the end of *AH*
4. 39. 1, cited in the previous note.

8: 29], and that, finally, man may be brought to such maturity as to see and comprehend God. (*AH* 4. 37. 7)

That Irenaeus can inscribe man's apostasy into the unfolding of the divine economy indicates that he did not consider the economy simply as a plan which progresses automatically. Rather, God created beings capable of initiative, as only such beings would be able to respond freely to God and to love him. The aim of the whole economy is twofold: first, the perfection of man, by, second, the realization and manifestation of the economies of God—a perfection which, at the same time, displays his goodness and realizes his justice. Finally, if *AH* 4. 37–9, in discussing the question of human freedom, has seemed to privatize the relationship to God of each human person by emphasizing the need for each to gain personal experience and to endeavour to love God more, the section nevertheless ends with the assertion that through this process the Church, a community, is conformed to the image of the Son, and in this way each is brought to such perfection as to see and comprehend God.

In *AH* 4. 38 Irenaeus approaches the same problem from a different angle. He argues that God could have created man perfect or as a 'god' from the beginning, for all things are possible to him. However, created things, by virtue of being created, are necessarily inferior to the One who created them, and so fall short of the perfect: they are of a later date, infantile, and so unaccustomed to, and unexercised in, perfect conduct.[40] Yet, just as it is possible for a mother to give an infant solid food, so too God could have made man 'perfect' from the beginning, but man, still in his infancy, could not have received this perfection.[41] It is not that the omnipotence of God is restricted by the nature of that on which he is working,[42] or

---

[40] *AH* 4. 38. 1.

[41] *AH* 4. 38. 1. Bacq interprets *AH* 4. 38. 4 (commenting on Ps. 81: 6–7 LXX) as stating that God did indeed bestow the power of his divinity on the human race, but that man, being unable to bear it, lost it, though it can now be regained through Christ's work of recapitulation (*De l'ancienne à la nouvelle alliance*, 384). However, in *AH* 4. 37–9 Irenaeus is speaking not of protology, but of the law of human growth which applies to all. Cf. e.g. *AH* 4. 39. 2: 'Oportet enem te primo quidem ordinem hominis custodire, tunc deinde participari gloriae Dei.'

[42] On this apparent flaw in Irenaeus's argument, see Minns, *Irenaeus*, 73–4.

that the infantile state, despite only beginning to grow towards its full perfection, is itself imperfect.[43] As a creature, man can never be uncreated, can never cease existing in the mode proper to a creature—that is, being created. But the aim of this creating or fashioning of man is that he should come to be ever more fully in the image and likeness of the uncreated God. There can be, for man, no end to this process, since he can never become uncreated; his perfection lies, instead, in his continual submission to the creative activity of God, through which he is brought to share in the glory of the Uncreated.[44] Finally, Irenaeus concludes *AH* 4. 38 by recapitulating the preceding discussion in a few brief strokes:

It was necessary, first, for nature to be manifest; after which, for what was mortal to be conquered and swallowed up by immortality, and the corruptible by incorruptibility, and for man to be made in the image and likeness of God, having received the knowledge of good and evil. (*AH* 4. 38. 4)[45]

Thus creation and salvation, the appearance of human nature and the conquering of mortality by immortality, belong to the same economy, the purposeful arrangement of history, in which the acquisition of the knowledge of good and evil has its place, contributing to the realization, in the end, of the original divine intention of making man in the image and likeness of God.

In *AH* 4. 37–9 Irenaeus speaks of God's patience in the face of the apostasy of man, and explains it, within the framework of God's overall economy, by the general principle of the need for newly created man to acquire experience, of both good and evil, in order to hold ever more firmly to the good and to continue indefinitely progressing towards God, becoming ever more fully in his image and likeness. Irenaeus treats the same

---

[43] On the relationship between the vocation of growth and the perfection of the human state of childhood, see esp. Wingren, *Man and the Incarnation*, 20, 26–35.

[44] *AH* 4. 38. 3; cf. *AH* 4. 11. 2. The whole tenor of Irenaeus's thought on this point is strikingly similar to that of Gregory of Nyssa: e.g. *On Perfection*, ed. W. Jaeger, in *Gregorii Nysseni Opera*, 8. 1 (Leiden, 1986), 214; trans. V. W. Callahan FC 58 (Washington, 1967), 122; cf. J. Daniélou, *L'Être et le temps chez Grégoire de Nysse* (Leiden, 1970), 114.

[45] Cf. 2 Cor. 5: 4; 1 Cor. 15: 53; Gen. 1: 26, 3: 5, 3: 22.

question of God's great patience in the face of man's apostasy
in *AH* 3. 20. 1–2, but this time he makes two points clearer:
first, how the vocation of growth, described in *AH* 4. 37–9,
relates to the specific economy of the Incarnation, the Passion,
and Christ's work of recapitulation;[46] and second, how the
general principle elaborated in *AH* 4. 37–9 relates to protology.

Irenaeus begins *AH* 3. 20 by asserting that God was patient
with man's apostasy, as he foresaw the victory which would be
granted to man through the Word; for, as strength is made
perfect in weakness, God could thus demonstrate his goodness
and magnificent power.[47] As an example of this, Irenaeus gives
the case of Jonah, who, by God's arrangement, was swallowed
by the whale, not that he should thus perish, but that, having
been cast out, he might be more obedient to God, and so
glorify more the One who had unexpectedly saved him.[48]
Irenaeus continues:

so also, from the beginning, God did bear[49] man to be swallowed up
by the great whale, who was the author of transgression, not that he
should perish altogether when so engulfed, but arranging in advance
the finding of salvation, which was accomplished by the Word,
through the 'sign of Jonah' [Matt. 12: 39–40], for those who held
the same opinion as Jonah regarding God, and who confessed, and
said, 'I am a servant of the Lord, and I worship the Lord God of
heaven, who made the sea and the dry land' [Jonah 1: 9], that man,
receiving an unhoped for salvation from God, might rise from the
dead, and glorify God, and utter the word prophesied by Jonah, 'I
cried to the Lord my God in my affliction, and he heard me from the

---

[46] This is not to suggest, however, that these themes are absent from *AH*
4. 37–9, or that the theology of growth described therein is absent from the
rest of Irenaeus's work; these themes are two aspects of one and the same
mystery. Cf. Bacq, *De l'ancienne à la nouvelle alliance*, 382.

[47] *AH* 3. 20. 1. Cf. 2 Cor. 12: 9.

[48] For a discussion of this passage, see G. Jouassard, 'Le "Signe de Jonas"
dans le livre IIIe de l'*Adversus haereses* de saint Irénée', in *L'Homme devant
Dieu: Mélanges offerts au Père Henri de Lubac*, 1: *Exégèse et patristique* (Paris,
1963), 235–46.

[49] Although the Latin is *fuit patiens*, Rousseau suggests that the Greek was
ἠνέσχετο and again translates this by 'a permis'; I have preferred 'bear', see my
comments above on *AH* 4. 37. 7. If the parallel with Jonah is indeed to hold,
God was more actively involved in this event than is suggested by 'a permis';
in Jonah 2: 1, it is said that the Lord appointed (προσέταξεν) a great whale to
swallow up Jonah.

belly of hell' [Jonah 2: 2], and that he might always continue glorifying God, and giving thanks without ceasing for that salvation which he has obtained from Him, 'that no flesh should glory in the Lord's presence' [1 Cor. 1: 29], and that man should never adopt an opposite opinion with regard to God, supposing that the incorruptibility which surrounds him is his own by nature, nor, by not holding the truth, should boast with empty superciliousness, as if he was by nature like to God. (*AH* 3. 20. 1)

So, for Irenaeus, God has borne man, from the beginning, while he was swallowed up by the whale.[50] Although God did not actually create the human race *in* this condition, there was, nevertheless, no period of time prior to which human beings were not engulfed: there is, for Irenaeus, no lost golden age of primordial perfection.[51] This is not to deny that man transgressed or apostatized, and that there was an 'author of transgression', an *agent provocateur* of the human transgression.[52] However, the law which God gave to Adam and Eve to obey was that of recognizing that they had as their Lord the Lord of all[53]—that is, the general law of human existence, confessed by Jonah in the above quotation. Had they kept this law, they would have remained immortal; but if they were to take up 'an attitude of self-conceited arrogance', to suppose

[50] For a similarly strong assertion, see Maximus the Confessor, who speaks of the first man inclining towards the senses, rather than following his natural desire for God, ἅμα τῷ γενέσθαι (*Quaestiones ad Thalassium*, 61; PG 90. 628a). For both Irenaeus and Maximus there is no protological age of original perfection: true human perfection is to be found only in the eschaton, realized by Christ 'in the last times', and anticipated by Christians in this present age.

[51] Irenaeus does, nevertheless, refer to the pre-lapsarian existence of Adam in occasional comments and discussion in *Against the Heresies*—e.g. *AH* 3. 22–3. The comments here, however, are made within the Pauline Adam–Christ framework. In *Dem.* 11–16, Irenaeus provides a sustained commentary on the creation and paradisiacal life of Adam and Eve, which will be analysed below, Ch. 2. But it is to be noted that the theology which Irenaeus develops out of the opening chapters of Genesis is that of the dependence of the human race on God and the need for grateful obedience, of human infancy and the need for growth: that is, it *functions*, within the *Demonstration*, to establish the framework within which salvation history unfolds, as e.g. *AH* 4. 14. 1 does with respect to 14. 2, dealt with in the previous section and the next respectively.

[52] For the Devil's role in man's apostasy, cf. *AH* 3. 23. 1–3; 4. pref. 4, 40. 3; *Dem.* 16.

[53] *Dem.* 15.

that this immortality which they enjoyed was theirs by nature,
as it is God's by nature, then, as they would no longer be
receiving the gift of existence from God, they would thus
become subject to death.[54] Hence the Devil's temptation,
according to Irenaeus, is to offer what he could not give:
Adam and Eve were beguiled under 'the pretext of immortality'.[55] Man's death is the result of apostasy, of turning away
from the one and only source of life; and at the same time it is
the expression of the Devil's dominion over the human race.

The newly created humans were inexperienced, however; so
they immediately gave way to temptation.[56] But, just as Jonah
was swallowed by the whale, so that he might learn the true
attitude to take towards God, so was man engulfed from the
beginning as part of the divine pedagogy, receiving an
unhoped-for, but none the less divinely foreseen, salvation,
accomplished by the Word through the 'sign of Jonah'. This
pedagogy, the whole of the divine economy, thus acquaints
man both with his own weakness, his total dependence on God,
and also with the strength and graciousness of God. As
Irenaeus explains:

Such then was the patience of God, that man, passing through all
things and acquiring knowledge of death, then attaining to the
resurrection from the dead, and learning by experience whence he
has been delivered, may thus always give thanks to the Lord, having
received from him the gift of incorruptibility, and may love him the
more, for 'he to whom more is forgiven, loveth more' [cf. Luke
7: 42–3], and may himself know how mortal and weak he is, but also
understand that God is so immortal and powerful as to bestow
immortality on the mortal and eternity on the temporal, and that he
may also know the other powers of God made manifest in himself
and, being taught by them, may think of God in accordance with the
greatness of God. For the glory of man is God, while the vessel of the
workings of God, and of all his wisdom and power is man. (*AH*
3. 20. 2)[57]

---

[54] *Dem.* 15.
[55] *AH* 3. 23. 5; 4. pref. 4.
[56] Cf. esp. *AH* 4. 40. 3, where Irenaeus mitigates the disobedience of
humans by attributing it to a lack of care and inexperience, in contrast to the
conscious sowing of tares by the Devil. Cf. *AH* 3. 23. 3.
[57] Cf. *AH* 5. 2. 3.

God was thus patient, while man learnt by experience of his own weakness and death in his ungrateful apostasy, knowing that having passed through this experience, and having an unhoped-for salvation bestowed upon him, man would remain ever more thankful to God, willing to accept from him the eternal existence which he alone can give. It is within this perspective that Irenaeus immediately cites Paul's assertion that 'God has consigned all to disobedience, that he may have mercy on all' (Rom. 11: 32). Both dimensions of this economy, the engulfing of the human and the salvation wrought by the Word, are represented by Jonah, who thus becomes a type of both the transgressing human race and its Saviour.

Thus, for Irenaeus, human death plays a pedagogical role within the divine economy, enabling man to experience to the uttermost his weakness and mortality in apostasy from God, the only source of life.[58] Irenaeus also follows Theophilus of Antioch in ascribing a positive, remedial value to death. In *AH* 3. 23. 6 Irenaeus describes the action of God in response to the apostasy:

Wherefore also he drove him [Adam] out of Paradise, and removed him far from the tree of life, not because he envied him the tree of life, as some venture to assert, but having mercy on him, that he should not continue a transgressor for ever, nor that the sin which surrounded him should be immortal, and evil interminable and irremediable. But he set a bound to his transgression, by interposing death and causing sin to cease, putting an end to it by the dissolution of the flesh into the earth, so that man, ceasing at length to live to sin, and dying to it, might begin to live to God [cf. Gen. 3: 22–4; Rom. 6: 2, 10]. (*AH* 3. 23. 6)[59]

---

[58] With regard to the problem of death in nature, apart from that of man, Irenaeus sometimes seems to consider death as a natural occurrence, for what comes to be will also cease to be; although it is also possible that he envisaged the abolition of all death in the Kingdom of the Son. Irenaeus never specifically attempted to tackle this point, but kept to Scripture, which clearly teaches that man was created for life, and that his death is the result of his apostasy. Cf. Wingren, *Man and the Incarnation*, 55–60, 193–7.

[59] Cf. Theophilus of Antioch, *To Autolycus*, 2. 26. This positive evaluation of death, as putting an end to sin through the dissolution of man into the earth, recurs in later patristic writings: e.g. Gregory of Nyssa, *Catechetical Oration*, 8; cf. P. Nellas, *Deification in Christ* (New York, 1987), 64–6. The

Thus, from this perspective, the subjection of man to death was
an act of mercy, for had man been created in such a way as to be
able to remain immortal after apostatizing from God (if, for
instance, he possessed a life of his own, other than the one he
receives from God), then sin and evil would also have remained
immortal and thus irremediable, and so God's economy would
have been frustrated, conquered by the serpent.[60]

It has to be noted, however, that despite the pedagogical
character of the apostasy and the pedagogical and remedial
characteristics of death, Irenaeus does not trivialize either.
Whilst the apostasy and death can be seen positively from
the point of view of the unfolding of the economy, they are,
nevertheless, nothing less than a catastrophe: the being created
by God for communion with himself in his glory turned his
back on him; man, the image of God, created for life, rots in the
earth. This is the victory of the Devil over man; his power
consists of inciting to apostasy and transgression, and into this
he has enticed and imprisoned mankind.[61] It was not possible
for man, who had been thus conquered and destroyed by
disobedience, to fight back and obtain the prize of victory.
This could be done only by the Word of God becoming
incarnate, stooping low, even unto death, and so fulfilling the
economy of salvation.[62] Although one can discern two dimensions to the apostasy and death, pedagogical and catastrophic,
these remain a matter of perspective: for Irenaeus, there is but
the one economy of the one God, which is the history unfolded
in Scripture.

IV   THE UNFOLDING OF THE
ECONOMY

Irenaeus continues his analysis of the finality of the act of
creation in *AH* 4. 14. 1, which we considered earlier, with a

positive, pedagogical value of death within the whole economy seems to be
peculiar to Irenaeus.

   [60] *AH* 3. 23. 1.   [61] *AH* 5. 21. 3.
   [62] *AH* 3. 18. 2. Minns is probably right to consider *replasmare* here as a
misreading of ἀναπλησσεῖν rather than a translation of ἀναπλασσεῖν (*Irenaeus*,
101 n. 18); the same confusion is evident at *AH* 4. 24. 1, where for *reformasse*
the Armenian has 'to fight and strike' (TU 35. 2, 83. 3).

summary description, in *AH* 4. 14. 2, of the progressive unfolding of the economy:

Thus God, from the beginning, fashioned man for his munificence; and chose the patriarchs for the sake of their salvation; and formed in advance a people, teaching the uneducated to follow God; and prepared the prophets, accustoming man on the earth to bear his Spirit and to have communion with God; he himself, indeed, having need of nothing, but granting communion with himself to those who stood in need of it. To those that pleased him, he sketched out like an architect, the construction of salvation;[63] and to those who did not see, in Egypt, he himself gave guidance; and to those who were unruly, in the desert, he promulgated a very suitable Law; while to those who entered into the good land he bestowed the appropriate inheritance; finally, for those converted to the Father, he killed the fatted calf and presented them with the finest robe.[64] Thus, in many ways, he harmonized the human race to the symphony of salvation. (*AH* 4. 14. 2)[65]

This 'construction of salvation' encompasses the whole history of the human race unfolded in Scripture. In this passage, Irenaeus summarizes this history twice, in two parallel

[63] Bacq suggests that the reference is to Gen. 6: 13–16, where God describes the plan for the ark to Noah (*De l'ancienne à la nouvelle alliance*, 117).

[64] Following Rousseau's translation of *primam stolam*, which he interprets as a 'symbole du don de la vie éternelle aux hommes' (SC 100, 234). Others take the adjective *prima* to mean 'original' and identify the *stola* with the 'robe of holiness from the Spirit' (*AH* 3. 23. 5) with which Adam was clothed in Paradise, before he lost both the Spirit and the ὁμοίωσις. Cf. Orbe, *Antropología*, 214–18, esp. n. 126; H. J. Jaschke, *Der Heilige Geist im Bekenntnis der Kirche* (Münster, 1976), 254–6; and Andia, *Homo vivens*, 95–9. The place of the Holy Spirit in Irenaeus's anthropology will be examined in Ch. 2. Here, in *AH* 4. 14. 2, the context is clearly an exegesis of the parable of the Prodigal Son (Luke 15: 11–32), where the father simply bestows on his repentant son the best that he has, and no reference is made to what type of clothing he may have worn before his adventures; as Bacq notes, Irenaeus uses *donans*, not *restaurans* or *restituens* (*De l'ancienne à la nouvelle alliance*, 118 n. 1).

[65] Here I am following the Armenian, which suggests a musical context for 'harmonized'; cf. Bacq, *De l'ancienne à la nouvelle alliance*, 118 n. 2. The 'symphony' is a further reference to the parable of the Prodigal Son, who, as he approached home, heard music (συμφωνία, Luke 15: 25). The musical metaphor of a 'symphony' and the corresponding adjective occurs throughout Irenaeus's work. On the 'accustoming' between God and man, see P. Évieux, 'La Théologie de l'accoutumance chez saint Irénée', *RSR* 55 (1967), 5–54.

sequences. Following the initial munificent creation, God chose the patriarchs 'for their salvation'; that is, he selected those who were to be fathers of a race, individuals whose names were to have a universal significance. To these, he sketched out the construction of salvation, for in them and through them salvation was to be achieved. This was accomplished through the theophanies recorded in Genesis, in which the future Incarnation and the economy of the Passion were prophetically foreseen in the Spirit, and found a response in the patriarchs' faith and trust, thereby effecting salvation.[66]

Having chosen the heads of the race, God then formed a people for himself, a community grounded and unified by the guidance given in Egypt and the Law given through Moses. Irenaeus continues, in *AH* 4. 14. 3, by explaining how this community was founded not only upon the Word given in the Law, but also through the tabernacle and the temple, the sacrifices and the oblations, 'types' by which 'they learned to fear God and to continue in His service'. This formation of the people was nevertheless preparatory, anticipating the future economies and the establishment of the Church.

After the journey through the desert, God bestowed upon the people who entered the good land an appropriate inheritance.[67] The next stage of the economy was that of the prophets. Like the patriarchs, the prophets have a twofold significance: both individual, in that they were moved by the Spirit; and universal, for in them mortal man became accustomed to bear the Spirit and to hold communion with God. This stage still pointed forward: in the persons of the prophets the people learned to recognize those sent from God, and in their suffering to see the suffering of the One to come, who would also realize in perfection the communion between God and man, bearing and imparting the fullness of the Spirit.

Finally, for those who converted to the Father—that is, the Gentiles[68]—God sacrificed his Son, the 'fatted calf', and

[66] *AH* 4. 5. 5.

[67] The entry into the good land described in Joshua also plays a typological role, referring to the reign, in the resurrection of the just, of the patriarchs, to whom the promise was made, and their seed (the Church, through adoption), together with Christ on the earth into which they never entered. Cf. *AH* 5. 32. 2.

[68] The identification of the prodigal son with the Gentiles is made by Bacq,

bestowed upon them the 'finest robe'. Such, then, are the many ways by which God harmonized the human race in the symphony of salvation which is the divine economy: choosing his friends, forming a people out of them, and finally making those who were not a people into his people.[69]

Irenaeus continues by considering the multiplicity of ways whereby man is brought to salvation from the point of view of God, who, though himself simple,[70] nevertheless accomplishes his economy in a manifold fashion. In his idiosyncratic manner, Irenaeus immediately joins to the 'many ways of the symphony of salvation' a quotation from Revelation (1: 15): 'And his voice was as the sound of many waters.'[71] For 'the Spirit of God is like many waters', and the Father is 'both rich and multiple', and the Word also is 'rich and multiple', manifesting the Father in different forms or figures according to the particular economy.[72] The image of a symphony or melody occurs again in *AH* 4. 20. 7, where it harmonizes the various events and the 'richness' of God, bringing them all into their appropriate time, their *kairos*, for the benefit of man:

Thus, from the beginning, the Son is the Revealer [*Enarrator*] of the Father, since he is with the Father from the beginning: the prophetic visions, the diversity of graces, his ministries, the glorification of the Father, all these, in the manner of a melody, compositely and harmoniously, he has unfolded to the human race at the appropriate time for their advantage. For where there is a melody, there is a composition; where there is a composition, there is appropriate time; and where there is appropriate time, there is advantage. (*AH* 4. 20. 7)

It is for this that the Word, in the Incarnation, became the 'dispenser of the Paternal grace' for the advantage of men,

---

De l'ancienne à la nouvelle alliance, 117. The only other place where Irenaeus refers to this parable is *AH* 4. 36. 7, to demonstrate that both those called first, Israel, and those called later, the Gentiles, have one and the same Father. Cf. ibid. 249.

[69] *AH* 1. 10. 3; Hos. 2: 23; Rom. 9: 25.

[70] Cf. e.g. *AH* 2. 13. 3, 28. 5.

[71] The connecting word is the φωνή of Rev. 1: 15, which picks up on the συμφωνία, which itself is an allusion to the parable of the Prodigal Son commented on in the preceding lines; cf. Bacq, *De l'ancienne à la nouvelle alliance*, 118 n. 2.

[72] Cf. *AH* 4. 14. 2, 20. 11.

'revealing God to men and presenting man to God'.[73] There is a certain dialectic in this revelation, for the Word always preserves the invisibility of the Father, lest man despise God and so that he might always have something towards which to advance, yet reveals God to men, so that they should not cease to be.[74] Man can never see God by his own powers, but only as, when, and how God wills, for he is powerful in all things. Whilst God had earlier been seen prophetically in the Spirit, he is now seen adoptively in the Son; but only in the Kingdom will man see him 'paternally', having been prepared by the Spirit for the Son, who leads man to the Father, who bestows incorruptibility and eternal life.[75]

We saw earlier how the whole divine economy was undertaken to extend the inner trinitarian life of glory to the disciples by their contemplation of the Son of God in the flesh, glorified with the glory he had with the Father from before all time, and by this contemplation, their participation in his glory. Now, in *AH* 4. 20. 7, Irenaeus explains what this glory is:

For the glory of God is a living man, and the life of man consists in beholding God: for if the manifestation of God through the creation affords life to all living on earth, much more does that revelation of the Father which comes through the Word give life to those who see God.

This is perhaps the most profound and beautiful reflection of Irenaeus: the vibrant unity between the glory of God and the living man, the life-giving manifestation of God and the vision of God by his creatures.[76] Rather than seeing human life as

[73] *AH* 4. 20. 7.

[74] Ibid.

[75] *AH* 4. 20. 5.

[76] Irenaeus had already made the identification of life and the vision of God in *AH* 4. 20. 5. There is a pervasive trend in current scholarship to assert that the life that Irenaeus writes about in *AH* 4. 20. 5 is '[E]vidently . . . other than physical and is the true life of humans' (M. A. Donovan, 'Alive to the Glory of God', *TS* 49. 2 (1988), 289). Although Irenaeus does write about the created life, the breath of life, and uncreated life, the life-giving Spirit, the contrast between a 'physical' or natural life and a 'true', supernatural life, which is not physical, is utterly foreign to Irenaeus's thought and vitiates its dynamism: as man, for Irenaeus, is essentially physical, made from mud, it is difficult to see how he can possess or live a life in a manner other than physical, unless we spiritualize our notion of life and our understanding of the 'true' human being

governed by an injunction to glorify God, for Irenaeus it is
God who seeks to glorify man, bringing him to share ever more
fully in his own glory.[77] It is this desire of God that prompted
his initial creation of man, in a world specially prepared for
this, and that has guided his diverse dealings with the human
race throughout the one economy.

V AT THE END, THE BEGINNING

Having seen how the divine economy is directed towards the
growth of man into the life, incorruptibility, and glory of God,
and the way in which Irenaeus considered that the human race
apostatized and was engulfed from the beginning, we are now
in a position to consider the most striking question that
Irenaeus sets before the theologian in *AH* 1. 10. 3: why is it
that the Beginning, Christ, true God and true man, appeared at
the end?

We have had occasion to see how, for Irenaeus, God's self-
manifestation and self-communication refers exclusively to the
Incarnation. The Old Testament theophanies were prophetic,
proleptic events, always referring to the Incarnation, preparing
the human race for the reception of this event and training
them to follow God. Likewise, in the Old Testament, the
human race was gradually being accustomed to bear the
Spirit, who, in the economy of the Incarnation, at the Baptism,
was the unction with which the Father anointed Jesus to be the
Christ,[78] so that the Spirit himself might also 'with him
[Christ] become accustomed to dwell in the human race and
to rest in men and to reside in the handiwork of God'.[79] It is
only in the eschatological event, 'at the end of time', that God
fully reveals himself in Christ and fully communicates his
Spirit, and that the full perfection of man is manifested.
Thus, the truth of man is eschatological, not protological: it

---

in a Gnostic fashion. Cf. *AH* 5. 3. 3: when God provides life, we live: ἐκείνου
γὰρ παρέχοντος ἡμῖν τὴν ζωήν, ζῶμεν. On the significance and scope of 'life' in
Irenaeus's writings, see below, Ch. 2.

[77] Cf. A. Orbe, 'Gloria Dei vivens homo: Análisis de Ireneo, *adv. haer.*
IV. 20. 1–7', *Greg.* 73. 2 (1992), 263.

[78] Cf. *AH* 3. 6. 1, 9. 3, 12. 7, 18. 3; *Dem.* 40, 41.

[79] *AH* 3. 17. 1.

lies hidden with Christ in God (cf. Col. 3: 3). It is in this sense that Irenaeus understands the apostle Paul's description of Adam as the 'type of the One to come' (τύπος τοῦ μέλλοντος, Rom. 5: 14). The genealogy of Jesus given in the Gospel according to Luke demonstrates, according to Irenaeus, how Christ recapitulated all generations back to Adam, uniting the end to the beginning:

Hence, also, Adam himself was termed by Paul 'the type of the One who was to come', because the Word, the Maker of all things, prefigured in him the economy that was to come of the humanity in regard to the Son of God; God having established that the first man should be psychical, namely, that he should be saved by the spiritual. For, since he who saves already existed, it was necessary that he who would be saved should come into existence, that the One who saves should not exist in vain. (*AH* 3. 22. 3)[80]

In Adam the Word prefigured, sketched out in advance, the fullness of the human being that would be manifested in the economy of the Incarnation. Hence, Adam is a type of the One to come.[81] However, the One who was to come existed before Adam; it was by him and for him that Adam came into being. So, although only appearing at the end, this One is indeed the Beginning.

This passage from *AH* 3. 22. 3 also introduces a second great Pauline theme: that the first Adam was psychical, while the last is spiritual (cf. 1 Cor. 15: 45–8; Gen. 2: 7). Adam was established as a psychical being, animated by the breath of life, as a type of, and to be saved by, the Spiritual One, he who was vivified by the Spirit. In this schema, Irenaeus makes no mention of the apostasy: the apostasy rendered the creature who had been created for immortality mortal; it did not transform an originally 'spiritual' Adam into a merely 'psychical' being. Through the apostasy Adam and Eve lost the

---

[80] On this difficult text see Rousseau's note, SC 210, 371–2; J. A. de Aldama, 'Adam, typus futuri', *Sacris Erudiri*, 13 (1962), 266–80; and Noormann, *Irenäus*, 160–2.

[81] It is important to note the literalism of Irenaeus's understanding of τύπος, as an imprint or impression. As a type of Christ, Adam 'does not simply prefigure Christ, but bears in his own body the lineaments of the incarnate Son of God' (Minns, *Irenaeus*, 86). We will see more of this when considering Irenaeus's understanding of the 'image' of God; see Ch. 2.

'strength' of the 'breath of life'; they did not 'lose' the Spirit.[82]
The Spirit was certainly present with Adam in Paradise, yet
never ceased being present with the human race throughout the
foreseen apostasy.[83] But the Spirit was present with Adam and
the human race in a preparatory manner, typifying the fullness
which was, and still is, to come. The way in which the economy
unfolded includes the apostasy. Nevertheless, this fact does not
determine the relationship of salvation described in *AH* 3. 22. 3;
Irenaeus understands 'salvation' as the continuing process of
God's activity in his handiwork, man, bringing him, when he
allows himself to be skilfully fashioned, to the stature of the
Saviour.

Irenaeus draws a similar parallel between the first, psychical
Adam and the perfection of man in the Word and Spirit in the
last times, in *AH* 5. 1. 3. Here the parallel is made slightly more
complicated, as Irenaeus includes in the picture the apostasy of
Adam and man's state of death in him. Irenaeus is writing
about the Ebionites, for whom Christ was the human child of
Mary and Joseph, and who therefore denied the possibility of
the union of God and man, so rejected the possibility of a new
generation:

> they remain in that Adam who had been conquered and was expelled
> from Paradise: not considering that as, at the beginning of our
> formation in Adam, the breath of life which proceeded from God,
> having been united to what had been fashioned, animated man, and
> manifested him as a being endowed with reason; so also, in the end,
> the Word of the Father and the Spirit of God having become united
> with the ancient substance of Adam's formation, rendered man living
> and perfect, receptive of the perfect Father, in order that as in the
> psychical we all die, so in the spiritual we all may be made alive [1 Cor.
> 15: 22]. (*AH* 5. 1. 3)

Here the parallel is drawn between man's original formation in
Adam, as a psychical being, animated with the breath of life

---

[82] *Dem.* 14; mistranslated by J. P. Smith, *St Irenaeus: Proof of the Apostolic
Preaching*, ACW 16 (New York, 1952), who justifies his translation by the
later distinction between the natural life of the breath and the supernatural life
of the Spirit (ibid. 151–2 nn. 82–3). The relationship between the 'breath of
life' and the 'life-giving Spirit' will be dealt with below, Ch. 2.

[83] Cf. e.g. *AH* 5. 1. 3; 4. 33. 1, 7, discussed in the section on 'The
Handiwork of God'.

that comes from God, and the union of the Word and the Spirit with that formation, rendering man living and perfect. Encompassing this parallel is the observation that Adam was conquered and expelled from Paradise, becoming subject to death, as are those who remain in his formation, in its post-lapsarian state. But rather than a return to the pre-lapsarian state of the psychical formation, now, through the Incarnation, the union of the Word and Spirit with the ancient substance of Adam's formation, man has the opportunity to be made alive again— this time, however, in the spiritual One, himself also thereby becoming spiritual.

The Incarnation of the Word is thus central to the accomplishment of the divine economy, and although perhaps conditioned by human apostasy, the Incarnation was certainly not occasioned by it.[84] The goal of the economy is the manifestation of the glory of God in a fully living man, partaking of the life, incorruptibility, and glory of God. But how can the created become a partaker in the Uncreated, unless the Uncreated first joins himself to his creature? This requirement is decisive for Irenaeus's understanding of the Incarnation:

For it was for this that the Word [became] man, and the Son of God the Son of man, that man, joined (*commixtus*) to the Word and receiving adoption, might become the son of God. For by no other means could we participate in incorruptibility and immortality, unless we had been joined to incorruptibility and immortality. But how could we be joined to incorruptibility and immortality, unless, first, incorruptibility and immortality had become that which we also are, so that the corruptible might be swallowed up by incorruptibility and the mortal by immortality, 'that we might receive the adoption of sons'? [cf. 1 Cor. 15: 53–4; 2 Cor. 5: 4; Gal. 4: 5]. (*AH* 3. 19. 1)[85]

The growth and increase that God set before the creature from the beginning could not itself have brought about such an outcome; rather, the growth was intended to accustom man to

---

[84] D'Alès ('La Doctrine de la récapitulation en S. Irénée', *RSR* 6 (1916), 191–2), thought that he could discern in Irenaeus the future positions of both Duns Scotus and Thomas Aquinas, and so began a lengthy debate which, as Wingren observed, 'might lead one to ask if the main question is really whether Irenaeus followed Thomas or Duns Scotus!' (*Man and the Incarnation*, 92–3 n. 37). Orbe continues such speculation in a manner which simply defies credulity (*Antropología*, 495–502).

[85] Cf. *AH* 3. 10. 2, 16. 3, 18. 7; 5. pref., 1. 1; *Dem.* 31.

be able to receive this adoption. On the one hand, God himself needed to be incarnate, to become man, so that man, joined to or bearing the Word, might be adopted as a son of God; whilst, on the other hand, man needed to be trained in preparation for this 'ascent towards God'.[86]

However, as man's apostasy and death are not simply part of the unfolding of the economy, but also the catastrophic response of man, prompted by the Devil, and its result, so too the Incarnation does not function within the economy, as it actually unfolded in history, only to render the psychical being fully spiritual, to bring the created being into full communion with the incorruptibility and glory of the uncreated God, the event for which the pedagogy of the economy was but a preparation. As man, after the apostasy, is dead 'in Adam', enslaved by the Devil, so Christ came to set man free:

> For he fought and conquered; for, on the one hand, he was man contending for the fathers, and through obedience doing away with disobedience completely; and on the other hand, he bound the strong man, and set free the weak, and endowed his own handiwork with salvation, by destroying sin [cf. Rom. 5: 19; Matt. 12: 29]. (*AH* 3. 18. 6)[87]

The liberation of man from the tyranny of the Devil is effected by Christ, who, as man, fought the enemy, and loosened the knot of disobedience through obedience, and who, as God, set free the weak and gave salvation to his handiwork.[88]

As the two dimensions of the apostasy, the catastrophic and the pedagogic, are but a matter of perspective, so also are the two dimensions of Christ's work of salvation—liberating the weak man from the Devil and bestowing incorruptibility—a matter of perspective, relating to the human and the divine in the one Jesus Christ.[89] Jesus Christ, not Adam, is the first manifestation in history of the true, fully human being; thus,

---

[86] *AH* 3. 19. 1.

[87] For the image of Christ binding the strong one, see *AH* 3. 18. 2, 23. 1; 4. 33. 4; 5. 21. 3, 22. 1; *Dem.* 31.

[88] Irenaeus continues this passage by reflecting very profoundly, in *AH* 3. 18. 7, on the relationship between the human and the divine in Christ.

[89] On Irenaeus's Christology, the older works of Houssiau, *La Christologie de saint Irénée*, and Wingren, *Man and the Incarnation*, are still useful.

whereas man in Adam was inexperienced, weak, and so, from the beginning, easily led into apostasy, the man Christ, being strong, conquered the enemy by remaining obedient. Likewise, Adam was a psychical being, and, whilst obedient, he could have remained immortal, yet he could not have become a partaker in incorruptibility, or have been united to the Spirit, had God not united himself to man in Christ. These two aspects are, of course, inseparable: they were realized by the one historical Jesus Christ.

It is important to note that, in accordance with Irenaeus's general understanding of the human person, the focus of Christ's work is located in the flesh: it is in the flesh that Christ suffered, and through it that he reconciled the flesh which was in bondage, bringing it into union with God.[90] Nevertheless, the work of redemption is solely the work of God, the incarnate Son, throughout:

the Lord has redeemed us through his own blood, giving his soul for our soul, his flesh for our flesh, and has poured out the Spirit of the Father for the union and communion of God and men, bringing God down to men through the Spirit, and lifting man up to God through his incarnation, and by his granting to us incorruptibility, firmly and truly, through communion with him. (*AH* 5. 1. 1)

Again, it is God, who, in man, by himself becoming man, accomplishes the economy.

That God did indeed become man is thus the foundation upon which economy is built and salvation achieved. But this must not be understood in too mechanical or physical a manner, for the work of salvation was accomplished by Christ through his obedience, suffering, and death.[91] Both of these dimensions are expressed in Irenaeus's use of the idea of recapitulation. Christ, in becoming man, recapitulates the

---

[90] *AH* 3. 18. 6–7; 5. 14. 2, referring to Col. 1: 22; and A. Orbe, 'San Ireneo y la doctrina de la reconciliación', *Greg.* 61. 1 (1980), 5–50.

[91] It is the great merit of Wingren's *Man and the Incarnation* to have emphasized how the 'physical' and the 'moral' aspects of salvation are inseparably bound together, against the earlier, mainly German Protestant scholars, who criticized Irenaeus for having taught a 'physical' understanding of salvation, consequent upon his supposed lack of appreciation of the really catastrophic dimensions of sin. Cf. Minn's perceptive comments (*Irenaeus*, 89–91).

ancient formation of Adam, that he should be truly man, so that what had been created in the beginning might now be saved. The virgin birth, far from depriving Christ of a real human nature, is in fact the indication that, in this recapitulation, he became fully man:

And just as the first-fashioned Adam had his substance from untilled and yet virgin soil, 'for God had not yet sent rain, and there was no man to till the ground' [Gen. 2: 5], and was fashioned by the Hand of God, that is, by the Word of God, for 'all things were made through him' [John 1: 3], and the Lord took mud from the ground and fashioned man [Gen. 2: 7]; so, when the Word, himself, recapitulated Adam in himself, he rightly received from Mary, who was as yet a virgin, that generation which was the recapitulation of Adam. If then the first Adam had a man for his father, and was born from male seed, they would be right to say that the second Adam was begotten of Joseph. But if the former was taken from the mud, and fashioned by the Word of God, so the Word himself, when bringing about the recapitulation of Adam within himself, ought to have the likeness of generation itself. Why then did God not once again take mud, rather than work this fashioning from Mary? So that there should not be another fashioning, nor that it should be another fashioning which would be saved, but that the same thing should be recapitulated, preserving the similitude. (*AH* 3. 21. 10)[92]

That the manner of Christ's incarnation preserved the manner of Adam's formation is due both to the fact that Adam was a type of Christ and to the need for Christ's flesh to be that of Adam, if he is to recapitulate all in himself, so becoming the head of all those whose 'head' had been Adam.[93]

For Christ's work of recapitulation to be complete, He has to recapitulate not only Adam's formation, by becoming man, but also all the stages pertaining to human life: 'He therefore passed through every age, becoming an infant for infants, thus sanctifying infants', a child for children, a youth for youths, and an old man for old men, offering to each an example appropriate to their age.[94] Likewise, becoming 'man

---

[92] Cf. *AH* 1. 9. 3; 3. 18. 7, 21. 9, 22. 1; 5. 1. 2, 12. 4, 14. 1–3.

[93] Note the connection between the recapitulation of Adam and all his progeny in Christ and the description of Adam as 'type of the One to come' in *AH* 3. 22. 3. Cf. *AH* 3. 18. 1.

[94] *AH* 2. 22. 4. Cf. *AH* 3. 18. 7.

in order to undergo temptation',[95] he recapitulated Adam's temptation. But while Adam was defeated through disobedience, Christ reversed that defeat through his own obedience. The parallels between Adam's temptation and disobedience and Christ's temptations in the desert and his obedience are worked out in great detail in *AH* 5. 21. 2. Irenaeus extends the dynamics of typological parallelism to include many other features of the one economy: most importantly, the parallel between Eve, the wife who was yet a virgin and who, seduced by the angel, by her disobedience became the cause of death to herself and to the human race, and Mary, the obedient wife of Joseph, who, by obedience to the Word of God conveyed by the angel, became the cause of salvation to herself and the human race.[96] While Adam was disobedient with respect to the tree, and thereby brought about death, so Christ was obedient unto death on the tree and by it brought life.[97] Finally, Christ, in his work of recapitulation, waging war against the enemy, also recapitulated the enmity between the woman and the serpent, and between their offspring, trampling on the head of him who had led us away as captives in Adam.[98]

Christ's work of salvation culminated in his passion and resurrection, foreshadowed by Abraham's readiness to sacrifice his only son.[99] Although the incarnate Son was anointed as Christ at his baptism, it was not until his Passion and Resurrection, that his flesh was permanently transfigured by the glory of the Father and so made incorruptible:

Similarly [to Eph. 4: 6] does the Lord say, 'All things are delivered to me by my Father' [Matt. 11: 27], clearly by him who made all things. . . . For no one was able, either in heaven or in earth or under the earth, to open the book of the Father, or to behold him, with the exception of the Lamb who was slain [cf. Rev. 5: 3–12], and who redeemed us with his own blood, receiving power over all things from the same God who made all things by the Word and adorned them by wisdom, when 'the Word was made flesh' [John 1: 14], so that, as the

[95] *AH* 3. 19. 3.

[96] Cf. *AH* 3. 22. 4, in which Irenaeus explains that the 'recycling' from Mary to Eve (and Christ to Adam), by inverting the process which caused the bonds to arise, puts them asunder. For Mary–Eve, cf. *AH* 5. 19. 1; *Dem*. 33.

[97] Cf. *AH* 5. 16. 3; *Dem*. 34; referring to Phil. 2: 8.

[98] Cf. *AH* 4. 40. 3; 5. 21. 1; referring to Gen. 3: 15.

[99] *AH* 4. 5. 4.

Word of God had first place in the heavens, so he should have first place on earth, as the just man who 'committed no sin neither was guile found in his mouth' [Isa. 53: 9], and that he might have first place also of those under the earth, he became 'the first-born of the dead' [Col. 1: 18], so that all should see their King . . . and so that the paternal light might fall upon our Lord's flesh, and from his resplendent flesh come to us, and so that man might attain to incorruptibility, wrapped around with the paternal light. (*AH* 4. 20. 2)

By his real passion, Christ both destroyed death and put an end to corruption, whilst manifesting life, revealing truth, and bestowing incorruptibility.[100] Similarly, it is by hanging on the tree that Christ, who as the Word contains all things and inheres in the entire creation, recapitulates all things in himself.[101]

It is thus through Christ's recapitulation of the ancient formation of Adam and of the various aspects pertaining to human growth that salvation, the divine fashioning of man, is fully achieved. All the events of the Old Testament pertaining to the unfolding of the economy, from the initial fashioning of Adam onwards, typify, or refer to, that which was to happen in and through Christ.

We have already seen something of how the Church was established, when looking at the unfolding of the economy: how God called the Gentiles to the faith of Abraham, making 'his people' those who were not his people, and how the Church is conformed to the image of the Son through the pedagogy of the economy. In the context of exhorting his readers to flee from the doctrines of heretics and take refuge in the Church, be nurtured in her bosom and nourished by the Lord's Scriptures, Irenaeus describes the Church as having been 'planted as a Paradise in this world'.[102] The instruction 'to eat freely from every tree of the Paradise' (Gen. 2: 16) refers to man's freedom 'to eat from every Scripture of the Lord', but not with an uplifted mind or to touch any heretical discord, lest he be cast out of the 'Paradise of life',

---

[100] *AH* 2. 20. 3.

[101] Cf. *AH* 5. 18. 3; *Dem.* 34; and A. Rousseau, 'Le Verbe "imprimé en forme de croix dans l'univers"': A propos de deux passages de saint Irénée', in *Armeniaca: Mélanges d'études arméniennes* (Venice, 1969), 67–82.

[102] *AH* 5. 20. 2; referring to Gen. 2: 8.

into which the Lord has introduced those who obey his proclamation, 'recapitulating in himself all things which are in heaven, and which are on earth' [Eph. 1: 10]; but the things in heaven are spiritual, while those on earth are the arrangements concerning man. These things, therefore, he recapitulated in himself, uniting man to the Spirit and making the Spirit to dwell in man, becoming himself the head of the Spirit, and giving the Spirit to be the head of man: through him we see and hear and speak. (*AH* 5. 20. 2)

The Church is thus the Paradise which the Garden of Eden prefigured. The Church is also prefigured in all the 'prophets and righteous'[103] who desired to see the day of the Lord—that is, in all those who, at various stages of the one economy, feared and loved God, practised justice and piety, and desired to see Christ. In reverse, it is in their true descendants, those of the Church, that the patriarchs and forefathers receive their recompense.[104]

The fulfilment of the prefigurations of the Church effected by Christ in his incarnation, joining God to man, and through his work of recapitulation is described in *AH* 5. 20. 2 in terms of the bestowal of the Spirit, making the Spirit to dwell in man, to be his head as he is the head of the Spirit. The gift of the Spirit is itself placed in the relationship of type fulfilment in *AH* 3. 24. 1, where it is compared to the breath of life given in Genesis 2: 7: just as the breath animated man at the beginning, so also the Spirit vivifies those in the Church:

It is to the Church itself that this gift of God has been entrusted, as was the breath to the handiwork, for this purpose, that all the members receiving it may be vivified; and in it [the Church] is deposited the communion with Christ, that is, the Holy Spirit, the pledge of incorruptibility, the means of confirming our faith, and the ladder of ascent to God. (*AH* 3. 24. 1)[105]

The Church is the locus of the Spirit. So Irenaeus continues: 'Where the Church is, there is the Spirit of God, and where the

---

[103] *AH* 4. 22. 1–2, referring to Matt. 13: 17.

[104] *AH* 4. 22. 2.

[105] See Rousseau's notes on this text, SC 210, 390–3. See also *Dem.* 11, where Irenaeus describes how God fashioned man and breathed the breath of life into him, so that 'both according to the inspiration and according to the formation, man was like God', i.e. Christ. This passage will be discussed fully below, Ch. 2.

Spirit of God is, there is the Church, and every kind of grace, and the Spirit is truth' (*AH* 3. 24. 1). It is, thus, in the Paradise which is the Church, that man, trained to follow the Word and accustomed to bear the Spirit through the pedagogy of the economy, can, by being vivified by the Spirit, attain the fullness of human nature, which was prefigured by the psychical Adam, but realized for the first time by Jesus Christ.

Jesus, at his baptism, was anointed by the Father with the Spirit so that man might also share in the abundance of his Unction which made him Christ.[106] At first it was in Jesus Christ that the Spirit became accustomed to dwell in the human race, 'working the will of the Father in them, and renewing them from oldness to the newness of Christ'.[107] But after his passion and resurrection, the same Spirit was poured out on all the disciples at Pentecost, uniting all nations, bringing them to life and opening the New Covenant, so that with one accord they praised God in many languages, thus reversing the divisive consequences of Babel (*AH* 3. 17. 2). After Pentecost, entry into the Church is through baptism. Irenaeus was fond of using water imagery for the Spirit,[108] and he continues in *AH* 3. 17. 2 by describing the work of the Spirit at Pentecost and in baptism in such terms:

Wherefore also the Lord promised to send the Paraclete who would make us fit for God. For just as a lump of dough or a loaf of bread cannot be made from dry flour without water, so neither could we, being many, be made one in Christ Jesus without the Water from heaven. Just as dry earth, unless it receives water, does not fructify, so we, who formerly were dry wood, would never have borne, as fruit, life without the willing Rain from above [cf. Ps. 67: 10 LXX]. For, by the washing, our bodies have received that unity which is towards incorruptibility, while our souls have received it from the Spirit. Wherefore both being necessary, since both contribute towards the life of God, our Lord took pity on that unfaithful Samaritan woman . . . by showing and promising her living Water, so that she should thirst no more, nor occupy herself in acquiring the moistening water obtained in labour, having in herself a Drink welling up to eternal life [John 4: 14], [a Drink] which the Lord received as a gift from the

---

[106] *AH* 3. 9. 3.
[107] *AH* 3. 17. 1; cf. *Dem.* 6.
[108] Cf. *AH* 3. 17. 2–3; 4. 14. 2, 33. 14, 36. 4, 39. 2; 5. 18. 2; and Andia, *Homo vivens*, 205–23.

Father, and himself gives to those who are partakers of himself, sending the Holy Spirit upon all the earth. (*AH* 3. 17. 2)

Just as God established the creation by his Word and bound it together by his Spirit,[109] so, to be made one in Christ, human beings need the Water from heaven. Their bodies need to be washed in baptism to receive the unity or cohesion which opens out onto incorruptibility, whilst their souls receive it directly from the Spirit.[110] The Spirit is the author of communal unity in Christ, and of man's personal and bodily cohesion. The Spirit, as the willing Rain, is also the author of the fruitfulness of the baptized, enabling them to bear, as fruit, life. Having received the Water from heaven, the willing Rain, and having been washed in baptism, the believer also becomes a source of living Water, a Drink which wells up to eternal life, having received the Spirit from Christ, who himself received it from the Father.

Irenaeus seldom writes of baptism as being for the remission of sins.[111] Remission of sins, or a purificatory washing, would still leave man 'in Adam'. For Irenaeus, the primary content of baptism is the 'regeneration unto God' which accomplishes man's adoption as a son of God.[112] Thus, while in *AH* 3. 17. 2 he speaks of the baptismal washing in terms of reception of the unity which leads to incorruptibility, in the *Demonstration* Irenaeus defines baptism as: 'the seal of eternal life and rebirth unto God, that we may no longer be sons of mortal men, but of the eternal and everlasting God' (*Dem.* 3). Baptism is a 'regeneration unto God' which accomplishes adoption as sons of God. It is a regeneration, effected by the new generation of Christ from the Virgin, which liberates man from the 'genera-

---

[109] *AH* 3. 24. 2.

[110] In *Dem.* 41, however, both the soul and the body together are described as being 'cleansed by the baptism of water and the Holy Spirit'.

[111] An explicit connection is made only in *Dem.* 3, where Irenaeus asserts that the faith handed down to us reminds us first of all 'that we have received baptism for the remission of sins', and in *AH* 3. 12. 7, where he comments on Acts 10: 43. In a different context, in *AH* 5. 14. 2–3, Irenaeus writes about the remission of sins for those who have been reconciled to the Father by being incorporated into the righteous flesh of Christ, but no explicit mention is made of baptism. Cf. A. Houssiau, 'Le Baptême selon Irénée de Lyon', *ETL* 60 (1984), 45–59.

[112] Cf. *AH* 1. 21. 1; 3. 17. 1; *Dem.* 7.

tion of death'.[113] Yet, this regeneration itself is but a prelude to the 'second generation' of the human race at the resurrection after their dissolution into the earth.[114]

The full significance of the baptismal regeneration, for Irenaeus, is that through it believers are adopted as sons of God. Just as this relationship was not realized, nor could it have been, except by God himself becoming incarnate, the Son of God become the Son of man, so, conversely, their entry into the reality manifested in the incarnate Son of God is not achieved by the believers' own powers, but by adoption (υἱοθεσία), by sons of men *being established* as sons of God. In *AH* 4. 41. 2–3 Irenaeus, following one of his predecessors, notes that the term 'son' has a twofold meaning: it is according to nature or according to teaching.[115] According to nature, the word 'son' applies both to the offspring and to the work or product of a creator, with the difference that the offspring is begotten while the work is made. Inasmuch as all human beings were created by God, all are sons of God. With regard to teaching, if they keep the true belief and remain in filial obedience to God, they can also be called sons of God in a deeper sense. But just as such a son can be disinherited, so they will be regarded as sons only so long as they remain in filial obedience to him. If, turning aside from this filial obedience, they join the apostasy of the Devil and do his works, they become sons of the Devil. It is only through conversion and repentance that an apostate son can return to his filial inheritance. In *Dem.* 8, Irenaeus distinguishes three different relationships between God and man: whereas God is the Creator of all—of Gentiles, Jews, and believers—to the Gentiles he is the Maker and Creator (sons as created by their Maker), to the

---

[113] Cf. *AH* esp. 4. 33. 4; also 3. 19. 1; 4. 33. 11; 5. 1. 3. On the connection between the *nova generatio* of Christ and that of believers, see Rousseau's notes, SC 100, 269–70; 152, 205–7.

[114] Cf. *AH* 5. 15. 1, where Irenaeus refers 'the second generation' to the first resurrection of the just in the Kingdom of the Son. The connection between the παλιγγενεσία and the Kingdom of the Son is made in Matt. 19: 28. See also *AH* 5. 32. 1–2, 35. 1, 36. 3; and A. Orbe, *Teología de San Ireneo*, 2 (Madrid, 1987), 7–8.

[115] Irenaeus does not inform us who his source was. I have followed Rousseau in giving preference to the Armenian version of *AH* 4. 41. 2; see his comments, SC 100, 283–5.

Jews he is a Lord and Lawgiver (sons as slaves to his Law), but 'to the faithful he is as Father, since "in the last times" he opened the testament of the adoption of sons'. As a creature, man was clearly not begotten of God—nor can he be—in the same way as the only begotten Son of God. But, to be adopted as a son of the Father means more than God simply regarding him as his son; he has *established* the believer as his son, incorporating him into the sonship of the Son of God, who became the Son of man for this end.[116] Becoming thus true sons of God, Ireneaus does not hesitate to describe the faithful as gods: 'God stood in the congregation of gods, he judges in the midst of the gods' (Ps. 81: 1 LXX): [this text] speaks of the Father and the Son and those who have received the adoption, for they are the Church.'[117] It is, therefore, by adoption that believers become established as sons of God, as gods; and gathered together, in and through the Son, they form the Church, the congregation of God.

Regenerated and adopted as sons of God, believers are no longer subject to the law of slavery, the pedagogue that led us to Christ (cf. Gal. 3: 24), for Christ has cancelled it by the 'new covenant of liberty'.[118] The natural precepts of the love of God and justice towards one's neighbour, the free and willing observance of which were sufficient for those who were justified by faith, were implanted by God in the human heart.[119] These precepts were forgotten during the slavery in Egypt, and so, having been led out of Egypt, the Decalogue was instituted so that the people might once again be followers of God.[120] However, when they turned away to the golden calf, showing that in their hearts they preferred the slavery of Egypt, they were subjected to the 'yoke of slavery' through the various precepts promulgated by Moses.[121] It is these precepts that Christ has abolished in the 'new covenant of

---

[116] Cf. *AH* 3. 19. 1, cited above; and Minns, *Irenaeus*, 110–12.

[117] *AH* 3. 6. 1; cf. *AH*, esp. 4. pref. 4; 3. 6. 2; 4. 1. 1.

[118] *AH* 4. 16. 5. The whole section *AH* 4. 9–16 is an extended discussion of the relationship between the Law and the Gospel. Cf. M. F. Berrouard, 'Servitude de la Loi et liberté de l'Evangile selon saint Irénée', *LV* 61 (1963), 41–60.

[119] Cf. *AH* 4. 13. 1, 13. 4, 15. 1.

[120] Cf. *AH* 4. 15. 1, 16. 3.

[121] *AH* 4. 15. 1.

liberty' which he has inaugurated. However, Christ did not abrogate the natural precepts implanted in the heart, but has 'extended and fulfilled them'.[122] Whereas the Law prohibited adultery and murder, Christ forbade lust and anger. This must not be misunderstood as an 'interiorization' or 'spiritualization' of the Law.[123] Rather, if piety and obedience are required just as much from sons as from slaves, in sons it is expressed voluntarily, and they in turn possess greater confidence and liberty.[124] Paradoxically, however, the liberty given to the sons in the new covenant of liberty is also realized as a greater subjection to God.[125] As man is the handiwork of God, subject to his creative activity, the more ready he is to be fashioned by God, the more God can fashion him. As such, the 'extension and fulfilment' of the natural precepts in the words of the Lord do not indicate an interiorization, but a greater subjection to the creative activity of God, appropriate to those who have been adopted as sons.

Besides being nourished by Scripture (*AH* 5. 20. 2), in the Church believers are also nourished and prepared for incorruptibility by the reception of the eucharist, which, as the body and blood of Christ, is itself a union of flesh and Spirit:

For we offer to him his own, fittingly proclaiming the communion and union of the flesh and the Spirit. For just as the bread from the earth, when it has received the invocation of God, is no longer ordinary bread, but eucharist, consisting of two things, earthly and heavenly, so also our bodies, receiving the eucharist, are no longer corruptible, having the hope of the resurrection. (*AH* 4. 18. 5)[126]

---

[122] Cf. *AH* 4. 13. 1–4, 16. 4–5; *Dem.* 96.

[123] As e.g. Berrouard, 'Servitude de la Loi', 50–1. Cf. H. J. Jaschke, 'Pneuma und Moral: Der Grund christlicher Sittlichkeit aus der Sicht des Irenäus von Lyon', *SM* 14 (1976), 272. 'Interiority' plays no role within Irenaeus's understanding of human life in the unfolding of the economy, and it is doubtful that it has any place in his anthropology.

[124] *AH* 4. 13. 2.

[125] *AH* 4. 13. 3. See the interesting article by B. Aland, 'Fides und Subiectio: Zur Anthropologie des Irenäus', in A. M. Ritter (ed.), *Kerygma und Logos: Beiträge zu den geistesgeschichtlichen Beziehung zwischen Antike und Christentum. Festschrift für Carl Andresen zum 70. Geburtstag* (Göttingen, 1979), 9–28.

[126] This text, which is preserved in Greek, is presented in parallel columns by P. Gächter, 'Unsere Einheit mit Christus nach dem hl. Irenäus', *ZKT* 58 (1939), 517, and slightly differently by Andia, *Homo vivens*, 242. For a

That flesh is nourished by the body and blood of Christ is evidence, for Irenaeus, that it can also partake of incorruptibility and life. As the eucharist is no longer common bread, so also by partaking of the eucharist the bodies of Christians are no longer corruptible flesh, but, as the eucharist is the 'union and communion of flesh and Spirit', so also do their bodies have the hope of the resurrection; that is, their flesh is nourished, even now, by that for which they are being prepared, the reception of incorruptibility.

Irenaeus develops this parallel in *AH* 5. 2. 3, where he uses the same image of the fecundity of the Spirit as in *AH* 3. 17. 2. He has been emphasizing that just as the believers' flesh 'has grown and [been] strengthened' by the mixed cup and the manufactured bread, which having received the Word of God is the body and blood of Christ, so also their flesh is capable of receiving eternal life from God. Furthermore, when the Apostle describes Christians as 'members of his body and of his flesh and of his bones' (cf. Eph. 5: 30), he is not speaking of a spiritual human being, 'for a spirit has neither flesh nor bones' (cf. Luke 24: 39), but of a genuine human being, made of flesh and blood, nourished by Christ's body and blood. Irenaeus then continues:

Just as the wood of the vine, planted in the earth, bore fruit in its own time, and the grain of wheat, falling into the earth and being decomposed, was raised up manifold by the Spirit of God who sustains all, then, by wisdom,[127] they come to the use of men, and receiving the Word of God, become eucharist, which is the body and blood of Christ; in the same way, our bodies, nourished by it, having been placed in the earth and decomposing in it, shall rise in their time, when the Word of God bestows on them the resurrection to the glory of God the Father, who secures immortality for the mortal and

summary of modern scholarship on the question of the 'two things' of *AH* 4. 18. 5, see Andia, *Homo vivens*, 254–5.

[127] The Greek, preserved in the *Sacra Parallela*, has διὰ τῆς σοφίας τοῦ θεοῦ, while the Latin and Armenian simply have 'by wisdom'. The context indicates a threefold process: the production of fruits by the Spirit, which are then made into bread and wine, and which then receive the invocation of the Word. Thus, at the beginning of *AH* 5. 2. 3, Irenaeus refers to τὸ κεκραμένον ποτήριον καὶ ὁ γεγονὼς ἄρτος. The wisdom in question would thus seem to refer to that of human art, so Rousseau translates 'grâce au savoir-faire'; see his note, SC 152, 213–15.

bountifully bestows incorruptibility on the corruptible [cf. 1 Cor.
15: 53], because the power of God is made perfect in weakness [cf. 2
Cor. 12: 9], that we may never become puffed up, as if we had life
from ourselves, nor exalted against God, entertaining ungrateful
thoughts, but learning by experience that it is from his excellence,
and not from our own nature, that we have eternal continuance, that
we should neither undervalue the true glory of God nor be ignorant of
our own nature, but should know what God can do and what benefits
man, and that we should never mistake the true understanding of
things as they are, that is, of God and man. (*AH* 5. 2. 3)[128]

There is clearly a close relationship between the dynamism and
fecundity of the Spirit and the action of the Word operative in
the processes that lead both to the eucharist and to the
resurrection. This relationship, however, is more than a
simple correspondence or parallelism.[129] It is *by receiving* the
eucharist, as the wheat and the vine received the fecundity of
the Spirit, that Christians are prepared, as they also make the
fruits into the bread and wine, for their own resurrection
effected by the Word, at which point, just as the bread and
wine receive the Word and so become the body and blood of
Christ, the eucharist, so also will their bodies receive immortality and incorruptibility from the Father. Christians themselves, therefore, need to use the fruits of the world
eucharistically, for it is by these that they are prepared for
the resurrection and the gift of incorruptibility. This understanding of the eucharist falls quite clearly within Irenaeus's
theology of the economy of God: it is within the temporal
things of this world that man is prepared, maturing in order to
be able to bear the fruit of immortality.[130] As such, the divine
economy can be seen as the eucharist of God the Father. This
relationship between the eucharist and the divine economy is
further emphasized by the role of death in both. We saw

[128] For the Greek text printed in parallel, see Andia, *Homo vivens*, 244.

[129] That is, it is not a correspondence between a merely natural process and
a mystical process. H. D. Simonin emphasizes that it is 'ce que l'on a appelé,
faute de mieux, le dynamisme de la sacramentaire grecque, dynamisme à la
fois cosmique et mystique' ('A propos d'un texte eucharistique de S. Irénée:
AH. IV. xviii. 5', *RSPhTh* 23 (1934), 285). Andia's analyses of the different
transformations seems somewhat scholastic (*Homo vivens*, 245–7).

[130] Cf. *AH* 4. 5. 1, discussed in the earlier section 'The Temporality of the
Economy'.

earlier, when looking at 'The Sign of Jonah', how death functions pedagogically within the economy, as the means by which man experiences both his own weakness and the strength of God deployed in such weakness. Irenaeus reiterates these themes in *AH* 5. 2. 3, adding that in this way man comes to learn the truth about both God and himself. However, in *AH* 5. 2. 3, man's death is not simply pedagogical or remedial, but functions within the 'eucharist' of God.

It is important to note that the human activity in the preparation of the eucharist corresponds to a passivity or receptivity with regard to the resurrection and the bestowal of incorruptibility. Christians are the ones who make bread and wine out of the fruits of the earth,[131] which, receiving the invocation (ἐπίκλησις, *AH* 4. 18. 5) and the Word of God, become the body and blood of Christ; while they themselves, prepared by their reception of the eucharist, will be raised by Christ and will be rendered immortal by the Father. It is, thus, as we have continually seen throughout our investigation of Irenaeus's theology of the economy, a matter of the receptiveness of man to the gifts of God and his thankfulness for them: his thankful use of the material things provided by God, in and through which he learns whence his life has its source, and an attitude of thankfulness, through which he comes to share ever more fully in that life.

As Israel, having passed through the Red Sea, sojourned in the desert, sustained by manna from heaven, before entering the Promised Land, so too believers, having passed through the waters of baptism and being nourished and strengthened by the eucharist, still have not entered the Promised Land. In the two passages concerning the eucharist that we have considered, the eucharist is said to provide 'the hope of the resurrection' (*AH* 4. 18. 5) or a nourishment which sustains and prepares believers for the resurrection (*AH* 5. 2. 3). It is also, as we have already seen, as a 'pledge of incorruptibility' that members of the Church have received the Spirit, so that, despite her

---

[131] Nicholas Cabasilas observes, in his *Commentary on the Divine Liturgy*, 3. 4, that man is essentially a cooking animal: 'We call human that which belongs to man alone. Now the need of baking bread to eat and making wine to drink is peculiar to man. That is why we offer bread and wine' (trans. J. M. Hussey and P. A. McNulty (London, 1960), 32).

members being dispersed throughout the world,[132] the Church, though in the world, is located in the Spirit (*AH* 3. 24. 1). It is in *AH* 5. 8. 1 that Irenaeus provides his most sustained analysis of the nature and function of this 'pledge':

For now we receive a certain portion of the Spirit towards perfection and preparation for incorruptibility, being slowly accustomed to contain and to bear God, which the Apostle called 'a pledge', that is, a part of the honour which God has promised us, saying, in the Epistle to the Ephesians, 'In him you also, having heard the word of truth, the Gospel of your salvation, and believing in him, have been sealed with the Holy Spirit of the promise, which is the pledge of our inheritance' [Eph. 1: 13–14]. This pledge, therefore, thus dwelling in us, renders us spiritual even now, and the mortal is swallowed up by immortality—for he declares, 'you are not in the flesh, but in the Spirit, if the Spirit of God dwells in you' [Rom. 8: 9]—and this is not by a casting away of the flesh, but by the communion of the Spirit, for those to whom he was writing were not without flesh, but those who had received the Spirit of God, 'in whom we cry Abba, Father' [Rom. 8: 15]; if then now, having the pledge, we cry 'Abba, Father', what shall it be when rising again we behold him face to face, when all the members shall burst forth in an effervescent hymn of exultation, glorifying him who raised them from the dead and gave them eternal life? For if the pledge, gathering man together into itself, makes him now say 'Abba, Father', what shall the full grace of the Spirit, which shall be given to men by God, effect? It will render us like unto him, and perfect the will of the Father: for it shall make man in the image and likeness of God. (*AH* 5. 8. 1)

Christians now receive a 'certain portion' (*partem aliquam*) of the Spirit towards their perfection and preparation for incorruptibility, when they will be able to contain and bear God. By this they are enabled to call on God as 'Abba, Father', and are made spiritual *even now*. Irenaeus is emphatic, as one would expect, that this takes place in the flesh: they become spiritual not by abandoning the flesh, but by being 'in the Spirit', having the Spirit dwelling in them. As Adam became a psychical being, flesh animated by the breath of life given from God, so too, by the imparting of the Holy Spirit, do Christians become spiritual beings, flesh vivified by the Spirit. Nevertheless, what they have received by being adopted and sealed

---

[132] Cf. *AH* 1. 10. 1; 4. 36. 2.

with the Spirit is but a 'pledge' of what is promised to them for when they are raised to see God 'face to face' and to receive the full grace of the Spirit. Just as the incarnate Son was anointed by the Spirit at his baptism, yet only through his death and resurrection radiated the glory of the Father in flesh rendered fully incorruptible, so also do those who have been baptized have the Spirit dwelling in them, 'working the will of the Father in them and renewing them from their oldness to the newness of Christ' (*AH* 3. 17. 1); but it is only through their own death, the dissolution of their flesh into the earth, like the wheat (*AH* 5. 2. 3), causing the cessation of sin (*AH* 3. 23. 6), that they are raised and fully receive incorruptibility from the Father, so becoming the image and likeness of God.

The cross of Christ, his suffering and death, is the same as that which his disciples must endure and undergo. A propos of Christ's words 'If any man would come after me, let him deny himself and take up his cross and follow me. For whoever would save his life, will lose it; and whoever loses his life for my sake shall find it' (Matt. 16: 24–5) and 'You will stand before governors and kings for my sake, and they shall scourge some of you, and shall slay you and persecute you from city to city' (cf. Matt. 10: 18; Mark 13: 9; Matt. 23: 34), Irenaeus comments:

He knew, therefore, those who would suffer persecution, and he knew those who would be scourged and slain because of him; and he did not speak of any other cross, but of the Passion which he should himself undergo first, and then his disciples afterwards. (*AH* 3. 18. 5)

Those who would be disciples of Christ must also take up his cross, deny themselves, and lose their lives for his sake, and this has no referent other than the Passion, which Christ and his disciples, following him, suffer. His disciples are those: 'who are slain on account of the confession of the Lord, and who endure all things predicted by the Lord, and who in this way strive to follow the footprints of the Lord's Passion, becoming martyrs of the suffering One' (*AH* 3. 18. 5). Irenaeus thus understands martyrdom in terms of Christ's own passion, his death and resurrection.[133]

---

[133] So the Cross is described as the 'tree of martyrdom' by which he draws all to himself and vivifies all (*AH* 4. 2. 7).

This identity between the death of Christ and that of the martyr extends to an identification between Christ and those confessing him. The idea that the martyr imitates Christ, and that Christ is united with the martyr in suffering, is a commonplace in the Acts of the Martyrs. It is vividly illustrated in the martyrdom of Blandina as recorded in the 'Letter of the churches of Vienne and Lyons to the churches of Asia and Phrygia', preserved in Eusebius's *Ecclesiastical History*, and which was quite possibly composed by Irenaeus himself.[134] According to this letter,

Blandina, hung on a stake (ἐπὶ ξύλου), was offered as food for the wild beasts that were let in. She, by being seen hanging in the form of a cross, by her vigorous prayer, caused great zeal in the contestants, as, in their struggle, they beheld with their outward eyes, through the sister, him who was crucified for them, that he might persuade those who believe in him that everyone who suffers for the glory of Christ has for ever communion with the living God. . . . the small and weak and despised woman had put on the great and invincible athlete, Christ, routing the adversary in many bouts, and, through the struggle, being crowned with the crown of incorruptibility.[135]

Blandina became an image, a living icon, of Christ for those who were suffering alongside her. It is in Blandina's weakness that the strength of God is victorious, and through her martyrdom that incorruptibility was bestowed upon her. The description is not simply a literary convention or *topos*, but is clearly inscribed within, and gives a very real sense of, Irenaeus's understanding of the economy: the strength of God being manifested in the weakness of man, bestowing incorruptibility on those who follow him, through martyrdom, and who become, in this way, the image and likeness of God.

Irenaeus picks up this theme of becoming in the image and likeness of God through martyrdom in *AH* 5. 28. 4. However, the framework used here is not that of following Christ and sharing in his passion, but that of the eucharist. Just as death, besides its pedagogical and remedial function, falls within the eucharistic understanding of the economy, so the sufferings of the martyrs prepare them for God in the same way that Christians prepare bread for the eucharist.

---

[134] As argued by Nautin, *Lettres et écrivains chrétiens*, 54–61.
[135] *EH* 5. 1. 41–2.

And therefore throughout all time, man, formed at the beginning by
the Hands of God, that is, by the Son and the Spirit, becomes after
the image and likeness of God: the chaff, that is, the apostasy, being
cast away, while the wheat, that is, those who bear as fruit faith in
God, being gathered into the granary. And therefore tribulation is
necessary for those who are being saved, that, in a certain way, having
been threshed and kneaded together, through endurance, with the
Word of God, and baked in the fire, they may be suitable for the
banquet of the King, as one of ours said, when condemned to the wild
beasts because of his testimony (μαρτυρία) to God: 'I am the wheat of
Christ, and I am ground by the teeth of the wild beasts, that I may be
found [to be] pure bread of God.' (*AH* 5. 28. 4)[136]

The perspective of this passage is oriented towards the fashioning of man in the image and likeness of God. Man, formed in
the beginning by the Word and the Spirit, is continually being
fashioned throughout all time into the image and likeness of
God.[137] We have seen how God bore the apostasy of man, that
man might come to learn of his own mortality and acknowledge
the one and only Source of life. Here the process of fashioning
man into the image, salvation, is described from a different
perspective: threshed by tribulation, the chaff or apostasy
being cast away, man is kneaded together with Christ, and
through fire the martyr is made into bread suitable for the
Father's celebration. Just as Christ's death and resurrection are
the basis on which Christians celebrate the eucharist, so the
martyr's death, kneaded together with the Word, and resurrection, as appropriate bread, are celebrated by God.

We saw earlier how through baptism believers receive a
'pledge' of the Spirit, rendering them spiritual even now,
absorbing what is mortal into the Spirit's own immortality,
and so preparing them for incorruptibility (*AH* 5. 8. 1). In the
same way as the Incarnate Word was anointed by the Spirit,

---

[136] Referring to Ignatius of Antioch, *Romans*, 4. 1. The eucharist frame-
work for understanding martyrdom is also demonstrated in *The Martyrdom of
Polycarp*, where the structure of the narrative closely parallels that of the Last
Supper.

[137] As Orbe points out, commenting on this passage, Irenaeus does not
think, as Philo and Origen do, of two distinct creations, Gen. 1: 26–7 and 2: 7,
but of one creation in two aspects: the initial, forming man from mud, and the
continual, historical fashioning of this creature into the image and likeness of
God (*Teología de San Ireneo*, 3. 192).

but in undergoing death was vivified by the Spirit to the point where his flesh became permanently incorruptible, transfigured by the glory of the Father, so also members of the Church, receiving a 'pledge' of the Spirit in baptism, are vivified by the Spirit in their martyrdom:

For it is testified by the Lord that as 'the flesh is weak', so 'the Spirit is ready' [Matt. 26: 41], that is, is able to accomplish what it wills. If, therefore, anyone mixes the readiness of the Spirit as a stimulus to the weakness of the flesh, it necessarily follows that what is strong will prevail over what is weak, so that the weakness of the flesh will be absorbed by the strength of the Spirit, and such a one will no longer be carnal but spiritual because of the communion of the Spirit. In this way, therefore, the martyrs bear witness and despise death: not after the weakness of the flesh, but by the readiness of the Spirit. For when the weakness of the flesh is absorbed, it manifests the Spirit as powerful; and again, when the Spirit absorbs the weakness, it inherits the flesh for itself, and from both of these is made a living man: living, indeed, because of the participation of the Spirit; and man, because of the substance of the flesh. (*AH* 5. 9. 2)[138]

The strength of God is made perfect in weakness; and so, paradoxically, it is in their death, their ultimate vulnerability, that the martyrs bear greatest witness to the strength of God. Not that they reckon death to be a thing of no importance, but that in their confession they are vivified by the Spirit, and live the life of the Spirit, who absorbs the weakness of their flesh into his own strength. When the Spirit so possesses the flesh, the flesh itself adopts the quality of the Spirit and is rendered like the Word of God.[139] It is thus not only in the resurrection that man comes to be fully vivified by the Spirit. Rather, our paradigm of the living human being—flesh vivified by the Spirit—is the martyr.[140]

As the patriarchs learnt to follow the Word, but did not enter the Promised Land before their death, so too their descendants,

---

[138] Cf. PO 12. 5, 738–9 (frag. 6); TU 36. 3, 14–19 (frag. 10).

[139] *AH* 5. 9. 3.

[140] Cf. Jaschke: 'Das Martyrium is die Grundform christlicher Existenz' ('Pneuma und Moral', 265); Y. de Andia, 'La Résurrection de la chair selon les Valentiniens et Irénée de Lyon', *Les Quatre Fleuves*, 15–16 (1982), 69; R. Tremblay, 'Le Martyre selon saint Irénée de Lyon', *SM* 16 (1978), 167–89.

the followers of Christ, do not receive the fullness of the promise until the resurrection. And as it was precisely *land* that was promised to the patriarchs, so it is the transfigured, though fully material, world that the human race will inhabit after the resurrection. The economy, which, as we have repeatedly seen, is centred upon the flesh formed from mud being fashioned into the image of God, culminates not in a mystical union of the soul with God, but in an earthly Kingdom, thus fulfilling the promises made to the patriarchs.[141] Irenaeus's emphasis on this fact is striking. As von Balthasar observes:

In his eschatology Irenaeus produces an important counterweight to the flight from the world and the failure to take seriously the resurrection of the flesh which marks the Platonizing Christian eschatologies of a later period and indeed the average Christian consciousness.[142]

Irenaeus's main thrust in *Against the Heresies* was to counter the teaching of the Gnostics, according to whose anthropology and soteriology there was, as he put it, nothing left of man to enter the Pleroma.[143] Yet he knew that his own views on the resurrection of the flesh in a fully material world were already under attack by some reputedly orthodox churchmen who despised the handiwork of God, denied the salvation of the flesh, so rejected the complete resurrection.[144] Although he tactfully refrained from mentioning his opponents by name, he did not shrink from responding with vivid, earthy descriptions of the Kingdom to come. Within a few decades, Dionysius of Alexandria began writing against those who, by a too literal

[141] Cf. *AH* 5. 30. 4, 32. 1–2.

[142] Balthasar, *Glory of the Lord*, 2. 93.

[143] *AH* 2. 29. 3.

[144] *AH* 5. 31. 1. Orbe identifies this group with those mentioned in *AH* 5. 2. 2–3. As Irenaeus, in *AH* 5. 1. 2–2. 3, has already tackled the Docetists (= Valentinians, cf. *AH* 5. 1. 2, line 59), the Ebionites, and the Marcionites, the group of *AH* 5. 2. 2, who do not deny the earthly reality of Christ, the divinity of his Person, or separate the Creator from the true God, are a group within the Church who deny the salvation of the flesh. Cf. A. Orbe, 'Adversarios anónimos de la s*alus carnis* (Iren. *adv. haer.* V. 2. 2s)', *Greg.* 60. 1 (1979), 9–53, and *idem*, *Teología*, 1 (Madrid, 1985), 129–30. Similar groups are also mentioned by Justin Martyr, *Dialogue with Trypho*, 80. 4, and Tertullian, *On the Resurrection*, 2.

interpretation of Scripture, especially the Book of Revelation, taught that the Kingdom of Christ would be on earth. Dionysius also adds the polemical slur that they dreamt that the Kingdom would consist of those things that were the objects of their own desires—eating, drinking, sexual desire, and marriage—for they were nothing but carnal lovers of the body.[145] According to Eusebius, the idea that 'there will be a millennium, after the resurrection from the dead, in which the Kingdom of Christ will be established in a bodily way on this earth' stems from Papias, who had presented this idea as an 'unwritten tradition', but had come to it by 'misunderstanding' the apostolic accounts, for he was a man of 'very little intelligence' and had not realized that such Scriptures were to be read symbolically ($\mu \nu \sigma \tau \iota \kappa \hat{\omega} s$). That Irenaeus followed Papias (cf. *AH* 5. 33. 4) was explained by Eusebius on the grounds that Irenaeus had been impressed by Papias's antiquity.[146]

The increasing distance placed by such churchmen between themselves and the theology of the flesh and the Kingdom of Christ on earth, as represented by Irenaeus, has, as its correlate, an increasing allegorization or mystical interpretation of Scripture and an increasing 'spiritualization' of the resurrection. Irenaeus, although not averse to the occasional allegory, emphasized that the resurrection and the Kingdom spoken of in Scripture cannot be allegorized.[147] However, it was the 'spiritualization' of man, rather than the legitimate scope of allegory, that was of greatest concern for Irenaeus, and which he attacked by maintaining a literal reading of Scripture. It was easy to pass from the teaching of the resurrection of the flesh to that of the 'body', a term which is open to many more interpretations than flesh, and thence to an understanding of the spiritual body as a *sui generis* body of the soul or the real, inner person, rather than the flesh which has been vivified by the Spirit.[148] With such an understanding of what is properly

[145] *EH* 7. 24–5. 5.

[146] *EH* 3. 39. 12–13. Eusebius inserts an extra generation between the apostle John and Papias (*EH* 3. 39. 2).

[147] *AH* 5. 35. 1–2.

[148] The most notable example of this is, of course, Origen. For a discussion of his understanding of the term 'body' in comparison with that of Irenaeus, see Orbe, *Antropología*, 25–7, and *idem*, 'Adversarios anónimos de la *Salus*

human, salvation concerns the soul or inner person alone in its ascent to a mystical union with God in a manner similar to Gnostic soteriology. Although later Church theologians never, as some of the heretics had reputedly done, regarded the body and material creation as inherently defiled, or deprived it of any function in salvation history, few theologians matched the central importance given to the flesh in the unfolding of the economy as described by Irenaeus.

The time before the resurrection and the coming of the Kingdom is a time of tribulation and martyrdom, separating the wheat from the chaff. Before Christ returns, the Antichrist will come and establish his kingdom, ruling at Jerusalem for three years and six months.[149] The Antichrist will recapitulate in himself all the diabolical apostasy and error, and every iniquity and deceit. Summed up in him, the whole apostasy can then be sent altogether to the eternal furnace.[150] This will be accomplished when Christ comes in the glory of the Father, casting the Antichrist into the lake of fire (cf. Rev. 19: 20) and bringing the just into the Kingdom which is the rest of the seventh day.[151]

For Irenaeus, the rhythm of the events of the last times is based on the opening verses in Genesis, for 'this is an account of what happened, as it happened, as also it is a prophecy of what is to come'.[152] As God finished his work on the sixth day and rested on the seventh (Gen. 2: 2), and as a day of the Lord is as 1,000 years,[153] so the completion of creation took 6,000 years. The seventh 1,000-year period will be the Kingdom of

carnis', 18–28. It is possible that Origen's comments may be directed at Irenaeus amongst others: 'We now direct the discussion to some of our own people, who either from poverty of intellect or from lack of instruction introduce an exceedingly base and abject sense of the resurrection of the body' (*On First Principles*, 2. 10. 3).

[149] *AH* 5. 25–6, 28–30; the three years and six months (*AH* 5. 30. 4) would seem to refer to the 'half week' of Dan. 9: 27.

[150] Cf. *AH* 5. 25. 1, 5; 28. 2; 29. 2; 30. 1. As a sign of this, the number 666 is said to recapitulate the apostasy which has taken place during the 6,000 years (*AH* 5. 28. 2; 30. 1).

[151] *AH* 5. 30. 4.

[152] *AH* 5. 28. 3.

[153] Cf. 2 Pet. 3: 8. Minns suggests that Irenaeus may simply have meant a long time (*Irenaeus*, 126).

the Son, in which the just will reign with him in a renewed earthly Jerusalem. This period is inaugurated by the first resurrection:

John, therefore, foresaw precisely the first resurrection of the just [cf Luke 14: 14; Rev. 20: 5–6] and the inheritance of the earth in the Kingdom, and the prophets have also prophesied concerning it in the same terms. For this is what the Lord also taught, promising to drink the new mingled cup with his disciples in the Kingdom [cf. Matt. 26: 29], and again when he said, 'the days are coming when the dead in their tombs will hear the voice of the Son of Man and those who have done good will rise to the resurrection of life, but those who have done evil will rise to the resurrection of judgement' [cf. John 5: 28–9], saying that those doing good will be raised first, going to the rest, and then those who are to be judged will be raised, just as the Book of Genesis has the completion of this world on the sixth day, that is, the sixth thousand years, and then the seventh day of rest, of which David says, 'this is my rest, the just shall enter into it' [cf. Pss. 131: 14, 117: 20 LXX], that is, the seventh thousand years of the Kingdom of the just, in which the just shall grow accustomed to incorruptibility, when the whole of creation will be renewed for those who have been preserved for this. (*AH* 5. 36. 3)[154]

The just who are raised in the first resurrection enjoy the land promised to the patriarchs and drink the fruit of the vine with Christ as he promised to his disciples (Matt. 26: 29).[155] Isaac's blessing on Jacob (Gen. 27: 27–9), is extended to the field of the world (cf. Matt. 13: 38), and so the blessing foreshadows the times of the Kingdom, when the just are raised and reign, and 'creation, also, having been renovated and set free, shall fructify with an abundance of all kinds of food, from the Dew of heaven and from the fertility of the earth'.[156] This earth, in the Kingdom of the just, provides a banquet at which God himself has promised to serve.[157] It is in this renewed creation that man is also further trained and accustomed to bear God, to partake of incorruptibility, and to receive the glory of the Father.[158]

[154] The portion running from 'and again when He said . . .' to the end of the quotation is preserved only in Armenian (TU 35. 2, 244. 23–5. 2).

[155] *AH* 5. 33. 1.

[156] *AH* 5. 33–4; the quotation is from *AH* 5. 33. 3.

[157] *AH* 5. 34. 3.

[158] Cf. *AH* 5. 32. 1; 35. 1–2.

At the end of the period of the Kingdom, those who are judged are raised and cast into 'the lake of fire, the second death', Gehenna or the eternal fire.[159] Irenaeus stresses that the meaning of the term 'judgement' is separation, and that as everyone has been created with free will and understanding, the choice whether to join the just or the judged rests with them, not with the God who 'makes his sun to rise on the evil and on the good' (Matt. 5: 45).[160] It is not the light that has blinded them, but they who have preferred the darkness, and as such, God's 'judgement' is simply a recognition of their own freely chosen separation.[161]

With death, the 'last enemy', thus destroyed, the Son will yield up his work to the Father, that he might be all in all.[162] The nature or the substance ($\dot{\upsilon}\pi\acute{o}\sigma\tau\alpha\sigma\iota\varsigma$, $o\dot{\upsilon}\sigma\acute{\iota}\alpha$) of the creation will remain, but 'the fashion of the world will pass away' (1 Cor. 7: 31): the fashion, that is, in which the apostasy took place and man grew old.[163] The fundamental characteristic of that which will replace the present fashion of the world is its continuing newness:

When this fashion passes away, and man is renewed and flourishing with incorruptibility so that he is no longer able to become old, 'there shall be a new heaven and a new earth' [Isa. 65: 17], in which the new man will remain, conversing with God in a manner forever new. (*AH* 5. 36. 1)

As to what it is that the Father will bestow on man, in a 'paternal manner' (*paternaliter*) after the completion of the Kingdom of the Son, Irenaeus does not dare speculate, but reminds his readers that of these things, 'no eye has seen, nor ear heard, nor the heart of man conceived'.[164] Only one, the

---

[159] *AH* 5. 35. 2; Rev. 20: 14.

[160] *AH* 5. 27. 1.

[161] *AH* 5. 27. 2, referring to John 3: 19–21; *AH* 4. 11. 2.

[162] *AH* 5. 36. 2; 1 Cor. 15: 24–8.

[163] *AH* 5. 36. 1.

[164] *AH* 5. 36. 3; 1 Cor. 2: 9. Orbe, undaunted, subjects this quotation to a lengthy analysis in terms of the vision of God with corporeal eyes (*Teología*, 3. 628–33, and more broadly, 646–51). The most profitable comparison with this passage is *AH* 4. 20. 5, which speaks of three different modes or means of seeing God (*prophetice, adoptive, paternaliter*). We do not ascend to a vision of God himself, the Father, for God has made himself manifest in the flesh of his Son, and the manifestation of God by the Son preserves the invisibility of the

Only Begotten, knows the Father, and only he has manifested the Father (cf. Matt. 11: 27; Luke 10: 22).

Irenaeus concludes his *Against the Heresies* by recapitulating his great work, summing up the whole economy in one sentence:

For there is one Son, who accomplished his Father's will, and there is one human race, in which the mysteries of God are wrought, 'which the angels desire to see' [1 Pet. 1: 12], not being able to search out the wisdom of God, through which his handiwork, conformed and incorporated with the Son, is perfected, [the Father's will] that his Offspring, the First-begotten Word, should descend to the creature, that is, to the handiwork, and be borne by it, and, on the other hand, [that] the creature should bear the Word and ascend to him, passing beyond the angels and becoming in the image and likeness of God. (*AH* 5. 36. 3)

This is the economy of God, the fashioning of his handiwork, bringing the creature made of mud to share in his own life, incorruptibility, and glory, in his incarnate Son, true God and true man. The unfolding of this economy, salvation history, is centred on, and culminates in, Christ: what has gone before typifies its realization in him, as he realizes what will be wrought in those who follow him. For Irenaeus, both protology and eschatology are Christocentric: man, from his initial formation and throughout the pedagogy of the economy, can be understood only in the light of Christ.

Father, so that we should always have something towards which we can continually advance. The vision of God *paternaliter*, in *AH* 4. 20. 5, has as its corresponding explanation the bestowal of incorruptibility and eternal life by the Father.

Chapter 2

The Human Formation

We have seen how, for Irenaeus, the divine economy is directed towards the becoming truly human of both God and human beings, first realized 'in the last times' in Jesus Christ, and to be fully realized for the adopted sons of God in the eschaton. Adam is a type of Christ, and the various events of the economy both typify and prepare the human race for the fulfilment achieved in Christ. It is a movement from animation to vivification: as Adam was animated by the breath of life, so the resurrected Christ is vivified by the life-creating Spirit. Yet, as the resurrection still lies in the future, those baptized into Christ and nourished by his body and blood have received a 'pledge' of the Spirit which will vivify them fully in the Kingdom, but which even now prepares them for the reception of incorruptibility and enables them to bear martyrdom as witnesses of the dynamics of salvation being wrought in them.

That Irenaeus's anthropology cannot be detached from this setting cannot be overemphasized: Irenaeus's reading of the verses in Genesis relating to the creation of man, his protology, just as much as his eschatology, is Christocentric, centred on Christ, true God and true man. Furthermore, the text we have been principally examining so far, *Against the Heresies*, while polemical, is also exegetical rather than analytical: it demonstrates, from Scripture, that there is but one God, one Christ, one Spirit, and one human race in which the one economy is enacted, as unfolded in Scripture, rather than analysing the human constitution in static, philosophical terms. Now that we have explored the perspective of Irenaeus's theology, the over-arching context for his anthropology, we can examine Irenaeus's most detailed and sustained discussion of the creation and formation of man, given in chapters 11–15 of the

Demonstration, supplemented with details taken from else-where.

Unlike Philo and those fathers who followed in his wake, Irenaeus does not distinguish between the two accounts of the creation of man given in Genesis.[1] There was a single creation of man, and Irenaeus cites Genesis 1: 26 and 2: 7 together to support this.[2] After having discussed the rule of truth and various matters pertaining to angels, Irenaeus begins his discussion of protology with the formation of man:

But he fashioned man with his own hands, taking the purest, the finest ⟨and the most delicate⟩ [elements] of the earth, mixing with the earth, in due measure, his own power; and because he ⟨sketched upon⟩ the handiwork his own form—in order that what would be seen should be godlike, for man was placed upon the earth fashioned ⟨in⟩ the image of God—and that he might be alive, 'He breathed into his face a breath of life' [Gen. 2: 7]: so that both according to the inspiration and according to the formation, man was like God. Accordingly, he was free and master of himself, having been made by God in this way, [in order] that he should rule over everything upon earth. And this great created world, prepared by God before the fashioning of man, was given to man as [his] domain, having everything in it. (*Dem.* 11)[3]

Irenaeus combines both creation accounts to give a continuous description of the creation of man. Not only is there no distinction between the 'making' (ποίησις) of Genesis 1: 26 and the 'fashioning' (πλάσις) of Genesis 2: 7, but Irenaeus explains how God made man in his image by the action of the Hands of God fashioning the earth.[4]

That it is from the earth itself that God took the material he used to fashion man was important to Irenaeus. In *AH*

---

[1] Philo had distinguished between Gen. 1: 26, the ideal human, neither male nor female, created in the image, the true man or νοῦς, and Gen. 2: 7, the fashioning of mud into the sensible and corruptible body. Cf. *Opif.*, 46, 134. The terms were changed by Origen into the Pauline contrast between the 'inner man' and the 'outer man', but the distinction remained; cf. e.g. *Homily 1 on Genesis*, 13.

[2] Cf. *AH* 4. 20. 1; Orbe, *Antropología*, 13–27, and Andia, *Homo vivens*, 62–3.

[3] In quotations from the *Demonstration*, words in ⟨ ⟩ indicate a correction of a probable corruption of the text printed in PO 12. 5; and words in [ ] are supplementary additions to the text.

[4] *AH* 4. 20. 1.

5. 15. 2–4 Irenaeus argues against the Valentinians' claim that man was not fashioned out of this earth, but from 'a fluid and diffused matter'.[5] According to Irenaeus, the healing of the blind man by Christ—spitting on the ground, making mud, and smearing it on his eyes—indicates the original fashioning of man, by the same Hand of God with the same earth. As 'the work of God is fashioning man', God omitted to form the blind man's eyes in the womb, 'so that the work of God might be made manifest in him'.[6]

The act of Christ spitting on the ground is paralleled in *Dem.* 11 by Irenaeus's introduction of a supplementary action of God into Genesis 2: 7, the mixing of his power with the dust from the earth, as a preparation for the formation of man. We have already seen, in connection with baptism, how, for Irenaeus, dry earth, unless it receives the 'willing Rain from above', can neither bear fruit nor be made into one body.[7] This connection has led various scholars to assert that the 'power' of God spoken of in *Dem.* 11 is the Spirit.[8] Irenaeus does not, however, write about the Spirit here. A more fruitful comparison may be made with *AH* 5. 3. 1–3, where Irenaeus comments on 2 Corinthians 12: 9: the power of God which is made perfect in weakness. Irenaeus claims that the flesh which, at the beginning, was skilfully formed by God into its various parts, will by the same power of God be raised from the dead. Irenaeus describes with wonder the physical constitution (or 'economy', *AH* 5. 3. 2) of man: the eyes, ears, arteries, lungs, and so on. He concludes:

It is not possible to enumerate all the [melodious] parts of the human organism (τῆς κατὰ τὸν ἄνθρωπον μελοποιΐας), which was not made without the great wisdom of God. Whatever participates in the art and wisdom of God also participates in his power. The flesh, therefore, is not without part in the art, the wisdom and the power of God,

[5] *AH* 5. 15. 4; cf. *AH* 1. 5. 5; Orbe, *Antropología*, 53–7.

[6] *AH* 5. 15. 2; referring to John 9: 3.

[7] *AH* 3. 17. 2; see also the parallel drawn between the formation of Adam from 'untilled and virgin soil' and Christ's formation from Mary (*AH* 3. 21. 10).

[8] Cf. Fantino, *L'Homme*, 157; Orbe, who takes the power here to refer to the Spirit of God mentioned in Gen. 1: 2, understood as an *anima mundi*, rather than a 'Personal Spirit' (*Antropología*, 59–61); Andia, *Homo vivens*, 75–6.

but his power, which produces life, is made perfect in weakness, that is, in the flesh. (*AH* 5. 3. 2–3)[9]

Although, as we will see later, it is indeed the Spirit who is life-creating, the idea behind both *Dem.* 11 and *AH* 5. 3. 1–3 seems to be that whatever is created receives, and so participates in, the art, the power, and the wisdom of the Creator.[10] This is especially so in the case of the fashioning of man, who is 'the vessel of the work of God and of all his wisdom and power'.[11] It is by receiving this power, or having it 'mixed in', that the dust taken from the earth becomes God's handiwork (πλάσμα). The form in which Irenaeus cites Genesis 2: 7 in *AH* 5. 3. 2, 'and God, taking dust from the earth, fashioned (ἔπλασε[12]) man', parallels the description of God's activity in *Dem.* 11: God, taking the dust, mixed his own power with it, and so produced his handiwork (πλάσμα).

Before going on to Genesis 2: 7b, Irenaeus, in *Dem.* 11, turns to Genesis 1: 27 in order to explain in what form God fashioned man: that is, in his own image. Elsewhere Irenaeus explicitly rejected the possibility of locating the image of God in an immaterial part or quality of man.[13] Arguing against the Gnostics, Irenaeus stressed that an image must have a form, and a form can exist only in matter.[14] Consequently, he is emphatic that the image of God in man is described quite concretely in the flesh.[15] An image also has a revelatory function: the image reveals the archetype of which it is an image. If the image of God is located in the flesh of man, then that very flesh must reveal God. But as God himself is immaterial, and therefore formless, the archetype of the image of God in man must be the incarnate Son of God. As Irenaeus puts it:

[9] While the context suggests that the primary referent of the very rare word μελοποιΐα is bodily limbs, the allusion to melody making can hardly be accidental. See Rousseau's note, SC 152, 218.

[10] Cf. *AH* 5. 17. 1, 18. 1.

[11] *AH* 3. 20. 2.

[12] The *Sacra Parallela* has ἐποίησε, but both the Latin and Armenian suggest ἔπλασε.

[13] Cf. Fantino, *L'Homme*, 87–9.

[14] Cf. esp. *AH* 2. 7, 19. 6.

[15] Stated most explicitly in *AH* 5. 6. 1: 'carni quae est plasmata secundum imaginem Dei'. Cf. Fantino, *L'Homme*, 94–106.

'For ⟨I made⟩ man ⟨in⟩ the image of God' [Gen. 9: 6 LXX] and the image of God is the Son, according to whose image was man made; and for this reason, he appeared in the last times, to render the image like himself. (*Dem*. 22)[16]

The Son reveals the true human form through his incarnation, demonstrating at the same time that man is indeed in the image of God.[17] Adam, as 'the type of the One to come' (Rom. 5: 14; *AH* 3. 22. 3), typifies, in his flesh, the incarnate Son. Thus the fashioning of the human flesh is intimately connected to Christ, the archetype of man, and his revelation of the image of God, the manifestation of both God and man.

Alongside this indelible image relationship,[18] located in the flesh, man is also like God in his possession of free will. That man was made 'free and master of himself' is mentioned in *Dem*. 11, and in *AH* 4. 37. 4 this fact is brought into a relationship of similitude with God: 'Because man is possessed of free will from the beginning, and God is possessed of free will, in whose similitude man was created, advice is always given to him to keep fast the good, which is done by means of obedience to God'. J. Fantino convincingly argues that we must carefully distinguish between two uses of the word *similitudo*, depending upon whether it translates ὁμοιότης or ὁμοίωσις.[19] We will have to wait until we have finished considering Irenaeus's protology to see what he meant by the latter sense, the ὁμοίωσις, the 'likeness' man lost in Adam and regained in Christ. In the former sense it refers to man's free will, which makes him like or similar to the Creator and

[16] Fantino (*L'Homme*, 145–54), points out that there is no other text in which Irenaeus describes the Son as 'the image of God' or 'the image of the Father' (cf. 2 Cor. 4: 4; Col. 1: 15), and that therefore this text should not be read as asserting that man was created in the image of the pre-incarnate Son, an invisible image of the invisible Father, but rather that this phrase should be understood in the light of what follows—viz. that man was made in the image of the incarnate Son. We have repeatedly seen the uniqueness of God's self-manifestation in the Incarnation, and it is this fact which makes the incarnate Son the image of the invisible God.

[17] *AH* 5. 16. 2.

[18] *AH* 3. 18. 1 might be taken to suggest that man lost the status of being in the image (cf. Grant, *Irenaeus*, 52); yet the context is that what we lost in Adam, being in the image *and* likeness, we regained in Christ.

[19] Cf. Fantino, *L'Homme*, 110–18.

Father.[20] It is a freedom which extends beyond actions to include a freedom of faith,[21] and, as the foundation for man's response towards God, it has always been preserved intact by God.[22] To be human is to be in the image of God, and this implies acting and behaving in a manner appropriate to the image of God, and so necessitates being free.

The final aspect of the fashioning of man as described in *Dem.* 11 is the animation with the breath of life, which renders man like to God in 'inspiration' as well as in his bodily formation. It is striking that Irenaeus does not speak at all of the soul and its role in the formation of man. Irenaeus is not interested so much in the soul itself, as a principle of interiority, as in its animation of the flesh. In one of his few comments on the soul itself, Irenaeus describes it as the intellect of man, 'mind, thought, mental intuition and such like'.[23] Inasmuch as the soul animates the body, it is the breath of life to the body. In the context of inquiring what it was that the Apostle described as the 'mortal body' which will be raised by the Spirit, Irenaeus denies that it refers to the soul, and continues:

But souls are incorporeal when compared to mortal bodies; for God 'breathed into the face' of man 'a breath of life, and the man became a living soul' [Gen. 2: 7], and the breath of life is incorporeal. But one cannot call it[24] mortal, since it is the breath of life. (*AH* 5. 7. 1)

The soul is the breath of life to the body, whilst itself being the locus of intellectual activity.[25] The soul does not simply

---

[20] Fantino (ibid. 118), suggests that while the 'image' refers to the Son, the 'similitude' refers to the Father, and through these is achieved the 'likeness' effected by the Spirit: the first two are anthropological categories, while the latter is a soteriological notion, the central axis of the relationship between God and man.

[21] *AH* 4. 37. 5. [22] *AH* 4. 15. 2.

[23] *AH* 2. 29. 3. Irenaeus makes this comment on the properties and activity of the soul itself only because he is discussing the Gnostic idea of the separate destinies for each 'part' of man.

[24] To what does this 'it' refer? The Latin has *ipsum*, referring back to the breath of life. Rousseau (SC 152, 236–7), thinks that this is a misinterpretation on the part of the translator, and that it should be *ipsam*, referring back to the soul (the Greek in either case being αὐτήν). I have left it open. However, an identification between the soul and the breath of life is made more explicitly a few lines later on, when Irenaeus writes about death: 'Hoc autem neque animae evenit, flatus est enim vitae.'

[See p. 92 for n. 25]

animate the body, but uses the body as an artist uses an instrument. Although the body may slow down the speed of the soul's own movement, the body enables the soul to operate in the material world.[26] When describing how the soul animates the body, Irenaeus is careful to maintain that the soul does not lose any of the operations proper to it, such as knowledge or memory: as he puts it: 'while, as it were, sharing life with the body, it does not itself cease to live'.[27] Whilst animating the body, the soul in return assumes the shape of the body, to the extent that its form can be recognized after the body and soul are separated at death.[28]

However, whilst taking the role of the breath of life in animating the body, and as such immortal,[29] soul does not possess life by nature. This is stated most explicitly in *AH* 2. 34. 2–4, an important passage which shows a marked dependency on Justin's *Dialogue with Trypho*.[30] Here Irenaeus argues against those who too rigidly apply to the soul the philosophical principle that what begins in time is subject to corruption and so must also end in time.[31] Irenaeus stresses that only God is without beginning or end, remaining ever the same, and everything else depends on him, both for its initial coming into being and for its continuance in existence. All things continue as long as God wills them to be and to continue. Irenaeus then comments on Psalm 20: 5 (LXX):

[25] The breath of life, bringing man to life, can also be described as showing man to be a rational animal, cf. *AH* 5. 1. 3.

[26] *AH* 2. 33. 4.

[27] *AH* 2. 33. 4.

[28] Irenaeus never says that souls possess a *sui generis* body (σῶμα), as did some Stoics (e.g. *SVF* 2. 790, 219. 24–8), but simply that they retain the form of the body. Cf. *AH* 2. 19. 6, and, apropos of the history of Lazarus and the rich man (Luke 16: 19–31), *AH* 2. 34. 1.

[29] For the immortality of the soul, see *AH* 5. 4. 1, 7. 1, 13. 3; and A. Rousseau, 'L'Éternité des peines de l'enfer et l'immortalité naturelle de l'âme selon saint Irénée', *NRT* 99 (1977), 834–64.

[30] The similarity is denied by Rousseau on the ground that the term 'life' in each signifies a different reality: for Irenaeus, the 'life of the Spirit'; for Justin, the 'natural life of the soul' (cf. SC 293, 348). The relationship between the two passages is upheld by van Winden, *An Early Christian Philosopher*, and Andia, *Homo vivens*, 271–3, who usefully prints both texts in parallel.

[31] A philosophical commonplace that goes back to Plato, cf. *Republic*, 8. 546a.

And again, he thus speaks of the man being saved: 'He asked life of thee, and thou gavest him length of days for ages and ages', as the Father of all bestowing also continuance for 'ages of ages' on those who are saved. For life does not arise from us, nor from our own nature; but it is bestowed according to the grace of God. And therefore, those who will have preserved the gift of life, and have given thanks to him who imparted it, will also receive 'length of days for ages of ages'. But those who will have rejected it, and will have proved themselves ungrateful to their Maker, inasmuch as they have been made and will not have recognized the Bestower, deprive themselves of continuance for ages of ages. And, for this reason, the Lord declared to those who showed themselves ungrateful towards him: 'If you have not been faithful in that which is little, who will give you that which is great?' [Luke 16: 11] indicating that those who, in this brief temporal life, have shown themselves ungrateful to him who bestowed it, shall justly not receive from him 'length of days for ages of ages'. (*AH* 2. 34. 3)

This passage contains many of the themes which we encountered in the study of the divine economy, primarily that man's existence should be one of thankfulness towards the God who has bestowed life upon him. What man learns through the economy, his experience of his own weakness and death, that 'we should not be puffed up as if we had life from our own nature',[32] is here stated as a general principle. God is the source of all life. If a man shows himself to be thankful, in his use of this 'gift of life' in this 'brief temporal life', towards him who bestowed it, he will receive from God 'length of days for ages of ages'—that is, continuance in the life bestowed by God.

Irenaeus concludes AH 2. 34 by bringing the discussion back to Genesis 2: 7:

But as the animated body is certainly not itself the soul, yet participates in the soul as long as God pleases; so also the soul herself assuredly is not life, but partakes in that life bestowed from God himself. Wherefore also the prophetic word declares of the first-formed, 'he became a living soul', teaching us that by participation of life the soul was made 'living' so that the soul is thought of separately, and separately also the life which is in her. With God therefore bestowing life and perpetual continuance, it comes to pass that even souls which did not at first exist should henceforth continue, since God will have both willed them to be and to continue. (*AH* 2. 34. 4)

[32] *AH* 5. 2. 3.

The soul, created out of nothing, does not in herself possess life, but participates in the life bestowed by God. Becoming in this way a 'living soul', the soul can also animate the body, and as such is a 'breath of life to the body'.[33]

A. Rousseau, in his desire to maintain the 'natural immortality' of the soul against H. Lassiat, seriously vitiates the profundity of Irenaeus's thought on this issue of the soul and her life.[34] According to Rousseau, Irenaeus's use of the word 'life' in *AH* 2. 34. 3–4 is determined by the mention of 'salvation' introducing the quotation from Psalm 20: 5.[35] Rousseau asserts that Irenaeus is not speaking of the physical or biological life of man, but of 'la vie supérieure qu'instaure en nous l'Esprit Saint par sa présence sanctificatrice et divinisante'.[36] It is this 'life of the Spirit' which the first Adam enjoyed from the instant he left his Creator's Hands and, having lost it through his disobedience, regained it through the obedience of the second Adam.[37]

However, it is a mistake to isolate this passage from the discussion, which extends throughout *AH* 2. 34, concerning how it is that created beings might remain indefinitely in

---

[33] *AH* 5. 7. 1. In *AH* 5. 4. 1, Irenaeus might be suggesting that the soul lives by its own nature, 'a sua natura adest vivere'. This statement occurs in a sentence in which Irenaeus criticizes the Gnostic idea of a God who does not vivify the whole person, soul *and* body, but only the soul. As such, the statement that the soul lives by its own nature might refer to the Gnostic position; so Irenaeus would be emphasizing that the Christian God vivifies both soul and body. This was the position taken by H. Lassiat, *Promotion de l'homme en Jésus-Christ d'après Irénée de Lyon* (Tours, 1974), 165–6; *idem*, 'L'Anthropologie d'Irénée', *NRT* 100 (1978), 411–12, and criticized by Rousseau, 'L'Éternité des peines', 847–8. If Irenaeus is indeed affirming that it is the nature of souls to live, this is simply because his interest in the soul is primarily, if not exclusively, as a principle of animation for the body.

[34] Rousseau's article, 'L'Éternité des peines', and his 'notes justificatives' pertaining to this passage are directed against the thesis of H. Lassiat, *Pour une théologie de l'homme. Création . . . Liberté . . . Incorruptibilité . . .* (Lille, 1972), published in a shortened form as *Promotion de l'homme*. Lassiat responded to Rousseau in 'L'Anthropologie d'Irénée'.

[35] Cf. SC 293, 348–9.

[36] Rousseau, 'L'Éternité des peines', 854. Cf. ibid., 842–3; SC 293, 346.

[37] Cf. Rousseau, SC 293, 347, commenting on *AH* 2. 34. 4, and appealing to *AH* 3. 18. 1, 5. 16. 3 (*sic*), which, however, say nothing about what 'life' it was that Adam had; they speak only of the 'likeness' lost by Adam and re-established by Christ.

existence: all is from God, and all is maintained in existence by him as long as he wills. If Irenaeus upholds the 'natural immortality' of the soul, this is a point which must be carefully distinguished from the question of the life and immortality which belong to God alone and which are participated in by the whole human being, body and soul. According to Irenaeus, the soul certainly endures after death, as his commentary on the 'history' of Lazarus and the rich man at the beginning of this section demonstrates (*AH* 2. 34. 1); but Irenaeus never describes this continuance, nor that of the damned in the eternal fire, as immortality: it is possible for the soul to endure without life, just as it is possible, conversely, for the naturally corruptible body to participate in life, immortality, and incorruptibility. Furthermore, although the question of life, as we shall see, is connected with the life-creating Spirit, Irenaeus does not speak of the Spirit in this section.

It is similarly mistaken to equate the pre-lapsarian life of Adam with the life of the Spirit manifested by Christ. That they should be regarded as different modalities of life is demanded by, first, Genesis 2: 7, which speaks only of the first man becoming a 'living soul' ($\psi\nu\chi\grave{\eta}\nu$ $\zeta\hat{\omega}\sigma\alpha\nu$); second, the apostle Paul, who specifies that it is the last Adam who became a life-creating Spirit ($\pi\nu\epsilon\hat{\nu}\mu\alpha$ $\zeta\omega\sigma\pi\sigma\iota\sigma\hat{\nu}\nu$), in contrast to the first Adam who was a 'living soul' (1 Cor. 15: 45–6); third, the whole movement of Irenaeus's theology of the economy, which moves from 'animation' to 'vivification': as Adam was animated by the breath of life, so Christ was vivified by the Spirit, as also will be those who, as adopted sons in him, presently have the pledge of the Spirit.

Most important, however, is Rousseau's assumption that the 'life' in this section is somehow other than the physical or biological life of man.[38] Given Irenaeus's emphasis on the essentially physical, fleshly nature of man, it makes no sense to speak of man possessing a life which is not lived in the flesh, in a similarly physical and fleshly manner.[39] Irenaeus does not

---

[38] Cf. SC 293, 346; 'L'Éternité des peines', 843. This problem has already been referred to apropos of *AH* 4. 20. 5 and Donovan's comment in 'Alive to the Glory of God', 289; see p. 56 n. 76.

[39] Lassiat, 'L'Anthropologie d'Irénée', 405, criticizes Rousseau for 'gnosifying' the thought of Irenaeus.

make any such distinction in this passage. The only qualifica-
tion concerning 'life' that he makes, in *AH* 2. 34. 3, is that 'the
gift of life' given by God is presently a 'brief temporal life', in
which man is to demonstrate his readiness to accept it 'for
length of days for ages and ages'.[40]

In *AH* 5. 3. 3 Irenaeus explains further his understanding of
the relationship between the present temporal life and eternal
life. In this section, Irenaeus is arguing against those who deny
that the flesh can be vivified by God:

> But if they now live, and if their whole body partakes of life, how can
> they dare to say that the flesh is not able to partake of life, when they
> do confess that they have life at the present moment? . . . If the
> present temporal life, which is much weaker than that eternal life, is
> nevertheless able to vivify our mortal members, why should not
> eternal life, being much more powerful than this, vivify the flesh,
> already exercised and accustomed to sustain life? For that the flesh is
> capable of receiving life is shown from the fact of its being alive; for it
> lives as long as God wants it to live. It is manifest, too, that God has
> the power to confer life upon it, for when he grants life, we live. (*AH*
> 5. 3. 3)

Like *AH* 2. 34, this passage emphasizes that man lives as long
as God wants, or as long as God confers life on his flesh. It is
important to note that although it is God who provides life, it is
man who lives. Participating in this life provided by God, man
does not lose his identity; nor does the gift exist apart from him
or superadded to him; but, rather, the gift is 'personalized' by
each human being: the gift is life, yet it is the human being who
lives this life in their flesh.

The most significant feature of *AH* 5. 3. 3, however, is that
there is a direct continuity between the life which human
beings (even the Gnostics) presently live and the eternal life
which will vivify them in the resurrection. The only distinction
made between the two is that of 'weaker' and 'stronger', with
their correlates 'temporal' and 'eternal'.[41] There is no sugges-

---

[40] Cf. Fantino, *La Théologie d'Irénée*, 319–21, points out that for Irenaeus
'created life' is already a gift of God, a participation, in a certain (though,
according to Fantino, unspecified) manner, in the uncreated life of God.

[41] Cf. Noormann, *Irenäus*, 277, 486–7. In *AH* 4. 9. 2, Irenaeus states that
the adjectives 'more' and 'less' can only be applied to things of the same

tion that they are two different types of life: physical/biological and spiritual/the presence of the Spirit. That the flesh has become accustomed, in this present temporal life, to bear life demonstrates that it is capable of being vivified by eternal life. If it were a question of two different 'lives', Irenaeus's argument would be undermined.

The confusion seems to arise from a reluctance to accept that the Holy Spirit is present with creation, and especially with man, not only in the protological time of Adam's pre-lapsarian existence, but also throughout the apostasy, preferring instead to associate the presence of the Spirit with the 'likeness' which man lost in Adam and regained in Christ. This reluctance is combined with a desire to avoid the charge, first made in the sixteenth century by the Magdeburgian Centuriators, that Irenaeus taught that Adam was not created 'perfect'. The corollary of positing the full perfection of Adam in his original state was to turn the effect of the Incarnation into Adam's return to his pre-lapsarian state.[42] If one holds that the life-creating Spirit was not present to the human race during the course of the apostasy, then one must also postulate a separate source of life, a breath of life, which is merely physical and has nothing to do with communion with God. A consequence of this position would be to interpret the demand to deny oneself and take up the cross, losing one's life in order to find it (Matt. 16: 24–5), as referring to losing one's merely natural life in order to gain true life in communion with God.[43] But when looking at the economy, we have seen that Irenaeus does, in fact, envisage the continual nourishing presence of the Spirit, which, nevertheless, was bestowed in a new manner in Christ at the end of time, and therefore, in its fullness, remains an eschatological reality, of which the adopted sons, at present, receive a pledge.[44]

nature, such as water, light, and grace. All life is of the grace of God, and thus there is no distinction in 'nature' between the weaker and the stronger.

[42] Cf. Wingren's perceptive comments on the false perspective of the approach which wants to ask of Irenaeus if Adam was 'perfect' in his 'original state' (*Man and the Incarnation*, 28–9). Wingren also repeatedly stresses that all life is from God, is communion with God (ibid., esp. 14, 54 n. 36, 108, 120).

[43] This would also entail an appropriation of the cross as something other than that which Christ himself underwent; see Irenaeus's comments on this passage in *AH* 3. 18. 5, discussed above (see p. 76).

[*See p. 98 for n. 44*]

So far, following the sequence suggested by *Dem.* 11, we have considered Irenaeus's comments on the formation of the body, its animation by the breath of life, and the relationship of the soul to both the body and the life in which it participates. What, then, does Irenaeus have to say regarding the presence of the Holy Spirit in the human formation?

Irenaeus knows the philosophical definition of man as 'an animal composed of soul and body', but never uses it as a definition of a self-sufficient 'natural' man to whom the Spirit is somehow superadded. For the most part, when Irenaeus speaks of man as 'composed of soul and body', it is in the context of exhorting his readers to live righteously in both soul and body, or, alternatively, of defending the resurrection of both.[45] More important is the fact that only the body and soul, both created out of nothing, can, strictly speaking, be described as man or be called 'parts' of man—the life in which they participate, although integral to a living man, comes from God. Thus, although Irenaeus occasionally describes man as a 'compound being',[46] a 'mixture' or 'union' of flesh and soul,[47] because the soul, and through it the body, must participate in life to be a living man, such descriptions are not sufficient definitions of the living man.

When looking at the significance of martyrdom in the unfolding of the economy, we saw something of the role of the Spirit in the vivification of man: when the Spirit absorbs the weakness of the flesh, from both of these is formed a living man, 'living, indeed, because of the participation of the Spirit, and man because of the substance of the flesh'.[48] From this perspective, Irenaeus can, in the context of a discussion on the similarity between the formation of Adam and the birth of Christ, describe man as 'a body taken from the earth, and a soul receiving the Spirit from God'.[49] Similarly, Irenaeus asserts that death befalls neither the soul, for it is a breath of life, nor the Spirit, for it is simple and cannot be decomposed, and 'is itself the life of those who receive it'.[50] The Spirit is clearly

[44] Cf. *AH* 4. 33. 1, 7, 15 (all of which have the character of 'rules of truth'); 5. 1. 3, 28. 4.

[45] Cf. e.g. *Dem.* 2; *AH* 5. 20. 1.   [46] *AH* 2. 28. 4; cf. *AH* 2. 13. 3.

[47] *AH* 4. pref. 4; 5. 8. 2.   [48] *AH* 5. 9. 2.

[49] *AH* 3. 22. 1.   [50] *AH* 5. 7. 1.

connected to the life lived by man: the Spirit is indeed life-creating. Yet, in the same way that Irenaeus carefully distinguished, in *AH* 2. 34, between man, whose parts are the body and soul, and the life in which he participates, so too the Spirit must not be thought of as a 'part' of man.

That the Spirit is essential to Irenaeus's understanding of man, yet is not a 'part' of his constitution, is brought out by two passages, most clearly in *AH* 5. 6. 1, where Irenaeus is discussing the eschatologically 'perfect' man, made spiritual by the full bestowal of the Spirit in the manner newly made possible by Christ, and so made in the image and likeness of God. The passage is long, but its importance merits examining it fully:

Now the soul and the Spirit can be a part of man, but by no means a man; the perfect man is the commingling and the union of the soul receiving the Spirit of the Father and joined to the flesh which was moulded after the image of God. For this reason the Apostle says 'We speak wisdom among them that are perfect' [1 Cor. 2: 6], calling those 'perfect' who have received the Spirit of God . . . these the Apostle also calls 'spiritual'—being spiritual by a participation in the Spirit and not by a deprivation and removal of the flesh [and merely that itself alone]. For if anyone take away the substance [of the flesh, that is] of the handiwork, and merely considers only the Spirit itself, such is no longer what is a spiritual man, but the Spirit of a man or the Spirit of God.[51] But when this Spirit, commingled with the soul, is united to the handiwork, because of the outpouring of the Spirit man is rendered spiritual and perfect, and this is the one who was made in

---

[51] The words in square brackets are only in the Latin version, and seem to be an attempt to soften Irenaeus's words; I have followed the Armenian in my interpretation. Rousseau's translation of 'et nude ipsum solum Spiritum intellegat' as 'pour ne considérer que ce qui est proprement esprit' is misleading, enabling his interpretation of the following phrase, 'Spiritus hominis', as the human soul, distinct from the 'Spiritus Dei'. But Irenaeus never refers to the soul as 'spiritus', and the whole thrust here is that the Spirit of God is present in men to such an extent that it can be considered 'their Spirit', without it being a 'part' of man, as Rousseau notes in his comments on the quotation of 1 Thess. 5: 23 (ὑμῶν τὸ πνεῦμα) in *AH* 5. 6. 1; cf. SC 152, 233–4. Rousseau also interprets the phrase 'their Spirit[s]' in *AH* 2. 33. 5 in this way; cf. SC 293, 339–42. Only in *AH* 2. 31. 2 might Irenaeus use the term 'spirit' to refer to the 'soul', though the choice of words here probably reflects Luke 8: 55, cited earlier, which would thus be consistent with the interpretation of *AH* 5. 6. 1 given here and of *AH* 2. 33. 5 and 5. 18. 2, as we shall see.

the image and likeness of God. But if the Spirit is lacking from the soul, such a one, remaining indeed animated and fleshly, will be imperfect, having the image, certainly, in the handiwork, but not receiving the likeness through the Spirit. Likewise this one is imperfect, in the same manner again, if someone takes away the image and rejects the handiwork—one can no longer contemplate a man, but either some part of man, as we have said, or something other than the man. For neither is the handiwork of the flesh itself, by itself, a perfect man, but the body of a man and a part of a man; nor is the soul itself, by itself, a man, but the soul of a man and a part of a man; nor is the Spirit a man, for it is called Spirit and not man. But the commingling and union of all of these constitutes the perfect man. (*AH* 5. 6. 1)

The soul and the Spirit together are a part of man, but not the man—for this we need the flesh which has been formed in the image. Irenaeus's emphasis on this fact is striking: what is important for him is not so much the presence of the Spirit in man, but the reality of the flesh. Yet, while the body, soul, and Spirit cannot individually be called a man, the body and soul can be called 'parts' of man in a way in which the Spirit cannot—for it is the Spirit, something other than man. In this passage, it is no longer a question of the flesh being animated by the breath of life, but of the flesh which is fully vivified or made spiritual by the Spirit; that it is an eschatological description is made clear by the citation of 1 Thessalonians 5: 23 towards the end of the section.[52] If we take away the Spirit, as it is given in Christ (for this is the context), then we are left with an animated and fleshly being. We have seen how the soul animates the flesh by participating in the gift of life and, as such, belongs to the handiwork which is animated by the breath of life.[53] Thus, if we take away the substance of the handiwork—flesh animated by the soul—we are left with 'only the Spirit itself', which Irenaeus describes as 'the Spirit of a man or the Spirit of God'. The Spirit itself is not a man, nor even a part of a man, but is itself given to man in such a manner that it can be legitimately described as his Spirit.

[52] Cf. Andia, *Homo vivens*, 84–5.

[53] In *AH* 5. 8. 2, in a very similar context, the human *substantia* is said to be the 'union of soul and body', which is perfected by the addition of the Spirit.

This fact is brought out by the second passage, *AH* 2. 33. 5, where Irenaeus discusses the resurrection:

all those who have been enrolled for life shall rise again, having their own body, their own soul, and their own Spirit, in which they had pleased God. Those, on the other hand, who are worthy of punishment, shall go away into it, they too having their own souls, and their own bodies, in which they stood apart from the goodness of God.[54]

Here we see the same dynamics as are operative in Irenaeus's discussion of life in *AH* 2. 34 and *AH* 5. 3. 3: those who have been thankful for the gift of life in this temporal life, and are thus pleasing to God, will be raised and maintained in eternal life. But now this thought is expressed in terms of the Spirit, which is given to each in a manner that makes the Spirit 'their Spirit'. Thus those who have pleased God in their body, soul, and Spirit will be raised in their body, soul, and Spirit. The parallel dynamics of these texts, and the fact that it is *in* their body, soul, and Spirit that they have pleased God, demand that it is also in their body, soul, *and* Spirit that the others have shown themselves worthy of punishment, and so are raised in their body and soul for the punishment of an existence without the Spirit, without participation in life.[55]

So the Spirit is vital to a proper appreciation of Irenaeus's understanding of man. There is no 'complete' or 'perfect' man without the Spirit, but the Spirit is not a 'part' of man; just as man does not live without participating in life, yet he does not possess life in his own nature. Although we have seen, when looking at the unfolding of the economy, the continual nourishing presence of the Spirit in creation, the passages so far examined concerning the presence of the Spirit in man have been of limited scope: *AH* 5. 6. 1 speaks unambiguously of the 'perfect', spiritual, eschatological man possessing the fullness of the Spirit as it is given in Christ; *AH* 2. 33. 5 asserts that those who have pleased God will rise in their body, soul, and Spirit, though it can be inferred that those who did not please God had 'their' Spirit before their death.

[54] The words 'body', 'soul', and 'Spirit' are given in the plural in both the Latin and the Greek (from the *Sacra Parallela*). I have followed Rousseau in translating these terms in the singular; cf. SC 293, 341–2.

[55] Rousseau, however, prefers to restrict the possession of the 'Spirit' to those who have been justified (SC 293, 339–40).

There is one further passage which merits close attention. Having described in *AH* 5. 18. 1 how the creation 'which subsists by the power, the skill and the wisdom of God' is borne in an invisible manner by the Father, but itself bore the Word in a visible manner, Irenaeus, before going on to cite and comment on Ephesians 4: 6, continues in *AH* 5. 18. 2:

> And this is true. For the Father simultaneously bears the creation and his own Word, and the Word borne by the Father bestows the Spirit on all as the Father wills,

Due to the difficulties of translation, the remaining part of the sentence must be given in both versions:

> quibusdam quidem secundum conditionem, [quod est conditionis], quod est factum; quibusdam autem secundum adoptionem, quod est ex Deo, quod est generatio.

> ամնոցիկ, որ բատ աշխարՀիս են, զաշխարՀիս, որ է եղեալն, իսկ ամնոցիկ, որ բատ որդեգրութեանն են, զ ի Հայրէն, որ է ծնունդն Նորա:[56]

The perplexity of the Latin scribes at this sentence is clearly shown by the omission of 'quod est conditionis' from two of the main manuscripts and by the fourfold use of 'quod est' without a preceding neuter substantive. Not wanting to accept that the Spirit might be present in creation outside Christ, Massuet asserted that the 'Verbum praestat spiritum omnibus, quemadmodum vult Pater, sed non eundem',[57] and this view has since predominated. Rousseau explains the use of the neuter relative by suggesting a careless translation from the Greek (in which $\pi\nu\epsilon\hat{\upsilon}\mu\alpha$ is neuter),[58] and translates as follows:

> ... et le Verbe, porté par le Père, donne l'Esprit (esprit) à tous, de la manière que veut le Père aux uns, en raport avec leur création, il donne l'esprit appartenant à la création, esprit qui est une chose fait;

[56] The Latin words in square brackets are omitted in two main manuscripts, Claromontanus and Vossianus. The Armenian is found in TU 35. 2, 197. 3–5, following the emendation proposed by Mercier.

[57] Massuet, *Sancti Irenaei*, PG 7. 1173 n. 72.

[58] Cf. SC 152, 287. Rousseau refers to S. Lündstrom, *Übersetzungstechnische Untersuchungen auf dem Gebiete der christlichen Latinität* (Lund, 1955), for a survey of such examples. It is important to note that mistranslations can occur into any gender, cf. Lündstrom, 240–74.

aux autres, en rapport avec leur adoption, il donne l'Esprit provenant du Père, Esprit qui est la Progéniture de celui-ci.

Rousseau's reading of the text, and the whole of his lengthy 'note justificative' is intended to demonstrate that Irenaeus is using the word *Spiritum* to mean two different things: both a created 'spirit', which Rousseau identifies with the soul or the breath of life, and the Holy Spirit.[59] However, as we have seen, Irenaeus never calls the soul 'spirit';[60] nor, moreover, does he play with words to this extent. Furthermore, Rousseau's reading necessitates applying 'quod est generatio [eius]', or որ է ծնունդն նորա, to the Holy Spirit. Rousseau, acknowledging that the description of the Holy Spirit as 'Progéniture' is somewhat unusual in patristic literature, points to *AH* 5. 36. 3, where Irenaeus applies the term *progenies* to the Son, and to *AH* 4. 7. 4, where, in his interpretation, it is applied to both the Son and the Spirit.[61] Looking further afield, Rousseau can only adduce one passage, from Leontius of Byzantium, where the term γέννημα is applied to the Spirit.[62]

---

[59] Rousseau's interpretation is followed by both Jaschke, *Der Heilige Geist*, 206–7, and Andia, *Homo vivens*, 338–43. Orbe maintains that the 'created spirit' cannot be identified with the soul, but is the Spirit as an *anima mundi*, distinct from the personal spirit (*Teología*, 2. 211–18); but, as with his interpretation of the 'power of God' in *Dem.* 11, there is no reason, in Irenaeus's text, to think that this should be so. For a more considered discussion, see Fantino, *La Théologie d'Irénée*, 367–9.

[60] The only comparison that Rousseau can adduce is his interpretation of *AH* 5. 6. 1, discussed above.

[61] However, Rousseau's justification for this interpretation fails to persuade. In *AH* 4. 7. 4 Irenaeus explains that God did not need the help of the angels to bring creation into being and to form man: 'ministrat enim ei ad omnia sua progenies et figuratio sua, hoc est Filius et Spiritus, Verbum et Sapientia, quibus serviunt et subiecti sunt omnes angeli'. Where the Latin has *figuratio sua*, the Armenian has իւր ձեռքն, 'his own Hands'. Rousseau believes that ձեռքն ('hands') was mistranscribed as ձեւն ('figure'), and so translates the phrase as 'sa Progéniture et ses Mains'. The error occurring the other way around would, however, also explain why the Latin has *figuratio*, something for which Rousseau has no explanation. Cf. SC 100, 212–19; J. A. Robinson, 'Notes on the Armenian Version of *Adv. Haereses* IV, V', *JTS* 32 (1930–1), 156–7. These two cases (*AH* 4. 7. 4; 5. 36. 3) are the only instances of the term being applied in a trinitarian context; Rousseau also lists various other instances which have no bearing on *AH* 5. 18. 2; cf. SC 152, 294–5.

[62] Leontius, *De Sectis*, PG 86. 1220b; this is in fact the only occurrence of

The most striking aspect of this reading of *AH* 5. 18. 2 is its divisive interpretation of the 'Spirit'. The very structure of the passage demands that it is one and the same Spirit that is given to all—in different manners, certainly, as the Father wills, but the same Spirit nevertheless.[63] How then is the passage to be understood?

The Armenian word ծնունդ is used twenty-three times in the Armenian version of *Against the Heresies*. In the majority of cases it conveys the idea of generation or engendering (γέν-νησις), referring either to our natural birth or to a rebirth, a new or second birth.[64] Much less frequently does it refer to that which is born (γέννημα).[65] As such it makes sense to read ծնունդ as 'engendering', and so to refer որ է ծնունդ ('which is an engendering')[66] back to որդեգրութեանն ('adoption'), rather than զ՚ի Հաւրէն ('the [Spirit] from the Father'). The phrase 'the [Spirit] from the Father' is the only phrase in the clause with the definite object marker, զ, indicating that it is 'the [Spirit] from the Father' which is being given. Thus, the second clause should be translated: 'to others, who are according to adoption, which is an engendering, he gives the Spirit of the Father'. As the two clauses are clearly structured in

this application of the term given by G. W. H. Lampe (ed.), *A Patristic Greek Lexicon* (Oxford, 1961, repr. 1989), 312.

[63] For the Spirit being given as the Father wills, see also *Dem.* 7, and Irenaeus's claim that though the Spirit is present in all generations (*AH* 4. 33. 1), the Spirit is nevertheless given in Christ, in a *new manner*; cf. e.g. *AH* 4. 33. 15, *Dem.* 6.

[64] The following list is based on B. Reynders (ed.), *Lexique comparé du texte grec et des versions latine, arménienne et syriaque de l'"Adversus Haereses" de saint Irénée*, CSCO, 141–2, subsidia 5–6 (Louvain, 1954), and gives the Latin equivalent: *nativitas AH* 4. 21. 3, line 37 (TU 35. 2, 77. 31); 5. 15. 2, 59 (189. 24); 5. 15. 3, 90 (190. 20); *generatio* 4. 21. 3, 42 (78. 3); 4. 33. 2, 43 (108. 28); 4. 33. 4, 81, 82 (110. 3); 5. 1. 3, 63, 68, 69, 70 (153. 13, 18, 19, 20); 5. 15. 1, 3 (188. 3); 5. 18. 2, 35 (197. 5); 5. 33. 1, 7, 13, 15, 19 (233. 19, 25, 27; 234. 1); *genesis* 4. 33. 4, 85 (110. 7).

[65] *AH* 4. 7. 4, 68 (26. 17) and 5. 36. 3, 70 (245. 17) of the Son of God; 4. 41. 3, 46 (148. 2–3); 5. 33. 4, 100 (236. 16).

[66] As the genitive demonstrative pronoun նորա ('of him') is in the singular in the clause as given above, it cannot refer back to 'the others', who are thus 'engendered'; so, on the basis of the Latin version, in which it is uniformly absent, and the evident parallelism between the two clauses, it seems reasonable to omit it. It is also possible that it is mistranscribed for the plural genitive demonstrative pronoun, նոցա.

parallel, the phrase որ է եղեալն ('which is made') refers back to the term աշխարհս ('the/this creation'), rather than the term զաշխարհս, which, with the definite object marker, refers to that which is given ('the [Spirit] of the/this creation'); so the first clause should be: 'to some, who are according to the creation, which is made, he gives the Spirit of creation'. Thus the sentence as a whole, translated a bit more freely, runs:

For the Father simultaneously bears the creation and his own Word, and the Word borne by the Father bestows the Spirit on all as the Father wills,
to some, who are in a created state, which is made, he gives the Spirit pertaining to creation,
to others, who are according to adoption, an engendering, he gives the Spirit of the Father.

This text, so rendered, affirms what has been evident throughout: that the Spirit of God, who was present with creation throughout the whole of the economy, was nevertheless bestowed in a special manner on those who have been adopted as sons of God: as sons, they can receive the Spirit from the Father. Those who have not been adopted as sons, but who remain in their created state, can receive only the Spirit as the Spirit is present throughout creation.

What, then, is the relationship between the Spirit and the breath of life? Irenaeus describes this relationship in *AH* 5. 12. 1–2, an important passage which needs to be described fully. This passage follows Irenaeus's exegesis of 1 Corinthians 15 that flesh and blood cannot inherit the kingdom, but can, nevertheless *be inherited* by the Spirit when vivified by the Spirit (1 Cor. 15: 50; *AH* 5. 9–10). Likewise, while working the deeds of the flesh, we have borne the image of the earthly one, but having been baptized and received the Spirit, we bear the image of the heavenly One, made alive by the workings of the Spirit (1 Cor. 15: 48–9; *AH* 5. 11). As in *AH* 5. 6. 1, the vivifying presence of the Spirit is that bestowed in baptism and the resurrection.

In *AH* 5. 12. 2 Irenaeus continues working backwards on the fifteenth chapter of 1 Corinthians, to explain verses 45–6. Irenaeus asserts that the breath of life, which made man an animated being, is other than the life-creating Spirit which

makes him spiritual. He then cites two passages from Isaiah
(42: 5; 57: 16) to demonstrate that, whilst the breath of life is
common to all people upon earth, the Spirit is peculiar to those
who tread down their earthly desires, and, furthermore, is
poured out upon the human race in the last times through
adoption. Picking up on Isaiah 57: 16, 'For the Spirit shall go
forth from me, and I have made every breath', and following its
terminology, Irenaeus describes the breath of life as something
'made', and thus to be differentiated from that which makes. As
something made, the breath is temporal, and in a short time
will leave its abode bereft of breath. But when the Spirit
pervades man inside and out, it is permanent, and remains
with the man. Irenaeus then cites 1 Corinthians 15: 46 to
demonstrate that as it is the 'animated' which is first, and only
then the 'spiritual', so, he argues, 'it was necessary first for man
to be fashioned, and having been fashioned to receive the soul,
and then to receive communion with the Spirit'. That Irenaeus
has changed from speaking of the 'breath' to the 'soul' is
because he is now commenting on 1 Corinthians 15: 46, and
follows his comments by citing 1 Corinthians 15: 45. He
concludes this section thus: 'Therefore, just as the one who
became a living soul turning to evil, lost life, so again, that same
one, in turning to what is better and receiving the life-creating
Spirit, finds life' (*AH* 5. 12. 2). In this whole passage, the
relationship between the breath of life and the Spirit is
characterized by the description of the Spirit as life-creating.
Those who have not received the Spirit through adoption
possess only the breath of life. Not being adopted sons of
God, they can receive only the Spirit in a manner pertaining to
their created state, and so, apropos of Isaiah 57: 16, Irenaeus
describes this as a created breath. Yet that which is created is
placed in a direct relationship to the One who creates it. It
would be a mistake to reify the breath of life, to treat it as
something which, once created, exists independently of its
source. Man, as we have seen repeatedly, does not have
independent life, but depends on God and his acknowledgement of God as the Source of life.

In *AH* 5. 12. 2 the breath of life is described not only as
temporal, but also as mortal. This is undoubtedly due to the
context, which contrasts life outside Christ with that given by

the Spirit in Christ. In his most detailed presentation of protology, the opening section of the *Demonstration*, Irenaeus asserts that man, animated by the breath of life, could have remained immortal by continuing to acknowledge God as the Lord of all (that is, as the source of all life).[67] When Adam and Eve transgressed this basic structure, the breath of life lost its 'strength', and they eventually died. But this life did not change from being the direct vivification by the Spirit to a 'mere' animation by the breath, for full vivification is possible only for the man adopted in Christ. In *AH* 5. 12. 2 Irenaeus similarly states that by turning aside to evil, the one who was a living soul lost life. But, he continues, when the same one returns to God, as an adopted son in Christ, he will receive the life-creating Spirit and find life. Those who through adoption possess the Spirit, either as a pledge in the present or in fullness in the resurrection, are vivified by the very One who creates life and never ceases from so doing. They are vivified 'inside and out' in a permanent fashion; the Spirit takes possession of its inheritance, flesh and blood, and the result is a living, rather than an animated, man. The former life, as Irenaeus says in the last lines of *AH* 5. 12. 1, is expelled, as it was given through the breath and not through the Spirit. Unlike those who are animated by the breath of life, created by the presence of the life-creating Spirit, the adopted sons of God receive the vivifying Spirit itself, 'communion with the Spirit'. Thus there are not two 'sources' of life, independent from each other; only the Spirit is life-creating. The difference between animation and vivification turns upon man's receptive capacity, either as a created being or as an adopted son of God, as described in *AH* 5. 18. 2.

Despite its inherent limitations, an analogy might be helpful. The created world is illumined and nourished by the light and warmth of the sun. The light and warmth which the world reflects or absorbs are a created state in the matter of the world, but are none the less continually dependent upon that source of light and warmth. If they are overshadowed, breaking that direct relationship between the source and its recipient, the matter will gradually lose its warmth and then turn cold. But the fading warmth of the matter, whilst overshadowed, is still

[67] *Dem.* 15.

that of the sun. Similarly, human life depends on God, who sustains and nourishes his creation. If man turns away from God, he will continue for a while and then die; the breath of life, with which God animated the human, will have lost its strength. Nevertheless, the life is still that which has been effected by the presence of God through his life-creating Spirit: it will have lost its strength, but it has not changed from being a 'spiritual' life to animation. As the light and warmth of the material world are but a pale reflection of those of the sun itself, so human life, outside Christ, is but a snatched breath compared to vivification by God himself. Yet, as God has become incarnate, he has enabled his sons, those adopted in Christ, to be illumined and warmed, or vivified, directly by his own life or life-creating Spirit.

As those outside Christ only have a breath of life which has lost its strength—that is, a life which has become mortal—Irenaeus occasionally describes such people as being dead. In *AH* 5. 9. 1, for instance, again in the context of a comparison between mortal life outside Christ and the possession of the Spirit, Irenaeus describes the soul as situated between the Spirit, that which saves and fashions, and the flesh, that which is saved and is fashioned: sometimes the soul follows the Spirit, and at other times it is persuaded to follow the flesh. Those who do not have the life-creating Spirit in themselves are mere flesh and blood, and it is these that Christ calls 'dead' (Luke 9: 60).

The idea that breath is common to all upon earth, whilst direct vivification by the life-creating Spirit belongs only to those adopted in Christ, yet there being but one Source of life as presented in *AH* 5. 12. 2, and the idea of the relative strengths of life discussed in *AH* 5. 3. 3, are brought together in *AH* 4. 20, in Irenaeus's favourite imagery, that of the vision of God. In *AH* 4. 20. 5, Irenaeus emphasizes that it is not possible to live without life, and that life is to be found in communion with God, which is to see God and enjoy his blessings.[68] After

---

[68] *AH* 4. 20. 5: Ἐπεὶ ζῆσαι ἄνευ ζωῆς [ἀδύνατον], ἡ δὲ ὕπαρξις τῆς ζωῆς ἐκ τοῦ θεοῦ περιγίνεται μετοχῆς, μετοχὴ δὲ θεοῦ ἐστι τὸ [ὁρᾶν] θεὸν καὶ ἀπολαύειν τῆς χρηστότητος αὐτοῦ. The words in square brackets mark Rousseau's emendations to the Greek text, as found in the *Sacra Parallela*, on the basis of the Latin and the Armenian.

describing the various prophetic visions of God in the Old Testament, Irenaeus continues:

For the glory of God is a living man, and the life of man consists in beholding God: for if the manifestation of God affords life to all living upon earth, much more does that revelation of the Father which comes through the Word give life to those who see God. (*AH* 4. 20. 7)

Again, there is only one Source of life, though it is bestowed upon man through two modes: all those upon earth live by seeing the Creator through the creation; while those who see the Father in the Son are vivified in a stronger fashion. Moreover, there is no suggestion that those who recognize the Creator have a mortal life. They become subject to death when they no longer acknowledge themselves as created beings, dependent upon God.

Returning to *Dem.* 11, Irenaeus states that God breathed the breath of life into his handiwork, so that 'both according to the inspiration and according to the formation, man was like God'. As the formation, the image of God located in the flesh, typifies Christ, so also the inspiration, the animation by the breath of life, typifies or prefigures the vivification of Christ, and those adopted in him, by the Spirit. Full vivification by the Spirit is eschatological, though manifest in the death of the martyrs who bear witness to salvation. Adopted sons now receive the pledge of the Spirit, possessing a 'part of the Spirit' (*AH* 5. 8. 1), which prepares them for the fullness to come. The rest of the people living on earth have received the breath of life, created by the presence of the life-giving Spirit in creation, as a type of the vivification to come. The whole process, the movement of the economy itself, is one of God and man becoming accustomed to each other: of man learning, throughout the unfolding of the Old Testament, to acknowledge and follow God; of the Spirit, in Christ, becoming accustomed to dwell in and to vivify man; and of man, as an adopted son in Christ, being prepared for vivification by the life-creating Spirit, and so for the incorruptibility and immortality of God.

Following the description of the creation of man in *Dem.* 11, and supplementing it with information gained from more detailed analysis elsewhere in Irenaeus's writings, we have looked so far at Irenaeus's understanding of the human body, fashioned in the image of God, its relationship to the soul, and the relationship between the breath of life and the life-creating Spirit. We need to follow Irenaeus's protological exegesis of the opening chapters of Genesis, in the subsequent chapters of the *Demonstration*, before we conclude this section by looking at Irenaeus's understanding of the 'likeness', that which was lost in Adam and regained in Christ.

Irenaeus presents us with a unitary account of the creation of man, combining Genesis 1: 26–7 and 2: 7 to describe the creation of a unified being, animated mud. Irenaeus continues, in *Dem*. 12, by suggesting that, as newly created, man was but an infant, who needed to grow to reach full perfection.[69] It was to nourish this growth, according to Irenaeus, that God prepared a place better than this present world, a beautiful Garden with a good climate, light and full of good things to eat and drink. So beautiful and good was this Garden, that

the Word of God was always walking in it; he would walk and talk with the man, prefiguring the future, which would come to pass, that he would dwell with him and speak with him and would be with mankind teaching them righteousness. (*Dem*. 12)

Irenaeus clearly refers the protological descriptions of the Garden in Genesis to the Church, a 'Paradise in this world' (*AH* 5. 20. 2), though located in the Spirit, and its fulfilment in the Kingdom of the Son. His understanding of the account in Genesis is, again, both Christological and eschatological.

Irenaeus extends the unitary account of the creation of man to the formation of Eve. In *Dem*. 13, Irenaeus paraphrases and extends Genesis 2: 18–23:

And he decided also to make a helper for the man, for in this manner, 'God said "It is not good for man to be alone, let us make him a helper fit for him,"' since among all the other living things no helper was found equal and like to Adam; and God himself 'cast a deep sleep upon Adam and put him to sleep,' and, that a work might be accomplished out of a work, sleep not being in Paradise, it came upon Adam by the will of God; and God 'took one of Adam's ribs and

---

[69] Irenaeus's depiction of Adam and Eve as children, and many of his protological descriptions, seem to be dependent upon Theophilus of Antioch (*To Autolycus*, 2. 20–8), either directly or through a common Asiatic tradition. Cf. Loofs, *Theophilus von Antiochen*, 58–72.

filled up flesh in its place, and he built up the rib which he took into a woman and, in this way, brought [her] before Adam'. And he, seeing [her], said, 'This at last is bone of my bones, and flesh of my flesh; she shall be called "woman", for she was taken from her man.' (*Dem.* 13)

Irenaeus keeps to the biblical text, and does not refer the formation of woman in any way to God's foresight of the apostasy and mortality, or even to the function of procreation. Irenaeus adds to the Genesis account of God putting Adam to sleep by stating that sleep did not yet exist in Paradise, and he explains this temporary 'suspension' of Adam's existence by the intention of God to 'accomplish a work from a work'.[70] This divine initiative reaches its conclusion in the formation of the woman. Bone from bone, Eve is of the same formation as Adam. The formation of man as a sexual being thus belongs to the arrangements of God for the growth and maturation of man: God prepares a 'helper' suitable, like and equal to Adam.

Irenaeus continues, in *Dem.* 14, by describing the life of Adam and Eve in Paradise:

And Adam and Eve, for this is the name of the woman, 'were naked and were not ashamed' [Gen. 2: 25], since there was in them an innocent and childlike mind and they thought or understood nothing whatsoever of those things which are wickedly born in the soul through lust and shameful desires, because, at that time, they preserved their nature ⟨intact⟩, since that which was breathed into the handiwork was the breath of life; and while the breath remains in ⟨its⟩ order and strength, it is without comprehension or understanding of what is evil: and thus 'they were not ashamed', kissing [and] embracing each other in holiness as children. (*Dem.* 14)

[70] Orbe, *Antropología*, 201–3, tries to find in this sleep a relaxation or slackening of the spirit, of the state of vigil, or an interruption of Adam's converse with the Word: had the initiative come from Adam, it would have been culpable, but coming from God it is acceptable, fitting in with his plan to fashion the woman. In this way, Orbe maintains, the woman is associated with the interruption of man's converse with God, and so becomes the occasion for the fall (ibid. 251–3). Orbe bases this curious interpretation on his earlier studies, 'El pecado de Eva, signo de division', *OCP* 29 (1963), 305–30; 'El sueño y el Paraíso: Iren., *Epid.* 13', *Greg.* 48 (1967), 346–9; 'La atonia del espiritu en los Padres y teólogos del s. II', *La Ciudad de Dios*, 181 (1968), 484–528. His argument is closely followed by D. Ramos-Lissón, 'Le Rôle de la femme dans la théologie de saint Irénée', *St. Patr.* 21 (Leuven, 1989), 163–74.

As long as the breath of life maintained its order and strength, and Adam and Eve retained their integrity and natural state, they were able to embrace each other in holiness, without the base thoughts which arise through desires and shameful pleasures. Similarly, in *AH* 3. 23. 5, Irenaeus describes Adam as having had a 'natural and childlike mind' (*indolem et puerilem . . . sensum*) which he lost when also losing the 'robe of sanctity which I [Adam] had from the Spirit' (*ab Spiritu sanctitatis stolam*).[71] As long as Adam and Eve continued in their orientation towards God, and the breath of life thus retained its strength and order, they remained in the holiness that is God's, clothed, as it were, in a robe of sanctity. Not only is bipolarity as male and female man's created state, but interaction between the two, in holiness, is clearly envisaged as a dimension of their life, growth, and maturation.

Later, in *Dem.* 17, Irenaeus follows Genesis, in a non-aetiological manner, by mentioning that Adam knew his wife Eve after their expulsion from Paradise (cf. Gen. 4: 1–2). Elsewhere, while describing the parallel between the disobedient virgin Eve and the obedient virgin Mary, Irenaeus has this to say as an aside:

in paradise 'they were both naked and were not ashamed', inasmuch as they, having been created a short time previously, had no understanding of the procreation of children: for it was necessary that they should first come to the adult age, and then multiply thenceforth. (*AH* 3. 22. 4)

It seems that Irenaeus understood the blessing of God in Genesis 1: 28, 'increase and multiply', in a sequential manner: grow/increase and (then) multiply. The procreation of children is part of God's economy for the human race, which would come into effect when the newly created 'children' have reached a suitable age and maturity. Accordingly, when they

---

[71] This text has become something of a *locus classicus* for Irenaean scholars, who see in it evidence that Adam 'possessed' the Holy Spirit in Paradise and lost this in the Fall. Cf. Andia, *Homo vivens*, 96–7; Fantino, *L'Homme*, 161–2; Jaschke, *Der Heilige Geist*, 254–7. According to E. Klebba, *Die Anthropologie des hl. Irenaeus* (Münster, 1894), 33, that Adam 'possessed' the Spirit as a 'robe' is taken to indicate the character of this 'possession' as a *donum superadditum*; though such language is avoided by contemporary scholars, the perspective remains.

attain such maturity, they would be able to conceive children whilst remaining in holiness, robed in sanctity. Elsewhere, speaking in a post-lapsarian context, Irenaeus asserts that God has foreordained the number to which the human race should increase. On the completion of this number, they shall cease from begetting and being begotten, from marrying and giving in marriage, so preserving the harmony formed by the Father.[72] Thus the intention of procreation is the same both in Paradise before the apostasy and after the apostasy in the human life of mortality. There is no suggestion, as for instance in Athenagoras, that the procreation of children is the human response to a life of mortality, an attempt to make the mortal immortal.[73] Procreation simply belongs, at the appropriate age, to the growth which God has set before man. Nor does Irenaeus, whilst speaking of adulthood as the age for procreation, ever restrict human sexuality to the function of procreation. Procreation shall cease once the foreordained number has been reached; human existence as male and female will not cease, for it is the condition and framework, as created by God, for the man's never-ending maturation and growth towards God.

A final aspect of Irenaeus's protology, discussed in *Dem.* 15, needs to be mentioned. God established man as the lord of the earth and everything in it (*Dem.* 12). In order to help man remain in the proper, thankful, attitude towards his Creator, and not to have thoughts of grandeur or assume an attitude of 'self-conceited arrogance' towards God, he was given a law by God, that he 'might know that he had as lord the Lord of all' (*Dem.* 15). It is thus that Irenaeus understands the function of the commandment of Genesis 2: 16–17.[74] If man were to keep this commandment, acknowledging God as his Creator, he would remain immortal; otherwise he would become mortal and return to the earth. But, being inexperienced children, Adam and Eve were easily misled by the Deceiver and so cast out of the Garden (*Dem.* 12, 16). Irenaeus thus places the tree

---

[72] *AH* 2. 33. 5, referring to Matt. 22: 30.

[73] Cf. Athenagoras, *On the Resurrection*, 12. 2. Athenagoras is here echoing a standard classical theme; cf. e.g. Plato, *Symposium*, 208e; van Eijk, 'Marriage and Virginity'.

[74] Similarly in *AH* 5. 20. 2, 23.

of the knowledge of good and evil within the context of life and death. As we saw when looking at the role of the apostasy within the unfolding of the economy, it is through the knowledge of both life (the good) and death (the evil) that man comes to be in the image and likeness of God.[75] The acknowledgement of the Creator which the law demands is the basic structure of human life, and its transgression is death.[76]

Having looked at Irenaeus's protology, the formation of man and woman and the character of their existence in Paradise, we can now turn to the final category of Irenaeus's theological anthropology, the notion of 'likeness' ($\delta\mu o\iota\omega\sigma\iota s$). So far, we have come across this term only once, in *AH* 5. 6. 1, where, in distinction to the image, located in the flesh, the likeness was said to be 'through the Spirit'. Irenaeus's most characteristic statement about the 'likeness' is that while man lost it in Adam, he has regained it in Christ. The most detailed and important text is *AH* 5. 16. 2:

For in times long past it was said man was made in the image of God, but it was not shown [to be so]; for the Word was as yet invisible, after whose image man was created; and because of this he easily lost the likeness. When, however, the Word of God became flesh, he confirmed both of these: for he both showed forth the image truly, himself becoming that which was his image, and he re-established the likeness in a sure manner, by co-assimilating ($\sigma\upsilon\nu\epsilon\xi o\mu o\iota\omega\sigma\alpha s$) man to the invisible Father through the Word become visible. (*AH* 5. 16. 2)

This text demonstrates what we have seen concerning the uniqueness of the manifestation of God in the incarnate Word, Jesus Christ, at the same time both God and man. The Word becoming incarnate, becoming himself the image, truly demonstrated what the image of God is: that is, the reality

[75] Cf. esp. *AH* 4. 38. 4, referring to Gen. 3: 5, 22.

[76] Orbe, recognizing that Irenaeus does not develop his exegesis of Gen. 2: 16–17, nevertheless, by a sophisticated analysis of the relationship between the two virgins (*AH* 3. 22. 4), concludes that for Irenaeus, as for Clement, Origen, and others, the prohibited object in Gen. 2: 17 was 'el uso del matrimonio carnal' (*Antropología*, 251): because the natural act of marriage distracts from God, Adam and Eve needed to practice a life of continence before they could engage in carnal union without detracting from their communion with God, and so God placed this prohibition (ibid. 252). It is difficult to see how this position can be deduced from the text of Irenaeus.

of man as the image of God. According to this passage, it was because this fact had previously been only asserted,[77] and not seen, that man lost the likeness easily. But Christ, being himself God made visible, 'the visible of the invisible Father' (*AH* 4. 6. 6), assimilates, in himself, man to the invisible Father, thus re-establishing the likeness in a steadfast manner.

What is this likeness, then, that man lost in Adam and regained, in a sure manner, in Christ? Although in *AH* 5. 6. 1, it is said to be 'through the Spirit', it cannot simply be, as Fantino suggests, the presence of the Spirit, for, as we have seen, the Spirit is present with creation throughout the unfolding of the economy; nor can it be the gift of the Spirit as it is received in baptism and adoption, for this was made possible only in Christ.[78] That which Adam lost in the apostasy was the strength of the breath of life, which would have kept Adam immortal, and his 'natural and childlike mind' or the 'robe of holiness from the Spirit', and both these are the expressions or results of man seeing God through the creation, recognizing the fact that he is created and therefore dependent upon his Creator, an attitude of thankfulness and obedience. It is this recognition and disposition that enables man to live, whether animated by the breath of life or vivified directly by the life-creating Spirit. The truly living man is the glory of God, and this is the one who was fashioned in the image *and likeness* of God. Having lost the strength of the breath, man's life is now mortal. But in Christ man has been given the possibility of living by seeing the Father, by receiving, as an adopted son, a pledge of the Spirit which prepares him to be fully vivified by the Spirit in a permanent fashion, thus rendering the likeness secure.

[77] Cf. *Dem*. 32, where this fact (or he?) is described as having been written: 'Thus, the Lord, recapitulating this man [i.e. Adam], received the same arrangement of embodiment as this one, being born from the Virgin by the will and wisdom of God, that he might also demonstrate the likeness of embodiment to Adam, and might become the man, written in the beginning, "according to the image and likeness of God".'

[78] Cf. Fantino, *L'Homme*, 117–18.

Chapter 3

Human Growth

'The work of God is the fashioning of man' (*AH* 5. 15. 2): this is the basic structure of Irenaeus's thought. It determines his theology at all levels: God has revealed himself, uniquely, as man, and, while God is life and life-creating, it is man who lives in the nature with which God has created him—that is, fleshly and sexual. As Berthouzoz admirably expressed it: 'tout est de Dieu, tout n'advient que par l'homme'.[1] This is not to question the independence of God, who had no need of the human race but created it for the enjoyment of his goodness and to come to share in his glory, but simply to state the truth which God has in fact revealed as he has revealed it. It demonstrates the realism and economic nature of Irenaeus's theology. The manifestation of God in Jesus Christ is also the revelation of the truth of man; so, to become truly human is to become that as which God has revealed himself.

How then, inscribed within this economy, is man to become truly human, to become a god? The answer is contained in the same structure: 'God makes, man is made' (*AH* 4. 11. 2). In *AH* 4. 38–9 Irenaeus argues against those who display ingratitude by refusing to accept that they are what God has created them to be, 'men subject to passions' (*homines passionum capaces*, *AH* 4. 38. 4), but want to be even as God. Such people betray, on the one hand, an ignorance of the divine economy, in which God has revealed himself as man, and, on the other, a lack of confidence in their Creator. They establish their own agenda for becoming what they want to be. To become truly human, to become a god, man must allow God to fashion him, and this requires that he be open and responsive. In *AH* 4. 39. 2–3, Irenaeus describes this interaction using various themes with which we are already familiar: the artistic

[1] Berthouzoz, *Liberté et grâce*, 240.

work of the Word of God, the presence of the Spirit, as Water, enabling the formation, and man's trust in God, letting him work in him:

How then will you be a god, when you are not yet made man? How perfect, when only recently begun? How immortal, when in mortal nature you did not obey the Creator? It is necessary for you first to hold the rank of man, and then to participate in the glory of God. For you do not create God, but God creates you. If, then, you are the work of God, await the Hand of God, who does everything at the appropriate time—the appropriate time for you, who are being made. Offer to him your heart, soft and pliable, and retain the shape with which the Fashioner shaped you, having in yourself his Water, lest you turn dry and lose the imprint of his fingers. By guarding this conformation, you will ascend to perfection; the mud in you will be concealed by the art of God. His Hand created your substance; it will gild you, inside and out, with pure gold and silver, and so adorn you that the King himself will desire your beauty. But if, becoming hardened, you reject his art and being ungrateful towards him, because he made you a man, ungrateful, that is, towards God, you have lost at once both his art and life. For to create is the character-istic of the goodness of God; to be created is characteristic of the nature of man. If, therefore, you offer to him what is yours, that is, faith in him and subjection, you will receive his art and become a perfect work of God. But if you do not believe in him, and flee from his Hands, the cause of imperfection will be in you who did not obey, and not in him who called you. For he sent messengers to call people to the feast; but those who did not obey deprived themselves of his royal banquet [cf. Matt. 22: 3]. (*AH* 4. 39. 2–3)

Rather than hardening himself, trying to become what he wants to be, which can only result in death, man must remain pliable, open, and responsive to the creative activity of God. As Minns puts it, 'What the earth creature [i.e. man] needs to learn above all is to relax in the hands of God, to let God be the creator.'[2] Irenaeus characterizes this readiness to accept the designs of God for man as faith and subjection, a trusting obedience, and specifies that it is this which man can and must offer.

Within this perspective, apostasy is a refusal to submit to the creative activity of God. In *AH* 3. 23. 5, Irenaeus describes the archetypal and paradigmatic example of such apostasy, that of

[2] Minns, *Irenaeus*, 64.

Adam, who hid himself from God and clothed himself with fig-leaves (Gen. 3: 7–8). Irenaeus is contrasting the repentance shown by Adam with the lack of repentance in Cain:

With Adam, however, nothing of this kind happened, but everything was the opposite. For having been beguiled by another under the pretext of immortality, he is immediately seized with terror, and hides himself; not as if he were able to escape from God, but confused, since having transgressed his command he is unworthy to appear before and to hold converse with God. Now, 'the fear of the Lord is the beginning of wisdom' [Prov. 1: 7 etc.], and the perception of transgression produces repentance, and God bestows his bounty upon those who are repentant. [Adam] showed his repentance in deed, by means of the girdle, covering himself with fig-leaves; while there were many other leaves which would have irritated his body to a lesser degree, he, nevertheless, made a garment conformable to his disobedience, being terrified by the fear of God: and resisting the lustful propensity of his flesh, since he had lost his natural and childlike mind, and had come to a knowledge of evil things, he girded a bridle of continence (*frenum continentiae*) upon himself and his wife, fearing God and waiting for his coming, and indicating, as it were, some such thing: 'Inasmuch as', he says, 'I have by dis-obedience lost that robe of sanctity which I had from the Spirit, I do now acknowledge that I am deserving of a covering of this nature, which affords no pleasure, but which gnaws and frets the body.' And thus he would no doubt have retained this clothing for ever, thus humbling himself, if God, who is merciful, had not clothed them with garments of skin instead of fig-leaves. (*AH* 3. 23. 5)

The state of continence which Adam adopted after his act of disobedience is, according to Irenaeus, one which is self-imposed. Furthermore, it is one which Adam imposes upon himself and his wife in his state of confusion, in which, having lost his natural and childlike mind, he feels unworthy to approach and hold converse with God. As such, one might describe it as an adolescent reaction of the disobedient man to his new situation.[3] Yet it is also Adam's attempt to express repentance, to make amends and cover up the mistake he made by conforming himself to what he supposed to be godlike. In *AH* 4. 39. 1, when describing why knowledge of both good and

---

[3] Cf. J. Behr, 'Irenaeus *AH* 3. 23. 5 and the Asectic Ideal', *SVTQ* 37. 4 (1993), 305–13; Minns, *Irenaeus*, 64.

evil are necessary for man in apostasy, Irenaeus explains that it is through repentance that man can cast away disobedience and return to hold more tenaciously to what is good: that is, life in obedience. In *AH* 3. 23. 5, the knowledge of evil is not referred to sexual activity, but to transgression of the commandment, which, as we have seen, is the refusal to acknowledge God as Lord. It is this transgression which results in the loss of the childlike mind and so the 'lustful propensity of the flesh', and it is this which the confused Adam, mistaking the symptom for the cause, then tries to control or negate by adopting a state of continence, one which 'gnaws and frets the body'. In such a state of repentant, but self-imposed continence, man would not have been able to receive the growth and increase which God has set before him: he has taken control of himself, no longer allowing God to act in him. Thus the economy of God, in this instance, is to replace these fig-leaves, the self-imposed continence, with garments of skin. The Gnostics, according to Irenaeus, taught that the garments of skin, the fleshly, sensible element of man, were added last, as the most exterior level, in the formation of man.[4] Irenaeus does not, himself, mention the garments of skin elsewhere in his writings, and it is difficult to ascertain exactly what he understood by them in *AH* 3. 23. 5. Two things, however, are clear: first, that they refer to the existence of Adam and Eve in apostasy, and second, that they are other than the bridle of continence. God replaces their self-imposed continence with a garment suited to life in apostasy, in which they can continue to live according to God's original plan of growth and increase.

A similar theme is developed in Irenaeus's discussion of the relationship between the Law and the law of bondage. As God, in Christ, has granted the abrogation of the precepts of the law of bondage, and has restored man to the ancient law of liberty extended into one suitable for sons, Irenaeus is extremely critical of those who prefer to keep zealously to the precepts of the law of bondage while neglecting the rationale of those precepts, the salvation realized in the law of love. Thus, Irenaeus asserts that God has assigned everlasting perdition to those who, as he puts it, 'pretend that they themselves

---

[4] *AH* 1. 5. 5. On the use of the 'garments of skin' by later Greek patristic writers, see Nellas, *Deification in Christ*, 43–91.

observe more than what has been prescribed, as if preferring their own zeal to God himself'.[5]

The same dialectic between the laws of bondage and the original Law, the freedom of which has been re-established in the New Covenant, is discussed in the *Didascalia Apostolorum*, probably composed in the early half of the third century. Those who have become disciples of Christ, 'through the Gospel yield to the Law and completely abstain from the second legislation'.[6] The author is extremely critical of those who then choose to keep to the practices of the second legislation:

But if there be any who are scrupulous and desire, according to the second legislation, to keep the habits of nature and fluxes and intercourse, first let them know that, as we have already said, together with the second legislation they affirm the curse against our Saviour and condemn themselves vainly. And again, let them tell us, in what days or in what hours they observe to pray and to receive the eucharist, or to reading the Scripture—let them tell us whether they are devoid of the Holy Spirit. For through baptism they receive the Holy Spirit who is always with those that work righteousness and does not depart from them by reason of natural fluxes and the intercourse of marriage, but always perseveres with those who possess him and keeps them.[7]

The author is emphatic that neither the workings of the solitary body, such as menstrual fluxes and male 'fluxes' or 'issues',[8] nor conjugal intercourse, defile the cleansing effected by baptism and as such are not a reason to abstain from prayer, the eucharist, or the reading of Scripture.

A similar example of self-imposed continence is described in the 'Letter of the churches of Vienne and Lyons to the churches of Asia and Phrygia', perhaps drafted by Irenaeus himself.[9] As a corollary to remaining open and responsive to the Creator, Irenaeus, as we have repeatedly seen, exhorts his readers to enjoy God's bounty and to use his gifts, the world

[5] *AH* 4. 11. 4.

[6] *Didascalia Apostolorum*, 26, ed. and trans. A. Vööbus, CSCO 402, 408; Scriptores Syri, 176, 180 (Louvain, 1979), CSCO 408, 237.

[7] Ibid. 238.

[8] Cf. ibid. 242. On this whole issue cf. D. Brakke, 'The Problem of Nocturnal Emissions in Early Christian Syria, Egypt, and Gaul', *JECS* 3. 4 (1995), 419–60.

[9] Cf. P. Nautin, *Lettres et écrivains chrétiens*, 54–61.

which he has prepared for man's nourishment and growth, with thankfulness. This was the lesson that one confessor taught another:

There was among them a certain Alcibiades, who was living a very austere life, and at first was not partaking of anything at all, but used merely bread and water and was trying to live thus even in the jail. But it was revealed to Attalus after the first contest which he underwent in the amphitheatre that Alcibiades was not doing well in not making use of the creations of God, and offering an example of offence to others. Alcibiades was persuaded and began to partake of everything without restraint and gave thanks to God; for they were not without help from the grace of God and the Holy Spirit was their counsellor.[10]

Alcibiades' action could have been deemed offensive if it was supposed to stem from a belief that the material world was tainted with evil. However, this was not the primary charge; it was, rather, that Alcibiades, by not using the material creation, was not doing well. The proper approach is not to impose restrictions upon oneself, but, as he was taught by another confessor, both under the counsel of the Holy Spirit, to partake of everything without (self-imposed) restraint and to give thanks to God.

Thus, if man is to grow and be fashioned by the creative activity of God, rather than harden himself in self-imposed and self-determined continence, he must remain open to God and his blessings. But it is important to note that this required responsiveness is not merely passive nor docile. Just as man does not have any life other than that which he receives from partaking in the Spirit, through different modalities, so it is not through his own strength that he performs the works of God, but the Spirit itself is the stimulus, capable of working out its own suggestions, so manifesting the strength of God in the weakness of man's flesh.[11] The life and the strength are of the Spirit, but it is quite unambiguously man, who is and remains free, that lives and works. Irenaeus, in *AH* 3. 17. 3, describes this relationship in terms of the parable of the Good Samaritan (Luke 10: 29–37):

[10] *EH* 5. 3. 2–3, following the translation of K. Lake, LCL (Cambridge, Mass., 1980).

[11] *AH* 5. 9. 2, a passage, discussed earlier, describing the spiritual strength of the martyrs.

Wherefore, we have need of the Dew of God, that we be not consumed by fire, nor be rendered unfruitful, and that where we have an accuser, there we may also have an Advocate, the Lord, commending to the Holy Spirit his own man, who had fallen among thieves, on whom he himself had compassion, and bound up his wounds, giving two royal denarii, so that we, receiving by the Spirit 'the image and the superscription' [Matt. 22: 20 etc.] of the Father and the Son, might fructify the denarium entrusted to us, counting out the increase to the Lord. (*AH* 3. 17. 3)

Man can only be fruitful, multiplying what God has given him, through the Dew of God, the Spirit. But it is nevertheless man, thus nourished, who acts, fructifying what God has entrusted to him. Similarly, in another context, Irenaeus writes: 'Wherefore, also, those who are in truth his disciples, receiving grace from him, do in his name act, for the benefit of others, according to the gift which each one has received from him' (*AH* 2. 32. 4). The gift which each one has received is put into practice for the benefit of others, through the grace received. The grace thus received finds its natural expression within the horizon of the community, each member using their particular gift for the welfare of all the others, rather than within the restricted perspective of the individual's own 'spiritual' life or development.

It is also important to recall that living and acting by the strength of God is an expression of freedom. As God is the One who fashions man, and the source of his life, the more man remains in subjection to God, the greater will be his freedom as a living human being. True freedom, and the proper exercise of that freedom, is found in subjection to God, freely performing the works of the Spirit in the flesh. The only possible alternative to this, the only thing that man can do of himself, is to perform the works of the flesh, a slavery which leads to death. This opposition is described repeatedly by Irenaeus in *AH* 5 in terms of the Pauline opposition between the spiritual and the carnal:

Those, then, who have the pledge of the Spirit, and who are not enslaved by the lusts of the flesh, but subject themselves to the Spirit and walk reasonably (*rationabiliter*)[12] in all things, does the Apostle

---

[12] This is the nearest Irenaeus comes to the dictum that one should live κατὰ τὸν λόγον. The word *rationabiliter* occurs only in three other places (*AH*

properly call 'spiritual', because the Spirit of God dwells in them: for spiritual men will not be incorporeal spirits, but our substance, that is, the union of the soul and flesh, receiving the Spirit of God, makes up the spiritual man. But those who reject the Spirit's counsel and are the slaves of fleshly lusts, and live unreasonably, and who, without restraint, plunge into their own desires, having no longing after the Divine Spirit, do live like swine and dogs; these does the apostle properly call 'carnal', because they have no thought of anything else except carnal things. (*AH* 5. 8. 2)

The opposition is not between works pertaining to man's being as a fleshly creature and 'spiritual' exploits, for he lives only in the flesh; rather, the opposition is between living in the flesh by the power of the Spirit and trying to live by the flesh alone. The first is the action of a truly free and spiritual person, whereas the latter is merely carnal, a slave to the flesh and its desires, and, as such, mortal. Authentic liberty is only truly realized in subjection to God, a life, which is participation in God and the presence of the Spirit, lived by man, with the strength of the Spirit overcoming the weakness of the flesh, and so rendering him spiritual, a truly living man.

The passage from *AH* 4. 39. 2–3 cited above also emphasizes that God does everything at the appropriate time—appropriate, that is, for the man who is being fashioned. The creative activity of God effects and matches the growth of man. When speaking of growth, Irenaeus emphatically distances himself from the idea of 'spiritual development' found in various representatives of Gnosticism, the idea that a 'divine seed' was deposited in men as in a womb, to grow therein until it is ready for perfect *gnōsis*.[13] Irenaeus does not even speak of man as possessing a 'seed' of the Spirit which grows within him until he receives the fullness thereof:[14] the Spirit is an eschatological gift, typified in the breath and given as a pledge to those adopted through baptism. Neither does Irenaeus speak of growth as 'becoming male'.[15] Virtue, for Irenaeus, does not

---

4. 37. 7; 5. 1. 1, 18. 3). It would perhaps be reasonable to translate the phrase as 'according to the Word', as Rousseau does in *AH* 5. 1. 1 (see his note, SC 152, 199–201), and 'contrary to the Word' later on in *AH* 5. 8. 2.

[13] Cf. e.g. *AH* 1. 5. 6.

[14] As Andia, *Homo vivens*, 336.

[15] As e.g. *The Gospel according to Thomas*, log. 114, 99. 18–26, ed. and

have a merely human character, let alone a male character; so he does not speak of the female becoming male in living a full Christian life. All virtue is of God, who deploys his strength in the weakness of human flesh, and is thus manifested in human beings when they lead their lives in obedience to the Spirit, who alone makes them spiritual.

Irenaeus does not speak of the growth of the interior, or spiritual, dimensions of the person.[16] From what we have seen, it is clear that Irenaeus is not interested in such interiority. Rather, when speaking of growth, Irenaeus, more simply and more realistically, focuses on the fashioning of the handiwork of God into a full human being. And this activity and growth has a pattern and rhythm:

By this order and such rhythms and such a movement the created and fashioned man becomes in the image and likeness of the uncreated God—the Father planning everything well and commanding, the Son executing and performing, and the Spirit nourishing and increasing, and man making progress day by day and ascending towards perfection, that is, approaching the Uncreated One. For the Uncreated is perfect, and this is God.

> Now, it was first necessary for man to be created;
> and having been created, to increase;
> and having increased, to become an adult;
> and having become an adult, to multiply;
> and having multiplied, to strengthen;
> and having strengthened, to be glorified;
> and being glorified, to see his Master;

for God is he who is yet to be seen, and the vision of God produces incorruptibility, and 'incorruptibility renders one close to God' [Wisd. 6: 19]. (*AH* 4. 38. 3)

This is the rhythm and pattern which God has arranged for the growth of man to his full perfection. It is clear that this arrangement is that of the course of each human life. It is no less clear that its progression unfolds with the divine economy, as we have traced it. Each human being, like the human race

trans. A. Guillaumont [*et al.*] (Leiden, 1959), 57. We will see this theme taken up by Clement of Alexandria in Part II; it later becomes a recurrent theme in Christian literature.

[16] Cf. Wingren, *Man and the Incarnation*, 32–5. On the whole question of growth in Irenaeus, cf. Noormann, *Irenäus*, 468–77.

itself, comes into being as an infant, who must grow to adulthood, the age for procreation, and then strengthen into the fullness of human maturity, before passing into the glory and vision of God. As the economy has unfolded, this includes death, which is followed by the Kingdom of the Son upon the earth, where we mature in the glory of the Son before everything is submitted to the Father.

One of the most noteworthy aspects of Irenaeus's historical sense of the unfolding of the economy is how it places a positive value upon man's experience of evil and his own weakness, which ultimately concludes in death. Within the framework of the progression of each individual life, this same perspective demands that, to become truly human, each person must fully engage themselves in their concrete lives and situations. One learns by experience. One cannot simply abstain, through a self-imposed continence, from anything that carries with it a risk that one might become ensnared thereby in apostasy.[17] Irenaeus does not exalt a state of primal innocence, or exhort his readers to recapture it through an evasive virginity; for, as the economy has unfolded, it is through a knowledge of good and evil, and the consequent rejection of evil, that man becomes like God.

A final point that must be noted is that, as adopted sons in Christ have received only a pledge of the Spirit, so the fullness of the vivification and liberty is, for them, yet to come. They are still being prepared and accustomed to bear the Spirit in full authentic liberty. Although Christ has abrogated the laws of bondage, this does not mean that everyone is already prepared to embrace fully the liberty which Christ has brought; those who are weak still need to be trained, that they too may come to know the fullness of liberty in life granted by God to his adopted sons. In *AH* 4. 15. 2, while discussing the dialectic between the ancient law of liberty and the new, extended law of liberty, in which the laws of bondage

---

[17] Well put by Berthouzoz: 'En conséquence, l'humanisation de l'homme demande un engagement de sa part, ce qui est évident à l'expérience, et comporte l'acceptation corrélative d'un risque, en particulier celui de se tromper. Par là se trouvent exclues l'éthique de l'abstention préventive, toute valorisation de l'innocence originelle et indifférenciée et, surtout, l'hétéronomie comme instance de conduite moral, adulte' (*Liberté et grâce*, 236).

are cancelled, Irenaeus demonstrates the unity of intent
between the original law of God and the precepts of Moses,
by pointing out how Christ explained that Moses had adapted
the initial Law of God (that 'he who made them from the
beginning made them male and female', so that the two might
be one flesh, not to be put asunder, Matt. 19: 4–6), to the
hardness of the Israelites' hearts (allowing divorce, Matt.
19: 7–9), so that they might be trained with what they could
bear, and so turn from their disobedience towards obedience to
God and his Law. Irenaeus points out that the same compassion is also shown in the New Covenant, when Paul makes his
'concessions', advice given 'from himself' to the Corinthians.
Such concessions were written with regard to human weakness
and incontinence, lest those who could not as yet bear the
freedom given in Christ should 'become hardened, and des-
pairing of their salvation, should become apostates from
God'.[18] As such, when seen within the context of the whole
economy, these concessions are not a true expression of the
fullness of liberty granted by Christ. Just as Paul places these
concessions within the context of the imminence of the parousia (cf. 1 Cor. 7: 29), so Irenaeus interprets these concessions
as a preparation for the full perfection and liberty which
adopted sons have yet to receive.

We can now see the significance of the eschatological dimension of Irenaeus's protological descriptions, reiterated by
Christ himself: 'He who made them from the beginning
made them male and female, and said: "For this reason shall
a man leave his father and mother and be joined to his wife, and
the two shall be one flesh" [Matt. 19: 4–5].' Irenaeus's
description of Adam and Eve 'kissing and embracing each
other in holiness' (*Dem.* 14) is not simply a quaint mythological
picture, but that towards which man is being trained: it does
not refer to a protological innocence, but to man's existence in

_____

[18] *AH* 4. 15. 2. Although Irenaeus cites many of Paul's concessionary
statements from 1 Cor. 7, he does not indicate whether he understood e.g.
1 Cor. 7: 5 as a concession to separate for prayer or as a concession to come
together again; but given that he begins this discussion by citing Christ's
word, that God made man from the beginning male and female so that they
might become one flesh, which no one shall divide, and that Moses'
concession is a weakening of this basic principle, the second alternative
seems improbable.

Christ and the law of love and freedom established by him. This is something to which, due to human weakness and incontinence, salvific concessions still need to be made, whilst man is trained by the pledge of the Spirit.

Irenaeus's anthropology and asceticism are both fundamentally theocentric and theophanic. Man's very body is fashioned in the image of the incarnate God, who, 'in the last times', has revealed both God and the truth of man to us, enabling man, through adoption, to be prepared by the pledge of the Spirit for the full vivification by the Spirit in the last times. Man's life, from the first breath to the last vivification by the Spirit, is a participation, in different modalities, in the very life of God. This particular understanding of man's being and life determines the outward expression of that life, its asceticism. Rather than subjecting himself to a self-imposed continence, undertaken either to conform himself to what he supposes to be pure, innocent, and godlike, or to avoid the demands that arise from his passionate nature, or to escape from the apparent annihilation of death, man is to engage fully with the concrete circumstances of his life, for it is only through his own experience, and ultimately through his own death, that he learns to hold ever more firmly to God. Man is still being trained by the pledge of the Spirit, and by salvific concessions, for the fullness realized by Christ, which for those adopted as sons is yet to come, the fullness of the authentic liberty, realized in full subjection to God, enabling the direct vivification of man, in the totality of his God-given, fleshly, and sexual existence, by the Spirit. This will be the truly living man—the glory of God.

Clement of Alexandria:
Tiptoeing on the Earth

PART II

Theon of Alexandria
Epidrome on the Earth

Clement of Alexandria intentionally, but also perhaps unintentionally, rivalled Paul's claim of being all things to all men: intentionally, in that his surviving writings are addressed to pagans, to the recently reborn children of Christianity, and to mature Christian Gnostics, in a dialogue with Greek philosophy and a confrontation with heretical (or falsely so-called) Gnosticism, whilst attempting to establish, for the first time, a systematic treatment of Christian theology; unintentionally, in that contemporary research has portrayed Clement as everything from a 'pure' Christian who, from evangelical motives, veils his true thought in philosophical language, to a thinker whose thought is no more than the fusion of the Jewish-Alexandrine tradition, the Platonic tradition, and Gnosticism, the only Christian element stemming from Christian Gnosticism.[1] The vexed Athens/Jerusalem question has to a certain extent been superseded by the more productive investigation of specific problems and themes raised within Clement's own work.[2] Yet, even within narrowly defined categories, his theological position is problematic, and there remains a lack of consensus in modern scholarship regarding him. This is undoubtedly due to the peculiar character of Clement's work itself. According to Jerome, he was the most learned of all the fathers.[3] His work abounds in a plethora of quotations and parallels, which he used to show how Christianity summed up all that was best in earlier traditions. Clement was a complex and subtle thinker, yet he was in no sense systematic, especially in his terminology. Indeed, in the *Stromateis* he deliberately aims to be obscure, 'to speak imperceptibly, to exhibit secretly

[1] For the most comprehensive representative of the first stance, see W. Völker, *Der wahre Gnostiker nach Clemens Alexandrinus*, TU 57 (Berlin, 1952), and for the latter, S. R. C. Lilla, *Clement of Alexandria: A Study in Christian Platonism and Gnosticism* (Oxford, 1971).

[2] Cf. E. F. Osborn, 'Clement of Alexandria: A Review of Research, 1958–1982', *Second Century*, 3 (1983), 219–44.

[3] Jerome, *Ep.* 70. 4, ed. by J. Labourt (Paris, 1953).

and demonstrate silently',[4] both to avoid divulging the mysteries of theology to those who are not prepared to receive them and to sweeten the delicacies of theology with the effort of application.[5] We must, therefore, pay careful attention not only to his overt assertions, but also to the movement of his thought, with all its tensions and apparent inconsistencies.

With regard to asceticism, Clement raises themes which prefigure much of the later developments in monastic spirituality: he writes extensively about inner peace, perpetual inward prayer, contemplation, *apatheia*, and detachment; he touches upon spiritual fatherhood, on the possibility of a second baptism of tears, on being a true presbyter and deacon without receiving ordination from men, and is perhaps the first to speak of the Christian as living in the city 'as in the desert'.[6] Yet his asceticism is not simply directed at a retreat from the world into the desert. Indeed, writing before the desert became a city, Clement advises socially responsible Christians, both married and single, how to direct their worldly affairs in a decorous manner according to God.[7] Furthermore, his works abound in affirmative statements about the beauty of the world and the need to use its pleasures thankfully and respectfully. This strain in his work has, since the study of Tollinton, earned him the title of the Christian Liberal or Humanist.[8] Yet, whilst these two tendencies in Clement are not confined to different works aimed at different audiences, the simple faithful, on the

---

[4] *Strom.* 1. 1. 15. 1; cf. *Strom.* 7. 17. 110. 4–111. 3. For Clement's work, I have used the edition of O. Stählin: *Clemens Alexandrinus I: Protrepticus, Paedagogus*, 3rd edn. rev. U. Treu, GCS 12 (Berlin, 1972); *Clemens Alexandrinus II: Stromata I–VI*, 3rd edn. rev. L. Früchtel, GCS 52 (Berlin, 1960); and *Clemens Alexandrinus III: Stromata VII, VIII, Excerpta ex Theodoto, Eclogae Propheticae, Quis Dives Salvetur, Fragmente*, 2nd edn. rev. L. Früchtel and U. Treu, GCS 17 (Berlin, 1970). I have occasionally referred to the Source Chrétiennes edition, where available, and have consulted the various available translations.

[5] *Strom.* 1. 2. 21. 1.

[6] Most of these themes can be found scattered throughout Clement's works; more specifically, for perpetual inner prayer, see esp. *Strom.* 7. 7. 39. 6–40. 3; contemplation, esp. *Strom.* 5. 6. 40. 1; spiritual fatherhood, *QDS* 41. 1; baptism of tears, *QDS* 42. 14; unordained ordination, *Strom.* 6. 13. 106. 2; living 'as in a desert', *Strom.* 7. 12. 77. 3.

[7] *Paed.* 3. 11. 78. 3.

[8] R. B. Tollinton, *Clement of Alexandria* (London, 1914).

one hand, and the mature Christian Gnostic, on the other, neither are they fully reconciled with each other. The constant oscillation between an attitude of openness towards the world and a rigorous demand for detachment can find its resolution only in the person of Clement and the task he set himself. He was, in the words of Wagner, a 'Verteidiger der Welt und Prediger der Weltflucht in einer Person'.[9]

Each of Clement's three main extant works addresses a particular stage of man's gradual progress towards God: first, the *Protrepticus*, an exhortation to pagans aimed at bringing about their conversion; second, the *Paedagogus*, which trains the newly baptized Christians in the life befitting their new calling; third, the *Stromateis*, which treats an assortment of subjects mainly pertaining to the higher levels of Christian perfection. Each of these stages corresponds to a particular activity, or appearance, of the Word of God, aiming, through its *paideia*, at man's salvation and perfection. And this gradual *paideia* is that of the economy itself:

Being eager, then, to perfect us by a salvific gradation, appropriate to efficacious discipline, the beautiful arrangement (τῇ καλῇ οἰκονομίᾳ) is observed by the all-philanthropic Word, first exhorting (προτρέπων), then training (παιδαγωγῶν), and finally teaching (ἐκδιδάσκων). (*Paed.* 1. 1. 3. 3)[10]

Clement thus understands the economy from the perspective of man's *paideia*, his training and education. The economy is not so much the activity of God unfolded in Scripture, or its overall arrangement, in which man is inscribed, as the arrangement of the threefold activity of the Word of God corresponding to the pattern of man's progression towards God. The economy itself is structured according to the progressive advancement of man in the *paideia* proposed by Clement

---

[9] W. Wagner, *Der Christ und die Welt nach Clemens von Alexandrien* (Göttingen, 1903), 78.

[10] Cf. *Paed.* 3. 12. 97. 3. The controversy concerning the relationship between the projected 'Didaskalikos Logos' and the *Stromateis* has somewhat abated; as C. Mondésert points out, the lack of substantial evidence makes a definitive solution impossible. Cf. *Les Stromates, I*, ed. C. Mondésert, SC 30 (Paris, 1951), 19–22. The question does not have any serious implications for this study: it is clear that the *Stromateis* are mainly concerned with Gnostic perfection, even if they are not notes for a projected 'Didaskalikos Logos'.

himself. The dominant note in Clement's writings is, as we shall see, that of *paideia*, both in the meticulous details of, for instance, how to live under the Logos-Paedagogus, as well as the overall pattern of advancement to God and man's own perfection. Inscribed in this particular economy, Clement's Christians continually progress in realizing their true dignity and rational nature, becoming what, for Clement, is properly man.

Chapter 4

Anthropology

Before looking at Clement's description of Christian life and the character of asceticism involved in the growth from faith to *gnōsis*, it will be useful to consider his description of Adam and Eve, their life in Paradise, and their Fall, together with his general anthropological framework.[1] Although Clement does not develop any sustained treatment of Adam and the character of his life, his comments will help us to understand the fundamental orientation of his anthropology. In common with Theophilus and Irenaeus, Clement represents Adam and Eve as children together in Paradise.[2] As a child of God, Adam played freely in Paradise, and, by reason of his simplicity, he was free from passions and their pleasures.[3] According to Clement, Adam enjoyed an immortal life in Paradise.[4] Man is a 'heavenly plant', constituted by nature so as to have fellowship with God.[5] Clement speaks of 'the innate original communion between men and heaven', obscured through ignorance, but which now shines clearly again.[6] There is no natural or ontological kinship between God and man, yet man is dear to God, since, unlike the other works of creation, man is

---

[1] Clement's thought about Adam is the subject of a monograph by T. Rüther, *Die Lehre von der Erbsunde bei Klemens von Alexandrien* (Freiburg im Breisgau, 1922), which is useful for the details it accumulates, but is somewhat anachronistic in its perspective.

[2] Cf. *Prot.* 11. 111. 1; *Strom.* 3. 17. 103. 1.

[3] *Prot.* 11. 111. 1. Cf. *Strom.* 7. 7. 46. 6, where some angels are described as falling due to their propensity for duplicity.

[4] In *Strom.* 2. 19. 98. 4 Adam is described as having exchanged an immortal life for a mortal one.

[5] *Prot.* 10. 100. 2–3. The image of man as a $\phi \upsilon \tau \grave{o} \nu$ $o \grave{\upsilon} \rho \acute{a} \nu \iota o \nu$ is from Plato, *Timaeus*, 90a.

[6] *Prot.* 2. 25. 3. Tatian had also spoken of an $\mathring{a} \rho \chi a \acute{\iota} a$ $\sigma \upsilon \gamma \gamma \acute{\epsilon} \nu \epsilon \iota a$, which it is now possible to restore. Cf. *Oration to the Greeks*, 20. 3.

the work of his own hands.[7] More than this, however, God
breathed into man what was peculiar to himself, and this works
as a 'love charm' in man.[8]

Although perfect as regards his formation, as a child Adam
needed to grow in order to acquire full perfection:

We say that Adam was perfect as regards his formation, for he lacked
none of the characteristics of the idea and form of man. Coming into
being he received perfection, and he was justified by obedience, and
this was growing to adulthood, which depended upon him. (*Strom.*
4. 23. 150. 3–4)

Thus Clement can answer the predicament posed by the
Gnostics when they ask whether God created man perfect or
imperfect:

They shall hear from us that he was not perfect in his creation, but
adapted for the acquisition of virtue, for it is of great importance in
regard to virtue to be made fit for its attainment, and it is intended
that we should be saved of ourselves (ἡμᾶς δὲ ἐξ ἡμῶν αὐτῶν βούλεται
σῴζεσθαι). (*Strom.* 6. 12. 96. 2)[9]

This stress on the 'perfect imperfection' of the child Adam, the
created man, and the need for growth as an active obedience in
freedom to realize the fullness of man's potential, to become an
adult, and achieve his own 'salvation', is Clement's response to
the Gnostics' ontological differentiation of the human race into
distinct groups. Whilst man, considered generically, is perfectly formed for the acquisition of virtue and full perfection,
the responsibility for this fulfilment lies with each person
individually, his individual character being determined by
the impression that his choices make on his soul.[10]

In his descriptions of the constitution of man, Clement's
statements vary considerably, using different schemas, biblical,
Platonic, and Stoic, in different contexts.[11] In one of his most
important descriptions, Clement, allegorizing the Decalogue,

---

[7] Cf. *Paed.* 1. 3. 7. 1; *Strom.* 2. 2. 5. 4–6. 3, 16. 74. 1–75. 3.

[8] *Paed.* 1. 3. 7. 3: τὸ φίλτρον. Cf. *Strom.* 5. 13. 87. 4, 88. 3.

[9] For man as created for the acquisition of virtue, see *Strom.* 1. 6. 34. 1–4;
6. 11. 95. 5, 12. 96. 3; 7. 3. 19. 3.

[10] *Strom.* 4. 23. 150. 2.

[11] Cf. M. Spanneut, *Le Stoïcisme et les Pères de l'Église de Clément de Rome
à Clément d'Alexandrie* (Paris, 1957), 166–76.

begins in a Stoic fashion, perhaps following Philo, by differ-
entiating the twofold spirit in man, the guiding principle (the
ἡγεμονικόν) and its subject (the ὑποκείμενον), corresponding to
the two tablets of the Law.[12] Clement then goes on to analyse
man in terms of a decad corresponding to the Decalogue:

And there is a ten in man himself: the five senses, and the power of
speech, and that of reproduction, and the eighth is the spiritual
principle received at his creation (τὸ κατὰ τὴν πλάσιν πνευματικόν)
and the ninth is the guiding principle (ἡγεμονικόν) of his soul; and
tenth, there is the distinctive characteristic of the Holy Spirit, which
comes to him through faith. (*Strom*. 6. 16. 134. 2)

Clement goes on to specify that the rational and ruling power is
the cause of the constitution of man, animating and incorporating the irrational.[13] The vital energy (τὴν ζωτικὴν δύναμιν), the
power of nutrition, growth, and motion, is assigned to the
carnal spirit (τὸ πνεῦμα τὸ σαρκικόν), while the power of choice
(τὴν προαιρετικήν), the ability to investigate, to study, and to
know, belongs to the guiding principle.[14] All the faculties are,
in the final analysis, placed in a Platonic hierarchical relation to
the guiding principle, and it is through this that man lives, and
has, moreover, the ability to live in a particular way.[15] This
close affinity between the guiding principle and the power of
choice is emphasized by Clement in a different passage, where
he maintains that the determining element in man's constitution is volition. Echoing Christ's recurring question, Clement
writes: 'Volition takes precedence over all, for the intellectual
powers are the servants of the will. "Will" it is said, "and you
shall be able." '[16] The emphasis on freedom as the determinative aspect in the constitution of man is distinctive to Clement,[17] and it determines, as we shall see, his discussion of
Christian life and asceticism.

[12] *Strom*. 6. 16. 134. 1–2. Cf. Philo, *Quis rer. div. her*. 25. 167.
[13] *Strom*. 6. 16. 135. 2.   [14] *Strom*. 6. 16. 135. 3–4.
[15] *Strom*. 6. 16. 135. 4.
[16] *Strom*. 2. 17. 77. 5; Stählin suggests that the reference is to John 5: 6.
[17] Cf. M. Müller, 'Freiheit: Über Autonomie und Gnade von Paulus bis
Clemens von Alexandrien', *ZNTW* 25 (1926), 218. This emphasis on the
determinative role of the will, a novelty in Christian literature, was a recurrent
theme in Stoicism and Hellenistic philosophy; cf. Epictetus, *Discourses*,
2. 10. 1.

The specific manner of life that Clement has in mind is living in obedience to the divine Logos, which, for Clement, is identical to living according to reason and to nature. Clement explicitly points to the similarity of his position to the Stoic doctrine of living according to nature, in which he claims that the term 'nature' has been impiously substituted for the term 'God'.[18] He describes an anthropocentric universe, in which 'Whatever in human actions is right and regular is the result of the inspiration of its rectitude and order', a description similar to that of Philo.[19]

In *Strom.* 6. 16. 134. 2 the Holy Spirit is counted as an element in the constitution of man. Elsewhere, in *Strom.* 2. 11. 50. 4, when analysing man into a decad, Clement enumerates the body, the soul, the five senses, and the reproductive and intellectual or spiritual faculties. Here the body has replaced the Holy Spirit as a constitutive element of man. This emphasizes the fact, mentioned in *Strom.* 6. 16. 134. 2, that the Holy Spirit is an addition *by faith* to created, 'natural' man.[20] This is further stressed by Clement when he distinguishes the possession of the Spirit from the divine breath breathed into man at his creation. According to Clement, 'the man, who, it is written in Genesis, received the breath, is far from destitute of a divine idea, partaking of a substance purer than that of other creatures'.[21] The 'breath' here refers to the rational soul (λογικὴ ψυχή) or the guiding principle (ἡγεμονικόν) breathed by God into man's earthly formation, which differentiates man from other creatures.[22] Clement then continues, distancing himself from the Greek

---

[18] *Strom.* 2. 19. 101. 1. For the Stoic background of Clement's thought on this point, see M. Pohlenz, 'Klemens von Alexandrien und sein hellenisches Christentum', *NAWG*, Phil.-Hist. Klasse, Fachgr. 5, NF 1. 5 (1943), 103–80. However, the more direct influence is likely to be Philo, who, in *Migr. Abr.* 23. 128, e.g., identifies the philosophical definition of 'living according to nature' with following after God (referring to Gen. 12: 4). Cf. Lilla, *Clement of Alexandria*, 92–4.

[19] *Paed.* 1. 2. 6. 6; cf. Philo, *Opif.* 1. 3.

[20] For an extensive discussion of the role of the 'S/spirit' in Clement's anthropology, see L. F. Ladaria, *El Espíritu en Clement Alejandrino* (Madrid, 1980), 113–247.

[21] *Strom.* 5. 13. 87. 4.

[22] *Strom.* 5. 14. 94. 3–4.

philosophical tradition, by distinguishing this divine portion from the gift of the Holy Spirit granted to believers: 'Hence the Pythagoreans say that the mind comes to man as a divine portion, as Plato and Aristotle also agree; but we say that Holy Spirit is additionally breathed into the believer' (*Strom.* 5. 13. 88. 1–2). Clement asserts that the Spirit is not present in us as a 'part' of God, but does not specify the mode of its presence, promising instead to develop this theme in other works.[23] For Clement, therefore, unlike Irenaeus, the Holy Spirit is not present in man from the beginning; this belongs, rather, to the mature adult, perfected, 'justified by obedience' (*Strom.* 4. 23. 150. 4) and 'saved of himself' (*Strom.* 6. 12. 96. 2). Such a gift is different from the intellect (*νοῦς*) breathed into man by God at his creation, a possession common to all mankind and itself divine. It seems from the passages cited above that possession of the Spirit would follow, in due course, for man on his attainment of full perfection.

Although Clement does not refer to the words of Genesis, that man was made in the image and likeness of God (Gen. 1: 26–7), in connection with his comments on Adam, it is this declaration that is the guiding motif for Clement's anthropology, and it is in his use of these words, 'image' (*εἰκών*) and 'likeness' (*ὁμοίωσις*), that Clement's vocabulary is especially unstable.[24] Clement uses these terms with different meanings on different occasions. For instance, 'image' by itself may denote man in his perfection, his complete assimilation to God: thus, 'the perfect inheritance belongs to those who attain to a "perfect man", according to the image of the Lord'.[25] When it is used by itself, however, 'image' most frequently has a strongly Philonic sense. In a polemic against the pagan cult of images in chapter 10 of the *Protrepticus*, Clement carefully defines what he means by 'image':

The image of God is his Word, the genuine Son of Intellect, the Divine Word, the archetypal light of light; and the image of the Word is the true man, the intellect which is in man, who is therefore said to

---

[23] *Strom.* 5. 13. 88. 3–4. The other works in question are *On Prophecy* and *On the Soul*, of which only fragments remain.

[24] A. Mayer, *Das Gottesbild im Menschen nach Clemens von Alexandrien* (Rome, 1942), remains the best treatment of this subject.

[25] *Strom.* 6. 14. 114. 4, referring to Eph. 4: 13.

have been made 'in the image and likeness of God', assimilated to the Divine Word in the affections of the heart and therefore rational (λογικός). (*Prot.* 10. 98. 4)

Here 'image' refers specifically to man's resemblance to God by virtue of his rational character, his intellect (νοῦς), which is then conversely used as the definition of the essential nature of man.[26] In this Clement is especially close to Philo, for whom the Logos is the true image of God and also the archetype for the true man, the intellect, which is thus the image of the image.[27] Clement also speaks quite distinctly of the Christian Gnostic as being a 'third image made as far as possible like the second cause',[28] and on one occasion he even extends the Platonic-Philonic perspective of the earthly reflecting its intellectual archetype to include the whole of creation.[29]

It is important to note, however, that Clement's use of the word 'image' in this sense does not denote a static, ontological given which itself makes man the image of God. It refers, rather, to a way of viewing man, which at the same time requires assimilation to the Divine Word 'in the affections of the heart' (*Prot.* 10. 98. 4). This essentially modifies the meaning of the word 'intellect': rather than being the rational faculty of man, as in the Platonic tradition, 'intellect', at least in this context, is now used as a term to describe the whole man considered in his relation to the Divine Word. Hence Clement can explain the scriptural saying that man was made 'in the image and likeness' thus: 'For the image of God is the divine and royal Word, the impassible Man; and the image of the image is the human intellect.'[30] As the human intellect has for its archetype the impassible Man, the word 'intellect' refers to the whole man, rather than just his intellectual capacities, whilst the image relation has an ethical dimension, demanding *apatheia*, a divine property, for man to be fully the image of God.[31]

Whilst the term 'intellect' is used to refer to the whole man

[26] *Strom.* 6. 9. 72. 2.
[27] Cf. Philo, *Quis rer. div. her.* 48. 231.
[28] *Strom.* 7. 3. 16. 6; cf. Plato, *Republic*, 10. 597e.
[29] *Strom.* 5. 14. 93. 4–94. 4.
[30] *Strom.* 5. 14. 94. 5.
[31] Cf. Mayer, *Das Gottesbild*, 25.

in his existence as the image, Clement is nevertheless quite definite that the scope of the image does not extend to the body: 'For conformity with the image and likeness is not meant of the body (for it were wrong for what is mortal to be made like what is immortal)'.[32] As the debate with Cassian in the third book of the *Stromateis* shows, Clement by no means disparages the body. He often speaks of the body and the flesh as being sanctified, clothed in immortality, and even itself receiving the Holy Spirit.[33] Yet, whilst the body, by virtue of the Incarnation, becomes 'conformed to the Lord' (σύμμορφον τοῦ κυρίου),[34] it essentially remains outside Clement's theology of the image.

It is, however, the use of the term 'image' in conjunction with 'likeness' that reveals the dynamic of Clement's anthropology. When they are so used, 'image' refers either to the final state of likeness to God, as described above, or to the basic starting-point for man, his created nature, whilst 'likeness' refers to the final perfected likeness of the Christian to God and includes the dynamic process by which man attains this end.[35] Clement explicitly identifies the biblical basis of this dynamic process, that of 'following God' (e.g. Deut. 14: 3), with the Platonic idea of assimilation and the Stoic idea of living according to nature.[36] Clement's clearest statement of

---

[32] *Strom.* 2. 19. 102. 6. Cf. *Strom.* 6. 14. 114. 4, 16. 136. 3.

[33] Cf. *Paed.* 1. 9. 84. 3; 2. 2. 20. 1; 3. 1. 2. 3; *Strom.* 4. 26. 163. 2.

[34] *Paed.* 3. 3. 20. 5. Marrou, *Le Pédagogue, I*, SC 70 (Paris, 1960), 37–8, enthusiastically overvalues this passage; the reference is probably to Rom. 8: 29, not Gen. 1: 26. Cf. Mayer, *Das Gottesbild*, 22.

[35] Clement refers this distinction between image and likeness to an earlier unnamed Christian writer: 'For is it not thus that some of our writers have understood that man straightaway on his creation received what is "according to the image", but that what is "according to the likeness" he will receive afterwards on his perfection?' (*Strom.* 2. 22. 131. 6). Irenaeus also distinguished between these two terms, although in a very different manner, so that if there is a relationship between him and Clement, it would seem to be grounded in a common struggle against the Gnostics and the distinction that they had already drawn between the image and the likeness. Cf. Irenaeus, *AH* 1. 5. 5 (referring to the Valentinians); Clement, *Exc. Th.* 54. 2.

[36] Cf. esp. *Strom.* 2. 19. 100. 3, 22. 131. 2–136. 6; 5. 14. 94. 5–96. 3. For a discussion of the Platonic background of Clement's thought on this point, see H. Merki, Ὁμοίωσις θεῷ: *Von der platonischen Angleichung an Gott zur Gottähnlichkeit bei Gregor von Nyssa* (Fribourg, 1952), 45–60.

the relation between the 'image' and the 'likeness' is given in
the first book of the *Paedagogus*:

It seems to me that he himself formed man of the dust, and
regenerated him by water; and made him grow by his Spirit; and
trained him by his Word to adoption and salvation, directing him by
sacred precepts; in order that, progressively transforming the earth-
born man into a holy and heavenly being, he might fulfil to the utmost
that divine utterance 'Let us make man in our own image and
likeness'. And in truth Christ became the perfect realization of what
God spoke, and the rest of mankind is only in the image. (*Paed.*
1. 12. 98. 2–3)

Christ is thus the first and perfect realization of Genesis 1: 26,
and opens the way, through rebirth and adoption, by the gift of
the Spirit, and training under sacred precepts, for all men to
acquire perfection and full likeness to God. Here, as we saw
earlier when discussing the constitution of man, possession of
the Spirit is the fulfilment and perfection of man as man. But,
rather than being considered as a possession which follows
naturally when man reaches maturity, possession of the Spirit
is now clearly seen as a gift consequent upon the incarnation of
Christ and man's subsequent rebirth and adoption.[37] Clement
now also speaks of this maturation as a transformation of the
'earth-born man' into a 'holy and heavenly being'.

Although Clement describes Adam as perfectly created for
growth towards full perfection, as we have seen, he does not
connect this dynamic to the process of developing the image
into the likeness. Clement does not speculate whether Adam
was only 'in the image', or whether he had the capability, of
himself, to become the likeness. It is important, however, to
note that in *Paed.* 1. 12. 98. 2–3 there are two aspects at work:
the gift of the Spirit and the regeneration by water, and,
corresponding to both of these, the reciprocal action of man,
guided and trained by the Word. Whilst in his original state
Adam was perfectly adapted for the increase of virtues and the
acquisition of the Holy Spirit, the misuse of his freedom made
this impossible. The Fall thus intervenes in what should have
been the natural development of man from his original created
state to his perfection in the possession of the Spirit, making

[37] Cf. Mayer, *Das Gottesbild*, 18–21; Ladaria, *El Espíritu*, 167–221.

the historical economy of Christ a necessity. The gift of the Spirit is now intimately connected with regeneration in Christ; but, whilst it is not to be separated from such regeneration, it is, in itself, distinct from it, in that possession of the Spirit was within the scope of man as he was first created. Thus, it would seem that 'likeness' is granted to man only through rebirth, made possible by the economy of Christ, whether man had fallen or not. This also suggests that, for Clement, Christ's incarnation is not determined solely by the Fall.

Although Clement seldom discusses the Fall, his work is dominated by the problems caused as a result of the Fall: man's weakness in the exercise of virtue and his ignorance of truth, and the corresponding need for training and instruction. It is, however, in his discussion of the Fall, that Clement describes the relationship between Adam and Eve prior to the Fall. In the third book of the *Stromateis* Clement is concerned to counter the Gnostic views which would connect the institution of marriage to the original sin. Clement is quite unambiguous about the pre-lapsarian state of Adam and Eve and the scope of their relationship:

And if the serpent took the use of intercourse from the irrational animals and persuaded Adam to agree to have sexual union with Eve, as though the couple first created did not have such union by nature, as some think, this again is blasphemy against creation; for it makes human nature weaker than that of brute beasts if in this matter those who were first created by God copied them. (*Strom.* 3. 17. 102. 4)

Such union was, therefore, natural to Adam and Eve. However, the sexual interpretation of the Fall, common to both his Gnostic opponents and to Philo, also had its influence on Clement.[38] All action is prompted by knowledge and impulse, and contrary to these are ignorance and weakness.[39] Adam, as a child, was vulnerable on both accounts: 'But if nature led them, like the irrational animals, to procreation, yet they were impelled to do it earlier than was proper because they were still young and had been led away by deceit' (*Strom.*

[38] For Philo, see *Opif.* 53. 151–2.

[39] Cf. esp. *Strom.* 6. 8. 69; 7. 16. 101. 6–7. The idea of ignorance and weakness as the root of sin has a diverse background: similar ideas are found in Plato (*Laws*, 9. 863c), Aristotle (*Nicomachean Ethics*, 5. 8. 6–7, 1135b12–19), Chrysippus (*SVF* 3. 256, 60. 29–33), and Philo (*Ebr.* 2. 6).

3. 17. 103. 1). Clement thus pictures the fall of Adam as consisting in premature engagement in sexual activity. The idea of the 'right time', the proper *kairos*, for sexual activity, both on the horizon of the individual's life and within that of the day, was a dominating determinant in cultural mores of the time, and also in Clement's own description of the right place and time for sexual activity.[40] It seems that Clement was convinced that the Fall must have had some connection with sexual activity, but that, not wanting to locate the misdeed in sexual activity itself, he had recourse to current assumptions about the 'right time' for an explanation which would safeguard both the naturalness of sexual activity and the link between such activity and the Fall.

Clement occasionally describes Eve as being tempted by the serpent, but does not suggest that it was Eve who led Adam into sexual activity.[41] Rather, Clement describes the incentive for the transgression in this way: 'the first-formed of our [race] did not bide his time, desired the favour (χάρις) of marriage before the proper hour and fell into sin . . . not waiting for the time of [God's] will' (*Strom.* 3. 14. 94. 3). It was the desire for the 'grace of marriage' that tempted Adam to anticipate the proper time ordained by God. Clement does not explain what he means by this 'grace'. It seems dubious, given Clement's strong insistence that sexual union should take place only for the sake of procreation,[42] to conclude from this passage, as Floyd does, that Adam and Eve were already enjoying sexual activity and that the serpent tempted the first parents with the joys of having a family.[43] It would appear more likely that this 'grace of marriage' is a euphemistic expression for Clement's opinion, which, as we have already seen, is that it was the immature desire for sexual activity which both prompted and, in its enactment, constituted the Fall (*Strom.* 3. 17. 103. 1).

This act effected a radical transformation both in the relation between man and God and also in man's own existence. Just as

[40] For a discussion of the idea of the 'right time' for sexual activity, see Foucault, *Le Souci de soi*, esp. 147–56; trans. 124–32.

[41] Cf. *Prot.* 1. 7. 6; 2. 12. 2; *Paed.* 2. 12. 123. 3.

[42] e.g. *Paed.* 2. 10. 83. 1.

[43] W. E. G. Floyd, *Clement of Alexandria's Treatment of the Problem of Evil* (Oxford, 1971), 52.

obedience had characterized Adam's original state of fellowship with God, so disobedience meant estrangement from
God.[44] Consequent upon this is death, the mortal life which
Adam exchanged for his immortal one.[45] For Clement, the
overriding meaning of death is the state of the soul separated
from the truth and its communion with the body in a state
of sin.[46]

It is, however, in his interpretation of the Lord's answer to
Salome's question, given in the Gospel according to the
Egyptians, 'Until when shall men die?', that Clement makes
his most interesting comments concerning death.[47] The aim of
these passages is to counter the radical eschatology of the
Encratites, who took the Lord's answer, 'As long as women
bear children', as grounds for the rejection of marriage and
procreation. Clement attempts to counter their argument by
spiritualizing the words involved: 'woman', 'man', 'birth',
'corruption', and 'death'. Clement points out that the word
'man' has two meanings: the outward man and the soul. It is
the latter that the Lord refers to in his reply 'As long as women
bear children', allegorizing 'women' as desire and children as
the various vices that spring from desire.[48] In this sense sin is
the death of the soul. But Clement goes on to speak of how
death applies to the outward man: 'By natural necessity in the
divine plan death follows birth, and the coming together of soul
and body is followed by their dissolution.'[49] Clement thus

---

[44] *Strom.* 4. 13. 94. 1.

[45] *Strom.* 2. 19. 98. 4.

[46] Cf. *Strom.* 2. 7. 34. 2; 4. 3. 12. 1. See also *Paed.* 2. 1. 8. 2; *Strom.* 2. 7.
35. 4; *QDS* 7. 3. Clement probably derives the distinction between the death
of the soul and the death of man as the separation of soul and body (cf. Plato,
Phaedo, 64c, 67d), from Philo, cf. *Leg. Alleg.* 1. 33. 105–8.

[47] *Strom.* 3. 6. 45. 3, 9. 63–7. For an analysis of these passages, and the same
theme as it was developed by other writers from Plato to Gregory of Nyssa,
see, van Eijk, 'Marriage and Virginity'.

[48] *Strom.* 3. 9. 63–4. Clement in fact adopts the Encratite interpretation of
'female' and 'woman' as desire (cf. *Strom.* 3. 9. 63. 2), but extends the scope of
the 'works' or 'children' that spring from desire to include, e.g. love of money
and gluttony, so modifying the Encratites' exclusively sexual understanding of
desire. Cf. D. G. Hunter, 'The Language of Desire: Clement of Alexandria's
Transformation of Ascetic Discourse', *Semeia*, 57 (1992), 98–9.

[49] *Strom.* 3. 9. 64. 2. Cf. *Strom.* 7. 4. 25. 2, where Clement links the
naturalness of man's death to that of the animals.

accepts the Encratites' premiss, that the connection between birth, and hence marriage, and corruption or death is natural and necessary; but, *contra* the Encratites, for Clement this connection is ordained by God, and as such there is no necessary reason to halt the process. There is, therefore, a disconcerting elision in Clement's thought. We have seen above that Clement described Adam's paradisal state as immortal, and that it encompassed marriage and procreation without, however, any inherent connection to death. Yet Clement now describes the connection between birth, marriage, *and death* as a divine arrangement.[50] Undoubtedly Clement, when speaking of the connection between birth and death, is referring to man's fallen condition and God's economical arrangement for man's fallen state of mortality. But Clement had no reason to accept the premiss itself: for Clement, marriage and procreation existed before the appearance of death.

Alongside death, the Fall effected the disordering of man's existential constitution:

As soon as the first man fell and disobeyed God, it is said that 'he became likened to the beasts' [Ps. 48: 13, 21 LXX]. As man sinned against the Word, it is natural that he should be considered as irrational and likened to the beasts. (*Paed.* 1. 13. 101. 3)

By asserting that man became irrational (ἄλογος) after the Fall, Clement does not mean to imply that he lost all capacity for rational thought. This statement must be understood in terms of Clement's hierarchical picture of the soul, as it was described above. All the lower powers and faculties of the soul should be subordinated to the guiding principle, or the intellect, for the right, or rational, functioning of man. If this order is upset or unbalanced, then the guiding principle of the soul is in danger of being dominated by the soul's irrational, animal part, and man thus becomes like the animals to whose nature he has succumbed.

No longer following the rule of nature and disobedient to the divine Logos, the passions take their rise in man. According to Clement,

[50] Cf. *Strom.* 4. 25. 160. 3.

Appetite (ὁρμή) is the movement of the mind (διανοίας) to or from something. Passion (πάθος) is an excessive appetite, exceeding the measures of the Word (τὸν λόγον), or appetite unbridled and dis-obedient to reason (λόγῳ). Passions then are a movement of the soul contrary to nature in disobedience to the Word. (*Strom.* 2. 13. 59. 6)[51]

For Clement it is the fleshly spirit (πνεῦμα σαρκικόν), which is intimately connected with the body and its sensations, and comprehends in itself all the irrational functions of the soul, including the capacities for desire (ἐπιθυμεῖν), pleasure (ἥδε-σθαι), and anger (ὀργίζεσθαι), which is the seat of the corres-ponding passions in man.[52] It would be mistaken to conclude from this, however, that the passions, desire (ἐπιθυμία), pleasure (ἡδονή), and anger (ὀργή), are the natural functions of the biological being of man. These passions are the manifestation of the natural appetites (ὁρμαί) when they exceed their natural and proper measure. Elsewhere, perhaps following Chrysippus, Clement refers to a similar differentia-tion between the impulses necessary for the functioning of man and desire:

Those skilled in such matters distinguish impulse (ὄρεξις) from desire and assign the latter, as being irrational, to pleasures and licentious-ness; and impulse, as being a rational movement, they assign to the necessities of nature. (*Strom.* 4. 18. 117. 5)

Here the impulses of the soul, which, as they relate to the 'necessities of nature', clearly refer to the functions of the fleshly spirit, are described as being 'rational', whilst 'desire' is now a purely irrational movement bound up with pleasure. Thus, while they have their origins in the 'fleshly spirit' and its natural functions and impulses, it is their excessive use

---

[51] Although I have translated the word λόγος with an article, as 'the Word', and without an article, as 'reason', such a distinction must not be taken as absolute; Marrou's comments on the *Paedagogus* are equally appropriate here: 'Toute le *Pédagogue* joue, page après page, sur l'ambiguité du mot grec *ΛΟΓΟΣ* . . .' ('Humanisme et christianisme chez Clément d'Alexandrie d'après le *Pédagogue*', *Fondation Hardt, Entretiens sur l'Antiquité Classique*, 3 (1955), 192). For similar Stoic formulations of the definition of passion, see Diogenes Laertius, 7. 110 (*SVF* 1. 205, 50. 22–3).

[52] Cf. *Strom.* 6. 16. 136. 1 and 135. 3. For the similarity of Clement's position to that of Middle Platonism and Philo, see Lilla, *Clement of Alexandria*, 84–92.

contrary to reason, brought about by pleasure and disobedience, that characterize the passions.[53]

Due to the role played by pleasure in the rise of the passions, Clement, in typically Stoic fashion, is severely critical of any pleasure attached to an action which is not governed by some natural need.[54] It is by keeping the pleasures under control that man can prevent desire.[55] Clement speaks of the unnecessary 'passion of pleasure' that accompanies certain natural needs, such as eating, drinking, and marriage. If it were possible to eat, drink, or beget children without it, then, Clement is convinced, there would be no need for the passion of pleasure.[56] Clement seems to suggest that it is only for the pleasure involved, a pleasure from which one should refrain, that man engages in such activities at all. This harsh strain produces an uncomfortable tension in Clement's thought, for he also wants to maintain that pleasure is good, as it was given by God. Whilst pleasure is to be given no admittance, it is nevertheless given by God for the necessity of procreation.[57]

It is through the senses that the passions have access to the intellect, producing evil fantasies which disturb man's peace even in dreams.[58] Such fantasies affect man's capacity for right judgement, and thus demand constant vigilance and discernment. Whilst this idea was common to both the Stoics and Philo, Clement adds a new twist by seeing behind this disruptive activity the work of the demons.[59]

Having succumbed to the passions and overturned the right ordering of his constitution, man nevertheless retains his intellectual capacities and his freedom, and is, therefore, still capable of grasping the truth and of moral effort. Clement's warm appreciation of Greek philosophy is well known. He describes the origin of philosophy in various ways, either as plagiarism from the Old Testament[60] or as being transmitted to men by an inferior angel[61] or, most importantly, as due to the

[53] Cf. Hunter, 'Language of Desire', 99–105.
[54] e.g. *Paed.* 2. 1. 5. 1, 8. 68. 1, 4; 3. 9. 46. 1; *Strom.* 2. 20. 106. 2.
[55] *Paed.* 2. 1. 9. 1.
[56] *Strom.* 2. 20. 118. 7–119. 1.
[57] *Strom.* 2. 20. 107. 3.   [58] *Strom.* 2. 20. 120. 3.
[59] Cf. esp. *Strom.* 2. 20. 110. 1–3; Völker, *Der wahre Gnostiker*, 127–43.
[60] *Prot.* 6. 70. 1; *Paed.* 2. 1. 18. 2; *Strom.* 1. 22. 150. 2–4.
[61] *Strom.* 1. 17. 81. 4; 5. 1. 10. 2; 7. 2. 6. 4.

divine inspiration present or sown in each man.[62] Clement did not feel these to be self-contradictory or mutually exclusive, for they essentially demonstrate the same fact: the fundamental harmony between philosophy and Scripture.[63] Ultimately for Clement, philosophy constitutes a gift of God to the Greeks, acting as a preparation for the Christian faith, a προπαιδεία τις.[64] As a covenant equivalent to the Law, Clement can speak of 'those who have been justified (or made righteous) by philosophy'.[65] Both these covenants lead to the Christian faith; it is faith which is the essential lacking in the righteous both of the Old Testament and of philosophy, although the latter must also learn to abandon idolatry:

For to those who were righteous according to the Law, faith was wanting. Wherefore the Lord, in healing them, said 'Your faith has saved you'. But to those who were righteous according to philosophy, not only faith in the Lord, but also the abandonment of idolatry was necessary. (*Strom.* 6. 6. 44. 4)[66]

It is this call to abandon idolatry and to turn to faith in the Lord that is the great theme of the *Protrepticus*.

When speaking of faith, Clement has three issues to tackle: first, the sceptical attitude of Greek philosophers towards Christian faith; second, the stance of the so-called Gnostics, especially the Valentinians, who sharply distinguished between the faith of the common believers and the *gnōsis* of the spiritual elect; and third, the unreflective attitude of some Christians towards their own faith.[67] In answer to the first, Clement

---

[62] *Prot.* 6. 72. 5, 7. 74. 7; *Strom.* 1. 7. 37. 1–2; 5. 13. 87. 2–4.

[63] For the origin of these views of Clement, and the similarity to ideas in contemporary philosophy and Philo, see Lilla, *Clement of Alexandria*, 9–59.

[64] *Strom.* 1. 5. 28. 1–3; 6. 5. 41. 7–42. 3.

[65] *Strom.* 1. 4. 27. 3. Only once, in *Strom.* 2. 2. 7. 1, does Clement suggest, in passing, that the righteousness taught by the Greeks is not 'according to truth'. And here it seems that this comment is determined by the context, in which Clement is trying to explain the δικαιοσύνη ἀληθής of Prov. 1: 3.

[66] Cf. *Strom.* 5. 13. 87. 1, where Clement insists that even those skilled in Greek philosophy must still learn the truth about Christ.

[67] For a good discussion of Clement's ideas about faith and its similarities especially with Middle Platonism, see Lilla, *Clement of Alexandria*, 118–42, to which the following paragraphs are indebted. T. Camelot, *Foi et Gnose: Introduction à l'étude de la connaissance mystique chez Clément d'Alexandrie* (Paris, 1945), remains useful.

points out that there is no knowledge of any kind without an acceptance, on faith, of the first principles of knowledge: demonstrations must, ultimately, rest upon undemonstrated principles.[68] Closely connected with this understanding of faith is the Stoic epistemological idea of 'assent' (συγκατάθεσις) and the corresponding Epicurean and Stoic idea of 'preconception' (πρόληψις).[69] For the Stoics, 'assent' referred to the acceptance by the mind of sense perception as the first step to knowledge, and had already been associated with 'faith' by Antiochus.[70] For the Epicureans, faith was a preconception of the mind in its acceptance of sense perception, a 'preconception' or 'anticipation' based on the memory of previous sense experience.[71] Clement combines the two ideas to define faith as 'a voluntary preconception, the assent of piety'.[72] As faith is now a matter of the will, it becomes the basis not only of knowledge, but also of action.[73]

As 'faith' refers to the acceptance of the first principles of knowledge, so too it is the acceptance of the conclusions arrived at by sure demonstration (that is, scientific demonstration, ἀπόδειξις ἐπιστημονική, as opposed to those of opinion, δοξαστική).[74] And it is with this distinction that Clement responds to the so-called Gnostics and to the simple Christians. Clement

---

[68] Cf. *Strom.* 2. 4. 13. 4; 8. 3. 6. 7–7. 2. The idea of the absolute ἀρχή ultimately goes back to Plato (*Republic*, 6. 511b6–7), was developed by Aristotle (*Posterior Analytics*, 1. 2, 71b, 20–3, 72a7–10; 1. 3, 72b19–25; 1. 22, 84a29–84b3), and became a part of the school tradition of Middle Platonism (cf. Alcinous, *Didaskalikos*, 5).

[69] For the use of these terms in Epicurean and Stoic epistemology, cf. A. A. Long and D. N. Sedley (eds.), *The Hellenistic Philosophers* (Cambridge, 1987), 1. 88–90, 249–53, respectively.

[70] Cf. Lilla, *Clement of Alexandria*, 128.

[71] Clement even refers for support to Epicurus (*Strom.* 2. 4. 16. 3), about whom he is otherwise severely critical, though he disagrees with him on the exact nature of this πρόληψις; for Epicurus πρόληψις is itself knowledge (cf. *Vita Epic.*, in *Epicurea*, ed. by H. Usener (Leipzig, 1887), 372. 6–7), but for Clement it is to be made into knowledge by instruction; cf. *Strom.* 2. 4. 17. 1.

[72] *Strom.* 2. 2. 8. 4. For faith as συγκατάθεσις, cf. *Strom.* 2. 12. 54. 5–55. 1 (which shows that Clement knew the Stoic doctrine) and 5. 13. 86. 1; for faith as πρόληψις, cf. *Strom.* 2. 4. 16. 3 (referring to Epicurus), 2. 6. 28. 1.

[73] *Strom.* 2. 2. 9. 2.

[74] For this distinction and the corresponding two kinds of faith, see *Strom.* 2. 11. 48. 2.

connects the two senses of faith by identifying the principle of demonstration with what is received in Scripture:

Therefore, as is reasonable, grasping by faith the indemonstrable first principle, and receiving in abundance, from the first principle itself, demonstrations in reference to the first principle, we are by the voice of the Lord trained to the knowledge of truth. (*Strom.* 7. 16. 95. 6)[75]

Thus the demonstration that Clement has in mind is the study and interpretation of Scripture. Since 'faith' can refer to the conclusions of such demonstration it is essentially also *gnōsis*.[76] As 'faith' now refers to both the acceptance of the principle of demonstration and the demonstration itself, Clement can speak of faith as the foundation of *gnōsis*, and also maintain their inseparability.[77] Thus Clement can insist on the intrinsic connection between faith and *gnōsis*, to counter the philosophers and Gnostics, on the one hand, whilst also insisting on the natural development of faith into *gnōsis*, by its own internal dynamic, to encourage the simple Christians, on the other. The twofold character of this faith, containing within itself the principles of its growth into *gnōsis*, which is not essentially different from it, clearly parallels Clement's description of Adam, whose initial 'imperfect perfection' was aimed at his growth to full perfection.

It is to this faith, the free assent of the will, that Clement calls the pagans in the *Protrepticus*: 'You, then, have God's promise, you have his love, become partakers of his grace.'[78] Clement stresses repeatedly that this requires only the exertion of man's will.[79] The motif running throughout the *Protrepticus* is that of the harmony to which man is called, when, having been tuned by the Holy Spirit, he becomes an 'instrument of many tones'.[80] Having seen the fundamental characteristics of Clement's anthropology and the dynamic conception of faith by which man is led to Christianity, we can now turn to this new harmony to investigate the character of Clement's asceticism.

---

[75] Cf. *Strom.* 2. 11. 48. 3; 7. 16. 93. 1, 96. 1.   [76] *Strom.* 2. 11. 49. 3.
[77] For πίστις as θεμέλιος, see *Strom.* 5. 1. 2. 5, 4. 26. 1; 7. 10. 55. 5. For their inseparability, see *Strom.* 5. 1. 1. 3. Cf. below, Ch. 6.
[78] *Prot.* 1. 6. 3.   [79] *Prot.* 9. 86. 1; 10. 106. 3–5; esp. 12. 118. 4.
[80] *Prot.* 1. 5. 3. Cf. *Paed.* 2. 4. 41. 5.

Chapter 5

Rebirth and Christian Life

The new life, entered by faith, to which man is called, is the subject of the *Paedagogus*. Two great themes stand out in this work: first, the significance of rebirth and the childhood of the new people of God, and, second, the divine *paideia*, or character formation (διάθεσις ἠθοποιΐας) consequent upon this.[1] The abundance of images which Clement uses to describe the Christian's new state of spiritual infancy—children, chicks, infants, colts, lambs, etc.[2]—is in stark contrast to a culture which had no real appreciation of the state of infancy.[3] The work certainly stands as an anti-Gnostic polemic, emphasizing the perfection of baptism and opposing the Gnostic division of men into separate categories. But the exuberance of Clement's words and the depth of his thought testify to much more than a polemical zeal; it is a warmth found also in the New Testament and later in the *Epistle of Barnabas* and *The Shepherd* of Hermas, to mention two works which Clement had to hand.[4]

Clement's predilection in the *Paedagogus* for images of infancy reflects the reality of regeneration: 'This is the one grace of the illumination, that we are no longer the same as we were before the washing.'[5] We have seen how Clement connects the gift of the Spirit, after Christ's incarnation, to baptism.[6] Clement also describes the regeneration as the work of the Father by the Spirit.[7] The water of baptism

[1] *Paed.* 1. 1. 2. 1.
[2] *Paed.* 1. 5. 14. 1–16. 3.
[3] Cf. H. I. Marrou, *Histoire de l'éducation dans l'antiquité*, 6th edn. (Paris, 1965), 325.
[4] *Barnabas*, 6. 11, 17; Hermas, *The Shepherd*, Mandate, 2. 1; *Similitude*, 9. 29. 1, 31. 3.
[5] *Paed.* 1. 6. 30. 1.
[6] *Paed.* 1. 12. 98. 2–3.
[7] *Paed.* 1. 5. 21. 2.

becomes a mother for Christians who are reborn by the Father, or is alternatively described as the 'rational water' which purifies them from the habits of custom.[8]

Clement's description of the effects of baptism is unreservedly categoric:

Being baptized, we are illumined; illumined, we become sons; being made sons, we are made perfect; being made perfect, we are made immortal. 'I have said', he says, 'that you are gods, sons of the Most High' [Ps. 81: 6 LXX]. This work is variously called grace, illumination, perfection and washing: washing, by which we cleanse away our sins; grace, by which the penalties accruing to transgressions are remitted; and illumination, by which that holy light of salvation is beheld, that is, by which we see the divine clearly. We call that perfect which wants nothing. For what is yet wanting to him who knows God? (*Paed.* 1. 6. 26. 1–3)

There are two remarkable features of this vivid description: first, that the newly baptized is unambiguously attributed with all the characteristics of perfection: illumined, adopted, perfected, and immortal. Clement, a little later, also speaks of baptism as granting *gnōsis*, the end of which, the final object of desire, is rest (ἀνάπαυσις).[9] The second striking point, consequent upon the first, is the immediacy of this perfection: it is a perfection which is granted here and now. Elsewhere in the same chapter, Clement stresses this even more strongly: 'Straightaway (εὐθέως) upon our regeneration we attain that perfection after which we aspired.'[10] Christians are already (ἐνθένδε ἤδη) practising the heavenly life, by which they are deified.[11]

We have already seen how Clement uses the term 'perfect' to refer to various states of perfection: Adam was created perfectly formed, yet called to grow to perfection; faith in itself is perfect, yet develops into *gnōsis*. It is in this sense that most scholars have interpreted Clement's comments on the perfection of the newly baptized: the neophyte possesses perfection in a seminal form, and is called to develop this seed into its full perfection, which will be achieved only after this life in the

---

[8] Cf. *Strom.* 4. 25. 160. 2; *Prot.* 10. 99. 3.
[9] *Paed.* 1. 6. 29. 3–4.
[10] *Paed.* 1. 6. 25. 1. Cf. *Paed.* 1. 6. 27. 1, 27. 2, 27. 3, 28. 1–2.
[11] *Paed.* 1. 12. 98. 3.

resurrection.[12] Alternatively, these claims are understood within the framework of a natural/supernatural distinction: the neophyte is granted eternal life here on earth, and thus possesses a twofold life, his natural life and a supernatural life in Christ.[13] Although Clement later, especially in the *Stromateis*, emphasizes the need for development and growth in the Christian life, his stress here on the complete perfection of the baptismal grace cannot, as is usually assumed, be reduced to an anti-Gnostic polemic. But neither does Clement, in these passages, speak of the perfection of the baptismal grace as seedlike, or as a supernatural life somehow added to the natural man. He does, however, explain how we are to understand this perfection of the neophyte, in terms which reverse such a perspective.

Clement provides an answer specifically for those who do not understand how one can speak of the neophyte as being already perfect:

But, say they, he has not yet received the perfect gift. I also assent to this: except he is in the light, and the darkness comprehends him not. There is nothing intermediate between light and darkness. But the end (τέλος) is reserved till the resurrection of those who believe, and it is not the reception of some other thing, but the obtaining of the promise previously made. For we do not say that both take place at the same time—both the arrival at the end and the anticipation (πρόληψις) of that arrival. For eternity and time are not the same, neither is the attempt (ὁρμή) and the final result (τέλος); but both have reference to the same thing, and one and the same person is concerned in both. Faith, so to speak, is the attempt generated in time; the final result is the attainment of the promise secured for eternity. (*Paed.* 1. 6. 28. 3–5)

The neophyte has not received the perfect gift as a present reality, but he has it by anticipation or in prior reception (πρόληψις). Yet there is nothing intermediary between the light and the darkness, and the neophyte is unambiguously in the light.[14] The most important aspect of this passage is that it

[12] Cf. F. Quatember, *Die christliche Lebenshaltung des Klemens von Alexandrinus nach seinem Pädagogus* (Vienna, 1946), 95; Völker, *Der wahre Gnostiker*, 452; M. Mees, 'Jetzt und Dann in der Eschatologie Klemens von Alexandrien', *Augustinianum*, 18 (1978), 127–37.

[13] Cf. Quatember, *Die christliche Lebenshaltung*, 89.

[14] Cf. *Paed.* 1. 26. 27. 3.

considers the neophyte from the point of view of what he will be, his final end (τέλος). In this eschatological existence, the neophyte is fully perfect. However, this state is not yet fully realized as a present reality; but neither is it solely a futural reality: it is in anticipation (πρόληψις) that the neophyte already exists as what he will be after the resurrection. After his regeneration in baptism, this eschatological existence in the light is his true being. It is faith which characterizes this eschatological existence generated or manifested in time.

In the *Stromateis*, Clement speaks repeatedly of such anticipation in terms of the Christian Gnostic's attainment of his futural reality in the present by *gnōsis*, by prayer, and by love.[15] In his discussion of baptism in the *Paedagogus*, Clement makes two further references to *prolēpsis* or, rather, to the corresponding verb:

Being perfect, he consequently bestows perfect gifts. As at his command all things were made, so on his bare wish to bestow grace ensues the perfecting of his grace. For the future of time is anticipated (προλαμβάνεται) by the power of his volition. (*Paed.* 1. 6. 26. 3)

If, then, those who have believed have life, what remains beyond the possession of eternal life? For nothing is lacking to faith, which is perfect and complete of itself. If anything were lacking to it, it would not be complete; lame regarding something, it would not even be faith. Nor after the departure from this world is there anything else waiting for the believers, those who have received here without distinction the pledge; but already having anticipated (προειληφότες) by faith that which is future, after the resurrection we receive it as present. (*Paed.* 1. 6. 29. 2–3)

In the first quotation Clement attributes the effective power of this anticipation to God, connecting it to the perfection of his

---

[15] Cf. *Strom.* 6. 9. 73. 4, 75. 2, 76. 4–77. 1; 7. 7. 43. 1, 47. 4, 47. 5. Cf. below, Ch. 6. In *Strom.* 2. 22. 131. 2–136. 6, Clement also expounds this anticipation through the use of Platonic 'participation'. For Plato the end is twofold: the 'Good' which exists first in the ideal form, yet is communicable, and second in the one who partakes of it and receives its likeness from it. In the same way, Clement understands Rom. 6: 22 to indicate a twofold hope: 'that which is expected and that which has been received, he [Paul] teaches the end to be the restitution of the hope'. For an analysis of this passage, see. E. F. Osborn, *The Philosophy of Clement of Alexandria* (Cambridge, 1954), 84–7, and *idem*, *Ethical Patterns in Early Christian Thought* (Cambridge, 1976), 67–8.

grace. In the second, the anticipation is described as the effect of faith, by which the neophypte receives here and now in faith what essentially belongs to the future and will be received as a present reality after the resurrection. In this way Clement's more abstract definitions of faith, which were considered earlier, are given substance as a living reality. Here Clement's understanding of faith clearly corresponds to that given in the Epistle to the Hebrews, as 'the substance of things hoped for' (11: 1); faith is a concrete 'substance', not simply an intellectual assent. It is also important to note that here the baptismal grace is considered as the bestowal of life ($\zeta\omega\eta$, $\zeta\omega\eta$ $\dot{\alpha}\dot{\iota}\delta\iota o s$), granted equally to all believers, to which nothing more can be added. This life as a present reality belongs to the future, but by anticipation in faith it is already ($\epsilon\dot{\upsilon}\theta\dot{\epsilon}\omega s$) lived here and now ($\dot{\epsilon}\nu\theta\dot{\epsilon}\nu\delta\epsilon$ $\ddot{\eta}\delta\eta$) by the baptized Christian.[16] It is this life which is the true existence of the Christian, and the Christian may therefore be said to live proleptically. Clement thus transposes the term *prolēpsis* from an epistemological context, in which, following Epicurus, he used it to define faith in terms of preconception, to an eschatological context, in which he uses it to describe the paradoxical state of the Christian whose true existence belongs to the eschaton, yet which is already lived in this world.[17] Clement's eschatology is therefore best characterized, at least in these passages, as a proleptic eschatology.[18] To describe this dynamic as the

---

[16] *Paed.* 1. 6. 27. 2.

[17] Lampe (ed.), *Greek Patristic Lexicon*, gives as one meaning of $\pi\rho\dot{o}\lambda\eta\psi\iota s$, 'anticipation', citing Clement as the first writer to use the word in this way. Liddell and Scott (eds.), *Greek–English Lexicon*, give $\pi\rho\dot{o}\lambda\eta\psi\iota s$ only in the sense of 'preconception', citing Epicurus and Chrysippus, though they give a wider range of meanings for the verb $\pi\rho o\lambda\alpha\mu\beta\dot{\alpha}\nu\omega$, esp. 'to take or receive beforehand'. Long and Sedley (eds.), *Hellenistic Philosophers*, do not suggest any usage similar to that of Clement. 'Anticipation' is perhaps not a satisfactory translation, since it does not necessarily involve a real content: one can dream of spending money one does not have, in anticipation of receiving it. Clement's use of the word $\pi\rho\dot{o}\lambda\eta\psi\iota s$ in this dynamic, 'realized' eschatological context is more concrete: we are already given the gift and live the life which itself essentially belongs to the eschaton. Camelot (*Foi et Gnose*, 45), hints at the eschatological nature of $\pi\rho\dot{o}\lambda\eta\psi\iota s$, but does not develop its significance; and likewise R. P. Casey, 'Clement of Alexandria and the Beginnings of Christian Platonism', *HTR* 18 (1925), 67–8.

[18] Mees, 'Jetzt und Dann', and O. Prunet, *La Morale de Clément d'Alex-*

bestowal of a seminal perfection at baptism, which must then be developed into full perfection, reverses the perspective of Clement's own explanation, and thereby overlooks the eschatological nature of the Christian's existence.

Although, in connection with baptism, Clement described Christ as being an 'example' (ὑπογραφή),[19] baptismal rebirth is not simply a matter of repeating the actions of Christ. Rather, baptism effects a grafting on to the body of Christ, bringing the Christian into union with him. Clement describes this in a passage in which he brings together the ideas of regeneration, incorporation, and nourishment:

For if we have been regenerated unto Christ, he who has regenerated us nourishes us with his own milk, the Word; for it is proper that what has begotten should forthwith supply nourishment to that which has been begotten. And as the regeneration, so analogously the food of man became spiritual. In all respects, therefore, and in all things, we are brought into union with Christ, and into relationship through his blood, by which we are redeemed; and into sympathy, in consequence of the nourishment which flows from the Word; and into immortality, through his guidance. (*Paed.* 1. 6. 49. 3–4)[20]

Here Clement was attempting to reconcile the words of St Paul, that adults are fed with solid food rather than the milk appropriate for children (1 Cor. 3: 2), to the image of the Promised Land as one running with milk and honey (Exod. 3: 8). For Clement, childhood in Christ is maturity compared to the Law.[21] As man's relationship to God will always be that of a child, so too, the food of Christians, Christ himself, is milk to them, yet inedible solid food to those outside Christ.[22] Clement's stress on baptism as the beginning of the Christian life and on the nourishment which sustains such life clearly shows the sacramental dimension of this life for Clement.[23] In

andrie et le Nouveau Testament (Paris, 1966), 234–6, underestimate this aspect of eschatological tension in Clement.

[19] *Paed.* 1. 6. 26. 1.

[20] Cf. *Paed.* 2. 2. 19. 4–20. 1.

[21] *Paed.* 1. 6. 34. 2.   [22] Cf. *Paed.* 1. 6. 32. 4–52. 3.

[23] Marrou rightly warns against the temptation to identify the nourishment spoken of in *Paed.* 1. 6 with the sacramental nourishment given in the eucharist (SC 70, 188 n. 2). Clement does not in fact speak here of the eucharist, but of nourishment by the Word, the milk of the Father.

this context, Clement also speaks of the Church as the locus of nourishment and life.[24] The Church is a virgin mother, who, before Christ's incarnation, was alone and not fully a woman, and so had no milk; but now, having brought forth her child, the milk, as virgin and mother, she calls all her children to her and nurses them with this holy milk.[25]

Through rebirth in Christ, Christians become a new race with new blessings and a new, eternally youthful life:

In contradistinction therefore to the older people, the new people are called young, having learned the new blessings; and we have the exuberance of life's morning prime in this youth which knows no old age, in which we are always maturing in understanding, are always young, always gentle, always new: for those must necessarily be new, who have become partakers of the new Word. And that which participates in eternity is wont to be assimilated to the incorruptible: so that to us appertains the designation of the age of childhood, a life-long spring-time, because the truth that is in us, and our habits saturated with the truth, cannot be touched by old age. (*Paed.* 1. 5. 20. 3–4)[26]

Participating in eternity, partaking of the eternal Word who has newly appeared, the new existence of Christians as children is untouched by time, an eternal springtime. Although they mature in understanding, they remain eternally young and eternally new; their childlike state in Christ is an eternal truth, their true existence.[27] In this state they live, as Clement puts it, on the boundaries of this life, already separated from death.[28]

Thus Clement, at least on a theoretical level, recognizes the profound ontological significance of baptism. Yet, as we noticed earlier, despite sharing certain premises with the Encratites, Clement also felt himself obliged to counter their radical conclusions: in particular, the claim that such rebirth effectively brings to a halt the course of everyday life, and especially marriage as the means through which this life holds sway. For Clement, although baptism transfers the ground of

---

[24] *Paed.* 1. 5. 18. 4, 22. 2; 6. 27. 2, 38. 2, 42. 1; 9. 84. 3.
[25] *Paed.* 1. 6. 42. 1–2.
[26] This 'new Word' probably refers to the incarnation of the Logos.
[27] *Paed.* 1. 5. 15. 2.
[28] *Paed.* 1. 6. 27. 1.

man's being, his ontology, to the eschaton, it does not imply such instantaneous mutation. Clement is deeply convinced that this eternal life, by which the Christian lives proleptically, is not to be thought of as separate or distinct from his or her day-to-day life: this ζωή can be manifested only within a βίος.[29] Clement visualizes this new existence within the terms of an 'art of living' (τέχνη περὶ βίον), an idea common to the popular philosophical and medical thought of his day.[30] Casting off the old man and abandoning the old forms of nourishment, Christians receive in exchange 'another new regimen, that of Christ'.[31] As a regimen, the Christian life is a long and rigorous process of training, required of each believer.[32] In this per-spective, baptism is now the entry into Christ's training: 'Having now accomplished those things, it is a fitting sequel that our pedagogue Jesus should sketch out for us the model of the true life, and train humanity in Christ' (*Paed.* 1. 12. 98. 1). It is the painstaking and compendious description of the manner in which the Christian should live that forms the bulk of the *Paedagogus*.

As there are two causes of sin, weakness and ignorance, so the life of the Christian has two aspects, training and in-struction. In the *Paedagogus*, Clement is concerned almost solely with the first aspect, the ceaseless exhortation of the Logos-Paedagogos urging the newly baptized to the 'energetic practice of our duties'.[33] The activity of the Logos as Teacher comes later, instructing those who have already been trained and disciplined.[34]

The essential characteristic of the life of the newly baptized Christian is obedience to the Logos, who, as a pedagogue, uses all his resources to encourage and exhort:

---

[29] Marrou's admirable formulation, SC 70, 28; cf. *idem*, 'Humanisme et christianisme', 193–4; *idem*, 'Morale et spiritualité chrétiennes dans le *Pédagogue* de Clément d'Alexandrie', *St. Patr.* 2, TU 64 (Berlin, 1957), 538.

[30] *Paed.* 2. 2. 25. 3. Cf. 1. 12. 99. 2. For a discussion of the idea of the 'arts of living' see Foucault, *L'Usage des plaisirs*, 16–19; trans. 10–13; and his *Histoire de la sexualité* in general; and, more recently, M. Nussbaum, *The Therapy of Desire: Theory and Practice in Hellenistic Ethics* (Princeton, 1994).

[31] *Paed.* 1. 6. 43. 1.

[32] Cf. *Strom.* 2. 21. 128. 4.

[33] *Paed.* 1. 1. 2. 1.

[34] *Paed.* 3. 12. 97. 3; 1. 1. 1.

With all his power then the Pedagogue of humanity, the divine Logos, using the resources of wisdom, devotes himself to the saving of the children, admonishing, upbraiding, blaming, chiding, reproving, threatening, healing, promising, favouring; and, as it were, by many reins, curbing the irrational impulses of humanity. To speak briefly, therefore, the Lord acts towards us as we do towards our children. (*Paed.* 1. 9. 75. 1–2)[35]

As passions took their rise from disobedience to the Logos, so, conversely, their defeat takes place through obedience to the Logos-Paedagogos. Alongside the Platonic image of the charioteer controlling the irrational impulses by means of reins,[36] the Logos-Paedagogos is also represented as a skilful doctor, who, with our co-operation, will heal our passions.[37] Clement also follows Plato in distinguishing two types of fear: one of reverence, which children show towards their parents, and the other of hatred, which slaves show towards cruel masters.[38] It is the first type of fear which should characterize our relationship to the Pedagogue, and prompt us to turn away from sin. Such fear is therefore described as 'salvific'.[39] Closely connected, in Clement's thought, to this fear is the hope inspired by the Pedagogue's promises, which is alternatively described as the reason for obedience, parallel to fear, and as the step succeeding fear.[40]

Playing on the multitude of possible meanings of the word *logos*, Clement extends this life of obedience to the Logos-Paedagogos to encompass both the correct reason in man and

---

[35] Cf. Plato, *Laws*, 7. 808d–e. See also the whole of *Paed.* 1. 9; 1. 8. 74. 3; and *Strom.* 6. 3. 28. 3.

[36] For the Pedagogue as ἡνίοχος, see also *Paed.* 3. 11. 53. 2; and Plato, *Phaedrus*, 247.

[37] Cf. *Paed.* 1. 1. 1. 2; 1. 1. 3. 1, 3; 1. 2. 6. 1, 2, 4; 1. 6. 51. 1. For an extended comparison of the passions to disease, see *Paed.* 1. 8. 64. 4–65. 2. For the background of this imagery in Chrysippus, Posidonius, and Galen, and for its use by Philo, who also spoke of the necessity of being healed by the Logos, see Lilla, *Clement of Alexandria*, 98. On the whole theme of 'therapy' in Hellenistic philosophy, see Nussbaum, *Therapy of Desire*.

[38] *Paed.* 1. 9. 87. 1; cf. Plato, *Laws*, 1. 646e–7c.

[39] *Paed.* 1. 9. 83. 2. Whilst Clement, following the Stoics (e.g. *SVF* 3. 378, 92. 16), includes fear in general as a passion, he nevertheless claims that such fear of the impassible God is itself impassible; cf. *Strom.* 2. 8. 40. 2: ὁ τοῦ ἀπαθοῦς θεοῦ φόβος ἀπαθής.

[40] Cf. *Strom.* 4. 7. 53. 1; 6. 12. 98. 3. See Völker, *Der wahre Gnostiker*, 278.

the natural ordering of the universe.[41] The idea of the 'correct reason' (ὀρθὸς λόγος) as the standard for human morality occurs repeatedly throughout the *Paedagogus*.[42] The Stoic background of this thought has been pointed out many times, and it is within a Stoic framework that Clement elaborates the theoretical aspects of his thought.[43] Thus, following a Stoic definition, Clement writes: 'Virtue is a disposition of the soul harmonious with the L/logos throughout the whole of life.'[44] This definition is augmented by a reference, in the *Stromateis*, to the Platonic idea of virtue as the harmony of the soul, the governing of her irrational parts by the reason, through which it is possible to lead an upright life.[45] The need for the rational part of the soul to be dominant, for the whole soul and life to be harmonious, also requires the ability to discern the fantasies conjured up by the passions. Thus Clement describes Christian conduct as being 'an operation of the rational soul in accordance with a correct judgement and desire for truth'.[46] Considered from this perspective, Clement can characterize the new Christian regimen in the following terms: 'The Christian life, in which we are now trained, is a system of rational actions, that is, of those things taught by the Logos, an unfailing energy which we have called faith' (*Paed*. 1. 13. 102. 4). Clement goes on to reduce the intellectualist tenor of this 'system of rational actions' by identifying it with the commandments of the Lord, written and adapted for mankind and for obedience.[47]

In the *Paedagogus*, Clement connects the idea of virtue as harmony with the 'correct reason' to the Aristotelian doctrine of virtue as moderation:

[41] Cf. Marrou: 'Toute le *Pédagogue* joue, page après page, sur l'ambiguité du mot grec *ΛΟΓΟΣ*' ('Humanisme et christianisme', 192). For the effect of the right ordering of the universe on human actions, cf. *Paed*. 1. 2. 6. 6.

[42] Not only does the ὀρθὸς λόγος act as the guide for Clement's descriptions of Christian behaviour, but it also becomes the measure of sin; cf. *Paed*. 1. 13. 101. 1: πᾶν τὸ παρὰ τὸν λόγον τὸν ὀρθὸν τοῦτο ἁμάρτημά ἐστιν.

[43] Cf. esp. Pohlenz, 'Klemens von Alexandrien', and Spanneut, *Le Stoïcisme et les Pères de l'Église*.

[44] *Paed*. 1. 13. 101. 2; cf. *SVF* 3. 197, 48. 4; 3. 262, 63. 34.

[45] Cf. *Strom*. 4. 4. 18. 1; Plato, *Republic*, 3. 410c. See Lilla, *Clement of Alexandria*, 61–72, for a comprehensive discussion of Clement's doctrine of virtue with regard to the contemporary philosophical background.

[46] *Paed*. 1. 13. 102. 3.

[47] *Paed*. 1. 13. 103. 1.

The medium is good in all things . . . since the extremes are dangerous, the middle courses are good. For to be in no want of necessaries is the medium, and the desires which are in accordance with nature are bounded by sufficiency. (*Paed.* 2. 1. 16. 4)[48]

As with most of his philosophical statements, this combination of Stoic and Aristotelian ideas is not original to Clement, but has its parallels in Middle Platonism and Philo.[49] The demand for self-sufficiency is also characteristic of the new regimen: Clement interprets the words 'Take no thought for the morrow' to demand that those dedicated to Christ should be self-sufficient, their own storehouse; for, requiring as few things as possible, they are assimilated to God, who alone is in need of nothing.[50] In the *Paedagogus*, at least, the aim of asceticism is therefore a moderation and harmony bounded by natural necessity: 'In a word, whatever things are natural to men we must not eradicate from them, but rather impose on them limits and suitable times.'[51] The most apt term to characterize this state, although Clement does not in fact use it in the *Paedagogus*, is moderation (μετριοπάθεια).[52]

Clement elaborates the practical details of this new regimen with an exacting strictness. Each of our acts is governed by a relentless concern for its modality, accordance with the correct *logos* (as the divine Logos, human reason and the natural order), and its finality, the limitation imposed by necessity. Although Clement does not mention Musonius by name, in the *Paedagogus* he treats the same subjects as Musonius, and frequently employs the same expressions.[53] At the beginning

---

[48] Cf. *Paed.* 3. 10. 51. 3; Aristotle, *Nicomachean Ethics*, 2. 6. 15–17, 1106b36–1107a8.

[49] For the Aristotelian influence on Clement, see, E. A. Clark, *Clement's Use of Aristotle* (New York, 1977), esp. 42–4, and for similar trends in Middle Platonism and Philo, see Lilla, *Clement of Alexandria*, 64–5.

[50] Cf. *Paed.* 1. 12. 98. 4; 3. 1. 1. 1; *Strom.* 2. 18. 81. 2.

[51] *Paed.* 2. 5. 46. 1.

[52] Clement uses this term in the *Stromateis* to distinguish the ethical state of the simple Christian from that of the Gnostics. μετριοπάθεια was commonly used by Philo and in Middle Platonism; see Lilla, *Clement of Alexandria*, 99–103.

[53] The parallel texts were established by P. Wendland, *Quaestiones Musonianae: De Musonio Stoico Clementis Alexandrini aliorumque auctore* (Berlin, 1886); see Marrou, SC 70, 52, for a brief comparison.

of the second book of the *Paedagogus*, Clement appropriates the old maxim that, whilst others may live in order to eat, the Pedagogue demands that we eat in order to live.[54] Every aspect of our nourishment is then systematically worked out from this principle, resulting in a clear preference for the most simple and frugal types of food, which are also, as a matter of principle, the foods most suitable for the body and which produce the strongest and noblest of men.[55] The same rationale is used to deduce what type of clothes Christians are permitted to wear, what objects they may have in their homes, and so on. Clement also spares us few details about the manner in which Christians ought to live their lives. For example, when discussing behaviour at the table, Clement enjoins his readers:

We must abstain from all slavish manners and excess, and touch what is set before us in a decorous way, keeping the hand and the couch and the chin free of stains, preserving the grace of the countenance undisturbed, and commit no indecorum in the act of swallowing. (*Paed.* 2. 1. 13. 1)[56]

The *Paedagogus* is full of such advice for every aspect of life—how to get up, walk, talk, laugh, go to bed, and sleep. The overall aim, according to Clement, was to fashion Christians so that they would be characterized by 'composure, tranquillity, calmness and peace'.[57]

Peter Brown admirably describes the significance of this comprehensive tableau:

He drew on the rules for disciplined deportment, commended by philosophers to the Greek elites of his age, in order to wrap the believer in a web of minute, seemingly insignificant patterns of daily living. But every detail of these codes unobtrusively communicated a view of the world, of the human person and of society, that was soundproof to the shrill claims of the 'born again' [i.e. the Encratites] . . . Clement's writings communicated a sense of the God-given

---

[54] *Paed.* 2. 1. 1. 4; cf. Musonius, 18b, ed. O. Hense (Leipzig, 1905), 103.

[55] *Paed.* 2. 1 *passim*; cf. 2. 1. 5. 2: πᾶν γὰρ τοὐναντίον οἱ ταῖς εὐτελεστάταις χρώμενοι τροφαῖς ἰσχυρότεροί εἰσι καὶ ὑγεινότεροι καὶ γενναιότεροι, with Musonius, 18b, ed. Hense, 104: πᾶν γὰρ τοὐναντίον οἱ ταῖς εὐτελεστάταις χρώμενοι τροφαῖς ἰσχυρότατοί εἰσιν.

[56] Cf. B. Leyerle, 'Clement of Alexandria on the Importance of Table Etiquette', *JECS* 3 (1995), 123–41.

[57] *Paed.* 2. 7. 60. 5.

importance of every moment of daily life, and especially of the life of the household.[58]

This 'system of rational actions' deliberately covers every aspect of life, awake and asleep, so as to leave no moment uninfluenced by the new regimen, but also so as to leave no crack through which the newly baptized Christian could be seduced by those who claimed that entry into the new life necessitated the abandonment, rather than the transformation, of the fabric of the old life, especially marriage.

It has been rightly stressed that Clement does not simply repeat the cultivated morality of his day, but transforms it by placing it in a Christian perspective.[59] The Stoic demand for a life lived 'according to the logos' becomes filled with a new meaning, that of obedience to the Logos-Paedagogos, Christ. The Stoic doctrine of the anthropocentric structure of the universe is placed in the context of a personal God who made the universe and all its goods for man. The enjoyment of the beauty of this world—for example, the fragrance and beauty of flowers—leads men to praise the Creator.[60] The right use of these goods therefore takes the form of thanksgiving, whilst the one who continually gives thanks no longer occupies himself with pleasures.[61] With regard to the good things of this world, Clement expands the Stoic doctrine of their communal possession into a perspective of love: the principle of κοινωνικόν is replaced by ἀγαπητικόν.[62] Further, whilst the *Paedagogus* was written to teach 'how each of us ought to conduct ourselves in respect of the body, or rather how to regulate the body itself', this now has as its goal 'to purify the flesh'.[63]

However, whilst Clement certainly places the common themes of Greek philosophical morality within a Christian context, there remains the problem of the motivation and modality. When discussing what drink is suitable for Christians, Clement begins with a categorical statement: 'The natural, sober and necessary drink for the thirsty is water.'[64]

---

[58] Brown, *The Body and Society*, 125–6.
[59] Cf. esp. Marrou, SC 70, 58.
[60] *Paed.* 2. 8. 70. 5.   [61] *Paed.* 2. 1. 10. 3.
[62] *Paed.* 2. 12. 120. 4; cf. Marrou, SC 70, 58.
[63] *Paed.* 2. 1. 1. 2.
[64] *Paed.* 2. 2. 19. 2.

He expresses his admiration for those who 'have adopted an austere life, and who are fond of water, the medicine of temperance, and flee as far as possible from wine, shunning it as they would the danger of fire'.[65] Christians are to eat their meals without any drink at all; if perchance thirst comes on, they are to satisfy it with water, but only in moderation.[66] In addition, Clement then writes several pages describing the dangers of wine. The conclusion of his argument—and one is left in no doubt that this would have been his preference—is complete abstinence from wine. But, as he reminds his readers, and himself, Christ himself drank wine.[67] There is, further-more, the fact that wine was blessed by Christ for the eucharist, which conversely gives a eucharistic character to each act of drinking wine.[68] Clement is forced to recall this in order to counter the Encratites, who would have prohibited the use of wine altogether.[69] Thus Clement is compelled to allow the use of wine, which he then restricts to older people, who, when they have finished their serious reading, and as the day becomes colder, may use a little wine to introduce some warmth into the body.[70] A similar dialectic can be seen in Clement's discussion of the eating of meat. Clement cites with approval Romans 14: 20, 'it is good not to eat meat nor to drink wine', pointing out that it is also a Pythagorean principle.[71] Whilst repeating passages from Romans 14 and 1 Corinthians 8, Clement does touch briefly upon the Pauline concern that the weaker brethren should not be scandalized by anyone's actions, but his main interest is shown in the following pages, where he describes the many virtues of eating only vegetables. Moreover, in the context of discussing the character of Chris-tian perfection, Clement suggests that a Christian Gnostic might abstain from meat both for the sake of his *ascēsis* and to weaken the sexual appetite.[72] However, the fact that Christ ate some fish in front of his disciples, and that Peter was

[65] *Paed.* 2. 2. 20. 2.   [66] *Paed.* 2. 2. 21. 2–3.

[67] *Paed.* 2. 2. 32. 2.

[68] Cf. Osborn, *Ethical Patterns in Early Christian Thought*, 59.

[69] *Paed.* 2. 2. 33. 1.   [70] Cf. *Paed.* 2. 2. 22. 1–2, 29. 2.

[71] *Paed.* 2. 1. 11. 1.

[72] Cf. *Strom.* 7. 6. 33. 6. For the ascetic principle of abstaining from meat so as to weaken the sexual appetite, as it was developed in later monasticism, see Rousselle, *Porneia*, esp. 205–26; trans. 160–78.

ordered to eat meat in his vision (Acts 10: 10–15), leads Clement to emphasize the need to use everything in moderation.[73] As Marrou points out, these passages indicate that the asceticism of Clement finds its limit in the incarnate Christ, and this, for Marrou, is sufficient to preserve its essentially Christian character.[74] But if Clement's asceticism is held in check by Christ, its motivation certainly lies elsewhere, in the ideal he establishes for Christian life, an ideal he found in the popular cultivated morality of his time. Christ's incarnation is consequently understood by Clement as enabling the exercise of the morality taught by the Greeks, who, despite having received a spark of the divine Word, were unable to practise it due to their own weakness.[75]

A parallel problem emerges from an analysis of the relation between God and man in the asceticism that Clement describes. There is a continual oscillation in this relation throughout Clement's works. Corresponding to the emphasis which, as we have seen, he places on freedom as the determinative element in the constitution of man, Clement stresses that the practice of this asceticism, the acquisition of virtue, falls within man's own ability. Man is by nature adapted for the acquisition of virtue;[76] if it were not so, the possession of virtue would be neither voluntary nor praiseworthy.[77] Clement repeatedly and expressly states that it is within man's power to train himself and to obey the commandments, for virtue is supremely a matter of man's own volition.[78] This significance and scope of human volition and ability is the result of God's plan for man: God adapted Adam for the acquisition of virtue, for God 'intended him to be saved of himself'.[79] Taken in isolation, the immense role ascribed to human volition would

[73] *Paed.* 2. 1. 10. 2–16. 4.
[74] Cf. Marrou, 'Morale et spiritualité chrétiennes', 543; SC 70, 60–1.
[75] *Prot.* 7. 74. 7.
[76] Cf. esp. *Strom.* 6. 11. 95. 5, and also *Strom.* 1. 6. 34. 2–4; 6. 12. 96. 3.
[77] *Strom.* 7. 3. 19. 3.
[78] e.g. *Strom.* 2. 15. 62. 4; 4. 19. 124. 1; 4. 24. 153. 2; 7. 2. 8. 6; 7. 7. 48. 7. Völker, commenting on *QDS* 18. 1, states that 'die Tugen fällt unter die Rubrik des τὸ ἐφ' ἡμῖν' (*Der wahre Gnostiker*, 457). See also J. Wytzes, 'The Twofold Way: Platonic Influences in the Work of Clement of Alexandria', *VC* 11 (1957), 226–48; 14 (1960), 129–53.
[79] *Strom.* 6. 12. 96. 2; cf. *Strom.* 7. 2. 6. 3.

seem to make Clement a forerunner of Pelagianism. But it seems to be balanced by an equal stress on the inadequacy of man's own ascetic labours:

For a man training and working for *apatheia* achieves nothing. But if he plainly shows himself very desirous and earnest about this, he attains it by the addition of the power of God. For God conspires (συνεπιπνεῖ) with willing souls. But if they abandon their eagerness, the Spirit which is bestowed by God is also restrained. (*QDS* 21. 1–2)

Man cannot attain the heights of *apatheia* without the aid of this power of God. God and man co-operate, enabling man to achieve the state of *apatheia*. However, this state of *apatheia* is not demanded of the simple Christians, who, for their salvation, are exhorted to remain in a state of moderation and self-sufficiency. As we will see, when looking at the life of the true Christian Gnostic, the goal of *apatheia* is for those who do not want simply to be saved, but to be saved in a 'fitting and becoming manner'.[80]

With regard to salvation, it is frequently asserted that the relationship between human asceticism and the grace or power of God, as Clement describes it, is one of 'synergy'.[81] As Jaeger noted, Clement is the first Christian writer to develop a fairly sophisticated vocabulary and theology of 'synergy'.[82] According to Jaeger, Clement's use of this term differs from that of Gregory of Nyssa and the later Greek patristic tradition, in that Clement never speaks of God, Christ, or the Spirit co-operating with man; it is, rather, man who is said to co-operate, 'who, when he feels that the grace of God is given him, seizes the opportunity to yield to it'.[83] In the eighth *Stromata*, Clement systematically analyses the various types of causes and provides a formal definition of what he means by 'synergy', by distinguishing the 'co-operative cause' (τὸ συνεργόν) from the related concept of a 'joint cause' (τὸ συναίτιον):

[80] *Strom.* 6. 14. 111. 3; cited and discussed below, Ch. 6.

[81] Cf. Völker, *Der wahre Gnostiker*, 121, 254–6, 458–60; T. Rüther, *Die sittliche Forderung der Apatheia in den beiden ersten christlichen Jahrhunderten und bei Klemens von Alexandrien* (Freiburg im Breisgau, 1949), 85; and Tollinton, *Clement of Alexandria*, 2. 82.

[82] Cf. W. Jaeger, *Two Rediscovered Works of Ancient Christian Literature* (Leiden, 1954), 103–6.

[83] Ibid. 103.

The joint cause is conceived of in conjunction with another, which is not capable of producing the effect by itself, being a cause along with a cause. The co-operative cause differs from the joint cause in this particular, that the joint cause produces the effect with the other, which by itself does not act. But the co-operative cause, while effecting nothing by itself, yet by its accession to that which acts by itself, co-operates with it, for the production of the effect in the intensest degree. (*Strom.* 8. 9. 33. 8–9)[84]

In this formal schema, the co-operative cause, which by itself is unable to act, co-operates with that which is capable of acting by itself, making the effect better and stronger. If one were to transfer this schema to the relationship between man and God, it would seem to imply that man is not able to achieve anything working by himself, but must accede to the power or grace of God.

However, Clement is less rigid in his application of this definition than Jaeger supposes. According to Clement, all causes, even co-operative causes, must effect something, of which they are then 'wholly' ($\pi\acute{a}\nu\tau\omega\varsigma$) the cause; otherwise they would not even be called a cause.[85] As such, Clement can also speak of co-operative causes as providing 'power' towards the desired effect.[86]

More specifically, in the context of Clement's descriptions of the relationship between man and God, it is not correct simply to assert that man 'co-operates' with the grace or power of God, or the Spirit. Clement is convinced that purity of soul is a prerequisite for the reception of the grace or the power of God.[87] For Clement, man is saved by his co-operation, not with the grace or power of God, but with the *paideia* of the commandments enjoined by God, which are always within his own capacity. In the seventh *Stromata* Clement provides a more detailed description of this relationship:

Nor shall he who is being saved be saved against his will, for he is not inanimate; but he will above all voluntarily and of free choice hasten to salvation. For man received the commandments so as to be self-

---

[84] See also the whole of *Strom.* 8. 9 and 1. 20, esp. 99.

[85] *Strom.* 8. 9. 33. 4. Clement here uses the same verb ($\pi\alpha\rho\acute{\epsilon}\chi\epsilon\iota\nu$) which he uses to contrast the $\sigma\upsilon\nu\alpha\acute{\iota}\tau\iota\upsilon\nu$ and the $\sigma\upsilon\nu\epsilon\rho\gamma\acute{\upsilon}\nu$ in *Strom.* 8. 9. 33. 8–9.

[86] *Strom.* 1. 20. 99. 4.

[87] Cf. *QDS* 16. 2; *Strom.* 3. 5. 42. 6.

impelled, to whatever he might wish of things to be chosen and things to be avoided. Wherefore God does not do good by necessity, but from his free choice he benefits those who turn to him of themselves. (*Strom.* 7. 7. 42. 4–6)

Man has been given the commandments that he might be self-impelled. Through his own free choice he has the possibility of choosing salvation and turning to God. His freely chosen application is then matched by God's grace, enabling the perfecting of his choice and the saving of those who by their own choice and application are already moving towards salvation. It is thus that Clement understands the Incarnation in terms of pedagogy: Christ 'came to show man what was possible through obedience to the commandments'.[88] In the fifth *Stromata* Clement describes the dynamic of this relationship in a similar fashion: Wisdom, the power of the Father, is given by God; it rouses our free will, and then repays the application of the elect with crowns of fellowship.[89]

This synergetic relationship is seen particularly clearly in the image of the Logos as a physician who, with our co-operation, heals our diseases, the passions:

As the physician provides health for those who co-operate with him towards health, so also God provides eternal salvation for those who co-operate with him for knowledge and right action; and the moment that we do any one of the things in our capacity, which are enjoined by the commandments, the promise also is also fulfilled (σὺν δὲ τῷ ποιεῖν, ὄντων ἐφ' ἡμῖν . . . καὶ ἡ ἐπαγγελία τελειοῦται). (*Strom.* 7. 7. 48. 4)

The fulfilment of the commandments, which are within man's capability, is simultaneously the fulfilment of the promise and the bestowal of salvation. It is in this sense that man is said to co-operate with God, helping him achieve his designs for mankind. Similarly, when Clement refers to Ephesians (2: 5) in *Stromata* 5, he makes his own characteristic addition: 'By grace we are saved, but not without good works.'[90] Likewise,

---

[88] *Strom.* 7. 2. 8. 6. It must be stressed that this pedagogic function does not exhaust Clement's understanding of the Incarnation. Cf. C. Bigg: 'For Clement's idea of the Saviour is larger and nobler—may we say less conventional?—than that of any other doctor of the Church' (*The Christian Platonists of Alexandria* (Oxford, 1886), 72).

[89] *Strom.* 5. 13. 83. 5.   [90] *Strom.* 5. 1. 7. 2.

when Clement reads 'your faith has saved you' (Mark 5: 34), he specifies that this does not simply mean faith, for it was spoken to the Jews—that is, to those who already kept the Law and lived blamelessly, lacking only faith.[91] The performance of these good works is thus not dependent upon, nor derived from, faith. This freely chosen ascetic labour is a prerequisite for the grace of salvation or the gift of *apatheia* (as in *QDS* 21. 1), rather than being the effect or manifestation of man's salvation.[92]

The relationship between man's efforts and the grace of God is, in Clement's thought, one of synergy. But it is a synergy which remains a purely external collaboration between two distinct actors. Man is created for the acquisition of virtue; he is aroused to this task by the God-given commandments or wisdom, and continually prompted to action by the threats and promises of the Pedagogue; yet the task remains one within the scope of man's free will and capacity, and it is his application to this task that is rewarded by the grace of God. There is no sense, in Clement's descriptions of the asceticism of the neophyte, of that asceticism being the application of the newness of life freely granted to those who turn to God in faith. The eschatological tension of the Christian proleptically living the life of the resurrection, which Clement described so vividly in the first book of the *Paedagogus*, has not penetrated into his description of the asceticism of Christian life. Clement's 'synergism' describes a relationship between God and man in which they co-operate to achieve man's salvation, rather than to enflesh man's freely given eschatological salvation in the present. It is, therefore, a synergy which does not result from our new relationship with God granted in baptism.

By his thoroughgoing analysis of the Christian life in terms of a system of rational actions, a life in which each act has a God-given importance, Clement, as Brown suggests, defends the value of every aspect of everyday human life against the 'born-again' Encratites. But his method of doing this involved changing the basis of the defence: the style of asceticism which

---

[91] *Strom.* 6. 14. 108. 4–5.

[92] Cf. Wytzes: 'In Clement the moral effort is a condition of salvation, in St. Paul moral effort proceeds from salvation as a task' ('Twofold Way', 237). See also Völker, *Der wahre Gnostiker*, 254.

he proposes, as we have seen, no longer has its motivation in Christ; nor does it stem from the new life granted by him. Rather, it is an *ascēsis* undertaken for its own sake,[93] which finds its limitation in Christ. Rendered secure, by a self-sufficient, self-assured composure and tranquillity, from attack by the Encratites, Clement's prescribed regimen for Christian life is also impregnable both to the newness of life granted in baptism and, as we will see when looking at his thought on marriage, to a full engagement with our concrete and interpersonal life.[94] Clement provides a particularly suitable image for the style of this asceticism: rather than a new life which penetrates every aspect of man's existence and his world, Clement's Christian pursues wisdom by inwardly stretching upwards; separated from the world and from sin, he touches the world on tiptoe only in order to appear to be in the world.[95]

The effects of this style of asceticism are seen, as I suggested, especially clearly in Clement's discussion of marriage. Clement is frequently praised for his warm appreciation of marriage.[96] He stresses, against the Encratites, that marriage is a matter of choice, for those who are suited for it and who are at the appropriate age.[97] In the final chapter of the second *Stromata*, a prelude to the celebrated third book, Clement presents a brief doxographical survey of the opinions of the philosophers about

[93] Cf. *Strom.* 7. 6. 33. 6, where Clement describes abstention from meat as being 'for the sake of *ascēsis*'.

[94] Marrou speaks of 'l'inspiration profondément chrétienne de la spiritualité du *Pédagogue*, ce que j'ai appelé son caractère "extatique": l'irruption de la transcendance divine dans notre vie la plus quotidienne' (SC 70, 39–40), referring to his article 'Morale et spiritualité chrétiennes', 544. Such divine irruption is certainly expressed by Clement in his description of the effects of baptism, but does not extend to his proposed framework for the Christian life.

[95] *Paed.* 1. 5. 16. 3; both Stählin and Marrou, in their respective editions, regard ὀλίγῳ ποδὶ ἐφαπτόμενοι τῆς γῆς as an unattributed quotation. Given that Clement believed that men's ideas about God correspond to their own character (*Strom.* 6. 17. 149. 4; 7. 4. 22. 2), it is perhaps no surprise that Clement on one occasion depicts Christ in somewhat docetic terms (*Strom.* 6. 9. 71. 2): a docetic Saviour is a suitable model for a 'docetic' asceticism.

[96] Most recently by J. P. Broudéhoux, *Mariage et Famille chez Clément d'Alexandrie* (Paris, 1970) and M. Mees, 'Clemens von Alexandrien über Ehe und Familie', *Augustinianum*, 17 (1977), 113–31; see also Quatember, *Die christliche Lebenshaltung.*

[97] *Strom.* 2. 23. 137. 3–4; 3. 9. 66. 3.

marriage. He cites Plato, without comment, as maintaining that marriage contrives immortality for the human race through the succession of children.[98] He refers to Democritus and Epicurus, who disparage marriage because of the many troubles that it brings. The Stoics regard marriage and the rearing of children as indifferent, whilst the Peripatetics believe it is a good.[99] He then refers to others, perhaps Hierocles and Antipatros, again without comment, for whom 'the childless man fails in the perfection which is according to nature, not having substituted his proper successor in his place'.[100] Finally Clement states his own position: 'Therefore we must by all means marry, both for our country's sake, for the succession of children, and as far as we are able, for the completion of the world' (*Strom.* 2. 23. 140. 1). This reference to the completion (συντελείωσις), does not seem to refer to the eschatological idea of the completion of the number of the elect, but rather to the continuity of the world as it is.[101] Clement then goes on to speak of the necessity of marriage, in a very self-centred manner, as being especially shown by the diseases of the body, for a wife's care far exceeds that of friends.[102] Likewise, marriage is shown to be necessary due to the help that a spouse and children can provide in old age.[103]

The emphasis of these stock themes is quite clearly on procreation, and that is, in fact, how Clement defines the content of marriage:

The goal of marriage is procreation, and its end is fair children. (*Paed.* 2. 10. 83. 1)

Marriage is the first coming together according to law of a man and a woman for the procreation of legitimate children. (*Strom.* 2. 23. 137. 1)

Every aspect of marital sexual activity is rigorously deduced from this principle; everything which does not conform to this

[98] *Strom.* 2. 23. 138. 2; cf. Plato, *Laws*, 6. 773e; *Symposium*, 207d.

[99] *Strom.* 2. 23. 138. 3–6. See Stählin's apparatus for suggested references.

[100] *Strom.* 2. 23. 139. 5; it is Stählin who identifies these as Hierocles and Antipatros, referring to Stobaeus, *Flor.* 67. 21. 25.

[101] Thus Clement refers to Plato's belief that those who do not marry dissolve the states and the world which is constituted by marriage: *Strom.* 2. 23. 141. 5; Plato, *Laws*, 6. 773e–4c. Cf. *Paed.* 2. 10. 83. 2; van Eijk, 'Marriage and Virginity', 220.

[102] *Strom.* 2. 23. 140. 2.

[103] *Strom.* 2. 23. 141. 1.

finality is severely condemned. Even the 'conjugal rights' which St Paul had defended against the Corinthians (1 Cor. 7: 3, 5), are restricted by Clement to the finality of procreation, something never mentioned by the Apostle.[104] In this context Clement speaks extensively about the need to 'follow nature', established as it is by divine providence.[105] Clement even cites with approval Epicurus's maxim that 'sexual intercourse does no one any good; one must be content if it does no harm', and adds that even lawful intercourse is perilous except in so far as it is undertaken for procreation.[106] Clement also aims to outdo Stoic morality in his rigorism: 'If, as the Stoics believe, reason recommends that the Sage does not even move a finger by chance, how much more necessary is it for those who seek wisdom to control the organ of intercourse.'[107]

Contrary to the Encratites, Clement extends the virtues of continence (ἐγκράτεια) and temperance (σωφροσύνη) to marriage.[108] A man who marries for the sake of procreation must abstain from desire for his wife, and practise continence in order to beget with a sober and temperate will.[109] Whereas the Encratites practise continence because of their pessimistic attitude towards the world,[110] and athletes have practised continence so as to keep their bodies in training,[111] Clement emphasizes that Christian continence, which sanctifies the shrine of the Spirit, should arise from a love of the Lord.[112] In defining continence as an 'ignoring of the body in accordance with the confession of faith in God', he also extends the range of continence, to include every aspect of man's relation to the world, limiting his use to the necessary.[113] That the virtue of continence describes man's inward disposition in his use of the world means that, in contrast to the Encratites, Clement views continence as an interior virtue, hidden in the soul.[114]

---

[104] *Strom.* 3. 17. 107. 5. Cf. Broudéhoux, *Mariage et famille*, 174.
[105] Cf. *Paed.* 2. 10 *passim*, esp. 87. 3, 90. 3–4, 95. 3.
[106] *Paed.* 2. 10. 98. 2; cf. Epicurus, Frag. 62, ed. Usener, 118. 22.
[107] *Paed.* 2. 10. 90. 2.
[108] Cf. Hunter, 'Language of Desire'.
[109] *Strom.* 3. 7. 58. 2.
[110] Cf. *Strom.* 3 *passim*, esp. 5. 40. 2 and 6. 45. 1.
[111] Strom. 3. 6. 50. 4.
[112] *Strom.* 3. 7. 59. 4.   [113] *Strom.* 3. 1. 4. 1.
[114] *Strom.* 3. 6. 48. 3.

For Clement, the virtue of continence is intimately linked with that of temperance, and both are invoked to describe a 'temperate' use of sexual dealings within marriage. Frequently the two terms are used indistinguishably by Clement; but when they are distinguished, temperance seems to lack the combative dimension of continence: temperance is concerned with the positive regulation of sexual activity towards its proper goal, while continence struggles against any impassioned activity, and so desensualizes marriage.[115]

There is the same synergetic ambivalence in Clement's description of the virtues of continence and temperance as we saw in his description of asceticism in general. In the third *Stromata* Clement stresses, against the Encratites and the athletes, that true continence and temperance are divine gifts.[116] Elsewhere, however, he maintains that the virtue of temperance is within the capacity of anyone who chooses it, and also compares licentiousness, which is to be thought of as the evil of the one who is licentious, with temperance, which is the good of the one capable of practising it.[117] Similarly, Clement exhorts his readers to cultivate temperance that there might be not only work, but also the grace of God.[118] Likewise, continence is defined as the state which does not overstep the boundaries of the correct reason (ὀρθὸς λόγος), and the one who exercises continence is described as curbing his desires, or curbing himself, so as not to indulge in desires contrary to the correct reason.[119] This ambivalence is clearly expressed in a statement in which Clement relates the two virtues: continence 'does not only teach us how to exercise temperance (σωφρονεῖν), rather it supplies temperance to us, being a divine power and grace'.[120] Continence is here described as a divine power, which teaches us how to practise and achieve the virtue of temperance: *we* attain or receive temperance by exercising that which is a divine gift.

[115] Cf. Broudéhoux, *Mariage et famille*, 122–3. This manner of using these terms seems to go back to Aristotle, *Nicomachean Ethics*, 3. 11. 8, 1119a (on the temperate person who keeps to the middle course), and 7. 7. 4, 1150a (on restraint which requires mastery). Cf. Foucault, *L'Usage des plaisirs*, 74–90; trans. 63–77.

[116] *Strom.* 3. 1. 4. 2, 7. 57. 2.

[117] *Strom.* 4. 8. 58. 4, 19. 124. 3

[118] *Prot.* 11. 117. 5.

[119] *Strom.* 2. 18. 80. 4.

[120] *Strom.* 3. 1. 4. 2.

Clement bases his procreative definition of marriage, something not heard of in the New Testament, on the divine command recorded in Genesis, 'Multiply!' (Gen. 1: 28). Thus, for Clement, the identification of marriage with procreation is not a restriction, but the fulfilment of God's designs. Clement even speaks of man becoming like God through his co-operation in the birth of another human being, while marriage is described as 'co-operation with the work of nature'.[121]

But, besides directing (in passing) the husband to love his wife,[122] Clement emphasized procreation to such an extent that he very rarely speaks of the mutual relationship between husband and wife. This stands out in sharp contrast to the description of marriage given by Musonius, an author otherwise extensively used by Clement. According to Musonius:

The husband and wife . . . should come together for the purpose of making a life in common and of procreating children, and furthermore of regarding all things in common between them, and nothing peculiar or private to one or the other, not even their own bodies. The birth of a human being which results from such a union is certainly something marvellous, but it is not yet enough for the relation of husband and wife, inasmuch as quite apart from marriage it could result from any other sexual union, just as in the case of animals. But in marriage there must be above all perfect companionship (συμ-βίωσις) and mutual love of husband and wife. . . . Where, then, this love for each other is perfect and the two share it completely, each striving to outdo the other in devotion, the marriage is ideal and worthy of envy, for such a union is beautiful.[123]

There is certainly no equivalent description in Clement.[124] Yet Clement undoubtedly had a high regard for the *style* of

---

[121] *Paed.* 2. 10. 83. 2. For the description of co-operation, see *Paed.* 2. 10. 93. 1; *Strom.* 3. 9. 66. 3. In *Strom.* 3. 12. 87. 4, Clement considers the relation to be one of a joint cause or a servant.

[122] *Strom.* 3. 7. 58. 2.

[123] Musonius Rufus, 13a, ed. Hense 67–8; trans. C. Lutz, 'Musonius Rufus', *Yale Classical Studies*, 10 (1947), 89.

[124] Cf. Broudéhoux, *Mariage et famille*, 174. On the dangers which Gregory of Nyssa perceived in such 'companionship', when it becomes a passionate attempt to find permanence and security in another, rather than in God; cf. M. D. Hart, 'Reconciliation of Body and Soul: Gregory of Nyssa's Deeper Theology of Marriage', *TS* 51 (1990), 450–78.

marriage he prescribes. He describes marriage as a 'sacred image' which must be kept pure from defilement, in which 'we are to rise from sleep with the Lord and go to sleep with thanksgiving and prayer, confessing the Lord in our whole life'.[125] It is the 'greatest bond of temperance' which breathes pure pleasures.[126] He expresses his admiration for monogamy, and proclaims the nobility (σεμνότης) of the single marriage.[127] Clement has such regard for the holiness of marriage, that on the rare occasions when he speaks of the espousal of Christ and the Church (cf. Eph. 5: 23–33), the value of this image arises, for him, from the given sanctity of marriage, a reversal of the usual perspective.[128] By the three gathered in the Lord's name (Matt. 18: 20), Clement understands the husband, wife, and child, the Christian household; for, as he explains, the wife is 'joined' to her husband by the Lord.[129] Furthermore, a marriage which is not given over to pleasure produces a harmony according to the Logos.[130]

Such marriage does not, according to Clement, hinder one from later attaining the heights of the true Christian Gnostic. Indeed, the discipline of marriage enables the married man to prove himself superior to the single man:

True manhood is not shown in the choice of a celibate life; rather, the prize in the contest of men is won by him who has trained himself by the discharge of the duties of marriage and procreation and by the supervision of a household, regardless of pleasure and pain, by him who in the midst of his solicitude for his family shows himself inseparable from the love of God and rises superior to every temptation which assails him through children and wife and servants and possessions. (*Strom.* 7. 12. 70. 7)

However, Clement's thoughts about the relative merits of marriage and the single life are not straightforward. For he continues by asserting that:

---

[125] *Strom.* 2. 23. 145. 1.
[126] *Paed.* 3. 12. 84. 1.
[127] *Strom.* 3. 1. 4. 3; 4. 20. 126. 1.
[128] *Strom.* 3. 12. 84. 2. Cf. Broudéhoux, *Mariage et famille*, 86–7.
[129] *Strom.* 3. 10. 68. 1. Broudéhoux sees in this passage 'une sorte de pressentiment de ce que la théologie postérieure appellera la grâce sacramentelle du mariage' (*Mariage et famille*, 84).
[130] *Strom.* 2. 23. 143. 1.

On the other hand, he who has no family is in most respects untried. Taking care for himself alone, he is inferior to the one who falls short of him as regards his own salvation (ἡττᾶται πρὸς τοῦ ἀπολειπομένου μὲν κατὰ τὴν ἑαυτοῦ σωτηρίαν), but who has the advantage in the conduct of life, as he truly preserves a faint image of providence. (*Strom.* 7. 12. 70. 8)

For Clement, the married man cannot dedicate himself to the service of God to the same extent as the single man, and so is inferior to the celibate 'as regards his own salvation'. But, on a purely human level, through his married state, the husband can develop possibilities, which are not open to the single man: his oversight of the family and household reflects, however faintly, God's providence within creation.[131]

As for the wife, Clement speaks of her as 'an aid in the faith'.[132] If she is married to an intemperate man, she must, according to Clement, persuade him to become 'her companion in virtue'. If such persuasion fails, she should then strive for virtue by herself, not doing anything against his will except for what contributes to virtue and salvation.[133] Commenting on the words of St Paul, that the single woman is free to care for the things of the Lord, while the married woman is burdened by her care for her husband (1 Cor. 7: 34), Clement rejects the Encratite interpretation, which would use this as grounds for the rejection of marriage:

Is it not permissible for both the married man and his wife to care for the things of the Lord together? But just as 'the unmarried woman cares in the Lord for the things of the Lord, that she may be holy in body and spirit', so also the married woman cares for both the things of her husband and the things of the Lord in the Lord, that she may be holy in body and spirit; both are holy in the Lord, the one as a wife, the other as a virgin. (*Strom.* 3. 12. 88. 2–3)[134]

Thus, although Clement does not value the conjugal bond itself as highly as does Musonius, he does see marriage as a mode of

---

[131] So Broudéhoux, *Mariage et famille*, 112–13. Clement here echoes the philosophical position he mentioned in the doxographical survey; cf. *Strom.* 2. 23. 139. 5.

[132] *Strom.* 3. 18. 108. 1.

[133] *Strom.* 4. 19. 123. 2; cf. 4. 20. 127. 1–2.

[134] Cf. *Strom.* 3. 12. 79. 5, where celibacy and marriage, both as service to the Lord, are described from the husband's perspective.

life which serves the Lord. This religious dimension of marriage indicates a certain originality in Clement's thought compared with his pagan contemporaries.[135]

However, Clement does not really integrate this religious dimension into his description of marriage; it is as a manner of each individual spouse serving the Lord that marriage is valued, rather than through the conjugal bond itself.[136] This is seen particularly clearly in *Strom*. 7. 12. 70. 7, where the married man is described as training himself in the duties pertaining to marriage, procreation, and the management of a household, yet falling short of the celibate in matters pertaining to salvation, and in *Strom*. 4. 19. 123. 2 and 4. 20. 127. 1–2, where the woman married to an intemperate husband is exhorted to strive after virtue and her own salvation. Similarly, in the first book of the *Paedagogus*, Clement maintains that as virtue belongs equally to men and women, so marriage is a 'common yoke' (συζύγιος), and those who have a common (κοινὸς) life have a common grace and a common salvation.[137] The common grace and salvation are a result not of a common, conjugal life, but of each spouse separately attaining virtue. The adjective 'common' does not denote any mutual relation between the two within the grace of God; rather, it denotes their simultaneous, yet individual, participation in the gifts of God.[138] The *style* of marriage Clement proposes is, despite or, rather, by virtue of his praise, one in which the conjugal bond is consistently subordinated to the finality of procreation.[139]

---

[135] Cf. Broudéhoux, *Mariage et famille*, 177.

[136] The most that even Broudéhoux can speak of is 'une communion au même idéal spirituel' (*Mariage et famille*, 154), or 'une communauté religieuse' (ibid. 197); lamenting, on the other hand, that 'ni l'amour, ni la sexualité ne sont réellement intégrés à sa vision du mariage' (ibid. 198).

[137] *Paed*. 1. 4. 10. 1–2; the identity of virtue between men and women was a Stoic theme; cf. *SVF* 1. 481, 107. 36.

[138] Given the overall discussion in *Strom*. 4. 19. 123. 2–20. 129. 5, it is difficult to see how, from *Strom*. 4. 20. 126. 1–127. 1, Mees can justly conclude: 'Daher sind Übereinstimmung und Leibe zu einander nicht nur Notwendigkeiten für ein glückliches Leben, sondern Gabe des Schöpfers und Gnade des Erlösers' ('Clemens von Alexandrien', 121). Broudéhoux, more realistically, speaks of 'une sorte de "sublimation" capable de compenser largement ses lacunes' (*Mariage et famille*, 153).

[139] Cf. Brown: 'As for the *charis*, the "graciousness" created by inter-

This emphasis in Clement's thought on the goal of marriage as procreation leads inexorably to the same attitude with regard to the sexual nature of man. Although Clement criticizes the Encratites for their use of Matthew 20: 30 and Luke 20: 34–5,[140] it is not so much their interpretation of this passage that he objects to, but its setting within an eschatology that sharply divides this world from the next.[141] In fact, Clement shares their interpretation:

'For in this world' he says 'they marry and are given in marriage', in which alone the female is distinguished from the male; 'but in that world it is so no more'. There the rewards of this social and holy life, which is based on conjugal union are laid up, not for male (ἄρρενι) and female (θηλείᾳ), but for man (ἀνθρώπῳ), the desire which divides him being removed. (*Paed.* 1. 4. 10. 3)[142]

It is desire (ἐπιθυμία) that divides mankind into male and female, a division which is limited to this present world.

It is again within a discussion about virtue being identical for men and women that Clement, in the fourth book of the *Stromateis*, expounds his thought on sexual difference further:

As far as respects human nature, then, the woman (ἡ γυνή) does not possess one nature and the man (ὁ ἀνήρ) exhibit another, but the same: so also with virtue. If, perhaps, temperance and righteousness, and whatever qualities are regarded as following them, are the virtue of the man, does it belongs to the man alone to be virtuous, and to the woman to be licentious and unjust? But it is indecent even to say this. Accordingly, the woman is to practice temperance and righteousness, and every other virtue, as well as the man, both free and bond, since it follows that one and the same virtue be of the same nature. (*Strom.* 4. 8. 59. 1–3)

As the same virtue is to be expected of the woman as of the man, due to the identity of the human nature of each, the

course—that indefinable quality of mutual trust and affection gained through the pleasure of the bed itself—which even the dignified Plutarch took for granted: Clement's stark insistence that intercourse should take place only for the begetting of children caused the delicate bloom of such a notion to vanish forever from late antique Christian thought' (*Body and Society*, 133). Clement speaks only once of a 'grace of marriage', *Strom.* 3. 14. 94. 3, in the context of discussing the Fall.

[140] Cf. *Strom.* 3. 6. 47–8. [141] Cf. Broudéhoux, *Mariage et famille*, 50.
[142] Cf. *Paed.* 2. 10. 100. 3.

difference between the two must be located elsewhere. Clement continues:

Therefore, we do not say that the same nature (τὴν αὐτὴν φύσιν) is of the female (τοῦ θήλεος) as [compared] to the male (τὸ ἄρρεν), inasmuch as she is female. For it is certainly fitting that some difference exist between each of them, by which one of them is female and the other male. Pregnancy and parturition, accordingly, we say, belong to the woman (τῇ γυναικὶ), inasmuch as she is female (θήλεια), and not inasmuch as she is a human being (ἄνθρωπος). For if there were no difference between the man (ἀνδρὸς) and the woman (γυναικός), both of them would do and suffer the same things. (*Strom.* 4. 8. 59. 4–5)

The identity of human nature in men and women requires of them the acquisition of identical virtue, whilst the bodily differences between the male and the female destines women to child bearing and housekeeping; as he explains in what follows: 'As, then, there is the same as regards the soul, by this sameness she will attain to the same virtue; but the difference with regard to the particularities of the body is towards child bearing and housekeeping' (*Strom.* 4. 8. 60. 1). Although Clement continually stresses the equality of virtue between men and women, he is ambiguous about a similar equality of gender. A few lines later he states that while women are 'to philosophize'—that is, practise virtue—alongside men, males are nevertheless superior at everything, unless they have become effeminate.[143] Here Clement is clearly using the idea of the masculine character of virtue. That virtue, by its virile character, produces both virile men and women, while its absence results in effeminate men and women, was a standard theme in Greek philosophical morality, which exerted a considerable influence in early Christian thought.[144] However,

[143] *Strom.* 4. 8. 62. 4. For Clement's ambiguous attitude towards women, see D. Kinder, 'Clement of Alexandria: Conflicting Views on Women', *Second Century*, 7. 4 (1990), 213–20.

[144] For the virile character of virtue, see Foucault, *L'Usage des plaisirs*, esp. 96–9; trans. 82–6. For the second century, including Clement, see M. W. Gleason, 'The Semiotics of Gender: Physiognomy and Self-Fashioning in the Second Century C.E.', in D. M. Halperin, J. J. Winkler, and F. I. Zeitlin (eds.), *Before Sexuality: The Construction of Erotic Experience in the Ancient Greek World* (Princeton, 1990), 389–415. The influence of this idea on early Christian thought has been discussed extensively in recent years; see the recent posthumous book of K. Aspegren, *The Male Woman: A Feminine Ideal*

Clement goes further to state that, despite the fact that souls are neither male nor female, and that the sexual difference is removed in the resurrection, the woman, when perfected in virtue, becomes a man:

For souls, by themselves equally souls, are not different, neither male nor female, when they no longer marry nor are given in marriage. And is not the woman translated into man (μετατίθεται εἰς τὸν ἄνδρα), when she is become equally unfeminine (ἀθήλυντος), and manly and perfect (ἀνδρικὴ καὶ τελεία)? (*Strom.* 6. 12. 100. 3)[145]

Interesting as such speculation might be, the important point about these comments on the sexual nature of men and women for our purposes, is that the finality of procreation, in terms of which marriage is understood, is, along with housekeeping, unreservedly applied by Clement to sexual difference itself.

As mentioned above, Clement shares the Encratite interpretation of Luke 20: 34–5, but, in the *Paedagogus* and *Stromata* 3, he refers the redundancy of marriage to the life hereafter. There is, however, one passage in *Stromata* 6 where he describes the married Christian Gnostic as already anticipating that state:

To such a one, his wife, after child bearing, is as a sister, and is judged as if of the same father, calling to mind her husband only when she looks on the children, as she will be a sister in reality after putting off the flesh, which separates and limits the knowledge of those who are spiritual by the peculiar forms (of the sexes). (*Strom.* 6. 12. 100. 3)[146]

in the Early Church (Uppsala, 1990). Clement, nevertheless, gives a positive value to femininity in his somewhat unusual attribution of femininity to God in *QDS* 37. 2: 'In his ineffable essence he is Father; in his compassion to us he became Mother. The Father by loving became feminine (ἀγαπήσας ὁ πατὴρ ἐθηλύνθη).' Here femininity is associated with 'compassion', which was not, however, counted amongst the virile virtues to be attained through asceticism. This dimension of God's dealings towards us does not seem to have had any noticeable effect on the asceticism proposed by Clement—not, at least, as regards human sexuality.

[145] Cf. *Exc. Th.* 21. 3.

[146] The context makes it clear that the 'forms' in question are those of the male and female. That Clement still refers to the woman as a 'sister' is probably to be taken as a necessity of style, rather than as an indication of continuing sexual difference.

This passage is reminiscent of the proleptic character of Christian existence which Clement describes in the context of baptism: after child bearing, husband and wife should be as brother and sister, for that is what they will be in reality after shedding the flesh with its sexual characteristics. It is clear, however, that this *prolēpsis* is active only after child bearing, and not, as earlier, after baptism. Thus we see the same problem as we saw in the discussion of his asceticism: the proleptic character of baptismal life does not actually influence Clement's description of Christian marriage. The newness of life granted in baptism does not have any effect on marriage, in which the spouses remain engaged in the pursuit of their own virtue.

Clement's description of Christian marriage is not, in fact, different from that which was prescribed by the Law, as Clement himself understands it. Countering those who, following Marcion, would separate the Old from the New Revelation and reject what belongs to the Old, Clement repeatedly emphasizes that 'the Law intended husbands to cohabit with their wives temperately (σωφρόνως) and only for the purpose of begetting children'.[147] Likewise, Clement explains the fact that we are no longer ordered to wash after sexual intercourse, by pointing to baptism, which encompasses the many washings of the Law. Clement is at pains to point out that it was not the emission of the generative seed that dictated the need to wash, for the seed of the holy is itself sanctified, but rather that the washings demanded by the Law prophesied our future regeneration.[148] Clement wanted to maintain a continuity of revelation between the New Covenant and the Old, and also with the ideals of Greek *paideia*. However, in doing so, he severely limited the effect of our regeneration in Christ. It is only to the extent that Clement defends the necessity of procreation that he defends marriage and differs from the Encratites.

Moreover, not even the necessity of procreation is absolute for Clement. In the *Protrepticus* he claims that 'men would not make love, nor beget children, nor sleep, if they were immortal and had no wants and never grew old'.[149] Similarly, amongst

---

[147] *Strom.* 3. 11. 71. 4; cf. *Strom.* 3. 6. 52. 1.

[148] Cf. *Strom.* 3. 12. 82. 6–83. 1; 3. 6. 46. 5; Broudéhoux, *Mariage et famille*, 47.   [149] *Prot.* 2. 36. 4.

the reasons why Christ did not marry, according to Clement, was that, being immortal, he did not need to beget children.[150] Granted immortality in baptism, Christians should have no need for marriage and procreation; they would be in Adam's pre-lapsarian state, which encompassed both marriage and procreation, without any inherent connection between these activities and death. The elision between Clement's descriptions of the pre-lapsarian and post-lapsarian states of Adam, and his tacit acceptance of the Encratite connection between birth, marriage, and death, thus result in a view of marriage governed by the finality of death, and hence the need for procreation, in which the conjugal bond itself plays no significant role.

Clement's characterization of the Christian life as 'tiptoeing on the earth' thus extends to his treatment of marriage and the relation between the sexes. Wanting, at all costs, to maintain the cultivated ideal which he establishes for the Christian, Clement advises:

Above all, it seems necessary that we turn away from the sight of women. . . . For it is possible for one who looks to slip; but it is impossible for one who looks not, to lust. (*Paed.* 3. 11. 82. 5–83. 1)

It is this self-imposed restraint, motivated by the desire for a life in accord with the ideal which he establishes for himself, that dominates the asceticism which Clement prescribes for those who have newly entered the Christian life. This style of asceticism, in its articulation, and especially in the ambivalent theology of synergy which it describes, severely curtails the effective power of the new life granted in baptism, which he nevertheless felt so keenly and described so vividly.[151] The problematics inherent in Clement's theology of 'synergetic' asceticism inevitably led to the idealization of a style of asceticism as a form of *self*-control, in which the virtues of continence and temperance are reduced to self-fashioning

---

[150] *Strom.* 3. 6. 49. 3.

[151] A similar attitude can be seen in the assumption behind Clement's rhetorical question to those Gnostics who understood Christianity as permitting a licentious life, any act being morally indifferent: 'If it is lawful to live any sort of life one likes, obviously one may live in continence; or if any kind of life has no dangers for the elect, obviously one of virtue and self-control is far less dangerous' (*Strom.* 3. 5. 40. 3).

techniques, and which ultimately results in the positing of a sexless (or exclusively male) existence, definitively in the age to come and by anticipation through this style of asceticism in this present world—unexpectedly, perhaps, given the unaffected warmth of Clement's praise for marriage.

Chapter 6

The Higher Christian Life:
gnōsis, apatheia, agapē

We have already seen how Clement defined the relation between faith and *gnōsis* in such a way that he could maintain their close dependence on one another whilst also insisting on the need to develop the common faith (κοινὴ πίστις) into a fully mature Christian *gnōsis*. The motivation for this twofold emphasis is usually seen in Clement's desire, on the one hand, to defend the integrity of faith against the scornful attitude of the philosophers, and the perfection of baptism and the sufficiency of faith against the disparagement, by so-called Gnosticism, of faith as an inferior form of Christianity, and, on the other hand, to maintain the need for growth and development in theological understanding and the ethical life.[1] So far we have considered the ambiguities and tensions between Clement's defence of the perfection of baptism and the corresponding style of asceticism which he prescribes for the neophyte, as described especially in the *Paedagogus*, together with the *Protrepticus* and various passages of the *Stromateis* (especially in Book 3). It is in the *Stromateis* that Clement develops his thought about *gnōsis* and describes the character of the Gnostic's life, and it is to this that we must now turn to complete our study of Clement.

Whereas the primary contrast in the *Paedagogus* was between the maturity of the new children of God and the immaturity of those outside Christ, one of the main themes of the *Stromateis* is the maturity of the true Gnostic compared with the immaturity of the simple believer. The milk of faith, which appeared

---

[1] For a clear summary of the various tacks in Clement's thought, see H. Chadwick, *Early Christian Thought and the Classical Tradition* (Oxford, 1987), 51–4.

as inedible meat to those outside the Church, is now seen to be only milk compared with the Gnostic 'meat': 'The apostle, in contradistinction to gnostic perfection, calls the common faith at times "the foundation" and other times "milk".'[2] Clement interprets Paul's words that 'the righteousness of God is revealed from faith to faith' (ἐκ πίστεως εἰς πίστιν, Rom. 1: 17) as admitting a 'twofold faith, or rather one which admits of growth and perfection', in which 'the common faith lies beneath as a foundation'.[3] It is as a 'superstructure' that gnōsis is built upon faith.[4] Whilst the Christian must progress in faith towards gnōsis, he never really leaves faith behind; although faith is more elementary than gnōsis, it is as necessary to the Gnostic as respiration.[5] Despite giving many passing definitions of gnōsis, Clement never really defines the content of gnōsis in a systematic and clear fashion;[6] what is more important for him, and us, is the style of the Gnostic's life, the ideal of the true Gnostic, and the means whereby this zenith is attained.

There are, fundamentally, two aspects of the ascent to gnōsis: ascēsis and instruction (μάθησις) or investigation (ζήτησις): 'As, then, the virtues follow one another, . . . faith hopes on repentance, and fear on faith; and patience in these, along with ascēsis and instruction, culminate in love which is perfected by gnōsis.'[7] This emphasis on the need for ascēsis in the attainment of virtue was a common theme in both Stoicism and Philo.[8] We have already seen how Clement regards ascēsis, following the commandments and the acquisition of virtue, as within man's own capacity, and the ambivalent synergetic relationship between God and man inherent in this. This

---

[2] Strom. 5. 4. 26. 1, referring to 1 Cor. 3: 11 and 1–3.

[3] Strom. 5. 1. 2. 4–5.

[4] Strom. 5. 4. 26. 4; cf. Strom. 7. 3. 20. 2.

[5] Strom. 2. 6. 31. 3.

[6] Cf. Camelot, Foi et Gnose, 96; Völker, Der wahre Gnostiker, 303–21; A. Méhat, Étude sur les 'Stromates' de Clément d'Alexandrie (Paris, 1966), 421–7.

[7] Strom. 2. 9. 45. 1; cf. Strom. 5. 1. 5. 2, 12. 2; 6. 7. 57. 2.

[8] Cf. SVF 3. 278, 68. 25. See also Philo's description of Jacob as the ἀσκητική quality, which, together with Abraham (teaching) and Isaac (nature), produce virtue: Migr. Abr. 11. 52 and Somn. 1. 27. 167, to which compare Strom. 1. 5. 31. 5.

problematic continues into Clement's description of the acquisition of *gnōsis* in the *Stromateis*. In the above quotation *gnōsis* is considered as the final perfecting of our labours in *ascēsis* and instruction. Clement is convinced that the perfection bestowed in *gnōsis* is a gift, but he maintains that it is given only to those who have made themselves worthy of it: after his departure from this life, the Gnostic hastens, by reason of his good conscience, to give thanks; and there with Christ, he himself worthy, through his own purity, to possess the power of God communicated by Christ.[9] A good conscience and purity are requisite for the dying if they are to depart with hope and confidence.[10] They are also essential, within the present life, for the reception of the grace or power of God.[11] Such asceticism makes the Gnostic 'worthy' (ἄξιος) of receiving the titles 'son' and 'friend'.[12] This stance is clearly revealed when Clement relates an old story with evident approval:

And what follows seems to me to be excellently said by the Greeks. An athlete of no mean reputation among those of old, having for a long time subjected his body to thorough *ascēsis* towards manly strength, on going up to the Olympic Games, looked upon the statue of the Pisaean Zeus, and said: 'O Zeus, if all the requisite preparations for the contest have been made by me, come, give me the victory, as is right.' For so in the case of the Gnostic, who has unblamably and with a good conscience fulfilled all that depends on him, in the direction of instruction and training (συνάσκησιν) and beneficence, and pleasing to God, the whole contributes to the most perfect salvation (τὴν τελειοτάτην σωτηρίαν). (*Strom.* 7. 7. 48. 5–6)

In this line of Clement's thought, then, the *ascēsis* of the Gnostic produces a boldness, a παρρησία, with which he can approach God and demand his due, for by himself he has made

---

[9] *Strom.* 7. 12. 79. 4.

[10] For the demand for a good conscience see *Strom.* 7. 12. 78. 3, 13. 83. 1. Clement also cites Socrates (Plato, *Phaedo*, 67bc) on the hope entertained by a man who dies with a purified mind (*Strom.* 4. 22. 144. 2). The idea of purification after death, an important theme in Clement, does not fall within the scope of this work; for this cf. K. Schmöle, *Läuterung nach dem Tode und pneumatische Auferstehung bei Klemens von Alexandrien* (Münster, 1974).

[11] Most explicitly stated in *QDS* 16. 2 and *Strom.* 3. 5. 42. 6.

[12] Cf. *Strom.* 3. 10. 69. 3–4; 7. 11. 68. 1; and also 6. 14. 114. 6.

himself worthy of receiving it.[13] It is important to note, however, that this merit does not compel God to comply:

> For, universally, God knows those who are and those who are not worthy of good things; whence he gives to each what is suitable. Thus to those that are unworthy, though they ask often, he will not give; but he will give to those who are worthy. And even if good things are given without claim, petition is not superfluous. (*Strom.* 7. 7. 41. 5–6)

The Gnostic's merit is therefore not sufficient for the gifts of God, but it is, none the less, necessary.

The framework for this line of thought is indicated by the concluding remark of the comparison between the Gnostic and the Olympic athlete: this *ascēsis* culminates in 'the most perfect salvation'. The implications of this are stated bluntly by Clement in a passage in which he distinguishes the salvation of the common believer from the more perfect salvation effected by the Gnostic's asceticism: 'Now to know is more than to believe, as to be dignified with the highest honour after being saved is a greater thing than being saved.'[14] These two different levels of merit are dependent upon two manners or styles of life. In a hypothetical speculation, Clement even suggests that if the *gnōsis* of God were distinguishable from eternal salvation, then the Gnostic would prefer such *gnōsis* over salvation itself.[15]

Whilst Paul had classified everything that does not proceed from faith as sin (Rom. 14: 23), Clement refines the classification by dividing the actions of the faithful into two levels:

> As, then, simply to be saved is the result of intermediate actions, but to be saved rightly and becomingly (ὀρθῶς καὶ δεόντως) is of right action (κατόρθωμα), so also every action of the Gnostic may be called right action; that of the simple believer, intermediate action, not yet performed according to reason (κατὰ λόγον), nor yet made right according to knowledge; whilst every action of the heathen is sinful. (*Strom.* 6. 14. 111. 3)[16]

---

[13] Cf. *Strom.* 7. 12. 72. 6 and *Strom.* 7. 12. 71. 1–3; cf. *Strom.* 7. 13. 81. 3: παρ' ἑαυτοῦ δὲ ἄξιον γενόμενον λαμβάνειν; *Strom.* 7. 13. 81. 4: ὁ τοιοῦτος ἀπαιτεῖ παρὰ κυρίου, οὐχὶ δὲ καὶ αἰτεῖ.

[14] *Strom.* 6. 14. 109. 2; cf. *Strom.* 4. 18. 113. 6–114. 1.

[15] *Strom.* 4. 22. 136. 5.

[16] For the Stoic background of the term κατόρθωμα and a similar definition, see *SVF* 3. 501, 136. 18–26; and Nussbaum, *Therapy of Desire*, 339.

Simply to be saved, the result of medium actions, is not enough for the Gnostic; he aims to perfect his life 'rightly and becomingly'. Whilst God has called all equally, he has nevertheless, according to Clement, assigned special honours for those who have believed in a specially excellent manner.[17] Thus Clement understands the perfection offered in Christ's question 'If thou will be perfect' (Matt. 19: 21) to demand an 'exceeding eagerness' of those who so choose, which in turn makes the gift of salvation their own (ἴδιον).[18] This zeal shows itself in an 'intensification of the righteousness according to the Law'.[19] According to Clement, all things which are created for man's use, such as marriage and procreation, are good, when used with moderation; yet it is 'better than good' to become free from passion (ἀπαθής). So the Gnostic does not reject such things as bad, but aims 'to do things that are better than good', which, not being essential, are also more difficult.[20]

Before examining further the state effected by this intensified *ascēsis*, we must consider the parallel demand for instruction required of those who would ascend to *gnōsis*. The instruction that Clement has in mind is primarily instruction in the inner, veiled meaning of the Scriptures. It is a knowledge which is naturally esoteric, limiting itself to those who show themselves worthy of it through their manner of life and diligence in study.[21] Clement refers to a number of philosophical schools to show how they also kept the most important aspects of their teachings hidden from the uninstructed.[22] Although Clement had, from evangelical motives, portrayed Christianity as a mystery religion in the *Protrepticus*, he now uses the same vocabulary in the *Stromateis* to heighten the sense of secrecy surrounding *gnōsis*.[23] Such hidden teaching is

[17] *Strom.* 7. 2. 7. 1.

[18] *QDS* 10. 2.

[19] *Strom.* 6. 18. 164. 3; cf. *Strom.* 6. 7. 60. 3.

[20] *Strom.* 4. 23. 147–149. 8.

[21] Cf. *Strom.* 1. 12. 55. 1; 5. 4. 19. 2–4, 6. 35. 5, 12. 80. 3; 6. 8. 70. 2, 15. 116. 1–2, esp. 15. 126. 1–3.

[22] *Strom.* 5. 9. 58. 1–5.

[23] Cf. *Prot.* 12. 118. 4, 120. 1, and e.g. *Strom.* 4. 1. 3. 1; 6. 12. 102. 2. These two applications cannot be conflated, so as to 'excuse' the use of mystery terminology in the *Stromateis*. Cf. H. G. Marsh, 'The Use of μυστήριον in the Writings of Clement of Alexandria with Special Reference to his Sacramental

most appropriately transmitted through oral teaching, and
Clement makes several references to such secret 'gnostic
traditions'.[24] However, as Völker notes, it is important not to
misinterpret the idea of the 'gnostic tradition' by contrasting it
with the 'ecclesiastical canon' of which Clement also speaks,[25]
for the essential content of both is the same.[26] Clement is
emphatic that all true *gnōsis* originates from the incarnate
Christ: 'Christ is both the beginning and the end, the foundation and the superstructure.'[27]

The content of this 'gnostic tradition' is essentially the
allegorical method of understanding the true sense of the
Scriptures, as it was taught, according to Clement, by Christ
and transmitted by the apostles. Through it the Gnostic is able
to understand the Scriptures in the same manner as Christ,
who gave it to the apostles.[28] In contrast to the Gnostic, simple
believers have insufficient understanding to comprehend the
Scriptures; not admitted to the secrets of the 'gnostic tradition', they have as little chance of understanding Scripture as
an ass has of playing a lyre.[29] Furthermore, their possible
misunderstanding of the true meaning of Scripture is poten-
tially harmful, and must, therefore, be avoided by veiling the
'salvific content' in parables.[30]

Whilst the Logos was the inspiration for both Greek philosophy and the Old Testament prophecies, both of which
prepared the way for Christianity, it is the full comprehension
of the Scriptures as taught by Christ that enables true *gnōsis*.
Clement's high appreciation of Greek philosophy, as a pre-

Doctrine', *JTS* 37 (1936), 64–80. For a similar emphasis on the esoteric
character of their higher teachings by Jewish-Alexandrine philosophy, Middle
Platonism, Neoplatonism, and Gnosticism, especially in their use of mystery
terms, see Lilla, *Clement of Alexandria*, 148–54; he concludes that this usage
reflects a literary dependence, rather than Clement's personal acquaintance
with the ancient Greek mystery rites.

[24] Cf. esp. *Strom*. 6. 7. 61. 3; and *Strom*. 1. 12. 55. 1–2; 5. 10. 63. 1–2; 6. 7.
61. 1–2, 15. 131. 5.

[25] e.g. *Strom*. 7. 7. 41. 3, 15. 90. 2, 16. 95. 1.

[26] Völker, *Der wahre Gnostiker*, 363–4.

[27] *Strom*. 7. 10. 55. 5.

[28] *Strom*. 4. 21. 130. 4.

[29] *Strom*. 1. 1. 2. 2; 6. 14. 112. 1.

[30] *Strom*. 6. 15. 126. 1–3, cited below.

paration for Christianity in a historical perspective, has already been noted. In the *Stromateis* Clement transfers the propaedeutic function of Greek philosophy, or, more precisely, the encyclical disciplines of the period (especially geometry, astronomy, and dialectics), to the instruction, which, if not absolutely necessary, is nevertheless very useful in achieving the necessary separation and abstraction from the material world required of the Christian before he can pass to true *gnōsis*.[31] Thus, for example, man is led to contemplate the heavens by his upright formation, and, through the contemplation of the harmony of the heavens, he raises his mind above the earth and approaches the power of the Creator.[32]

All these aspects are summed up in the following passage:

> For many reasons the Scriptures keep their meaning hidden; first, so that we may become inquisitive and ever on the watch for the discovery of the words of salvation; then, because it was not suitable for all to understand, so that they might not be harmed by taking in another sense the things declared for salvation by the Holy Spirit. Thus the holy mysteries of the prophecies are veiled in parables and preserved for the selected men, those admitted from faith to *gnōsis*; the character of the Scriptures is parabolic, whence the Lord came to men not as belonging to the world, but as of the world; he was clothed in all virtue, so as to lead man, the foster child of the world, by *gnōsis*, to the intellectual and authentic realm, from one world to another. (*Strom*. 6. 15. 126. 1–3)

The purpose of the Incarnation was to impart to those capable of *gnōsis* the correct manner of interpreting the symbolic nature of the Scriptures, and thereby to lead them from this material world to the intellectual realm. And for this purpose, the Logos was incarnate in a similarly 'symbolic' manner (οὐκ ὢν κοσμικὸς, ὡς κοσμικός).

It would, nevertheless, be wrong to restrict the Gnostic's ascent simply to the intellectual realm and the contemplation of intellectual realities, understood in a Platonic fashion. In many passages Clement certainly follows Plato in insisting that the contemplation of intellectual realities corresponds to

---

[31] *Strom*. 6. 10. 80. 1–83. 3. For a comparison of the use made of the encyclical disciplines by Clement and his pagan contemporaries, see Lilla, *Clement of Alexandria*, 169–73.

[32] *Strom*. 4. 26. 163. 1; 6. 10. 80. 3, 11. 90. 3.

the separation of the soul from the senses and the purification of the intellect.[33] This is linked, in Clement's thought, with the Socratic practice of death (μελέτη θανάτου), the discipline of severing the soul from the body, thereby enabling clear vision.[34] In the fourth *Stromata*, Clement develops this idea of detachment or practice of death in terms of a spiritualized or 'gnostic martyrdom': true martyrs bear witness through their detachment in all aspects of their daily life.[35]

However, for Clement, the Gnostic does not stop his ascent at the intellectual realm. Rather, he penetrates beyond this realm to the spiritual realities, of which men had no idea until they were revealed by Christ.[36] The idea of a realm transcending the intellectual level was a developing theme in Middle Platonism, which would ultimately culminate in the absolute transcendence of the One of Plotinus.[37] In Clement the aim of this transcendence is, in the last analysis, knowledge and contemplation of God.[38] Thus Clement writes of the aim of Scripture:

Scripture . . . gently admonishes us to seek God and to know him as far as possible; which is the highest contemplation, vision, and true knowledge, which is unshakeable by reason. This alone is the *gnōsis* of wisdom, from which the right conduct can never be separated. (*Strom*. 2. 10. 47. 4)

As this passage illustrates, Clement develops his treatment of the Gnostic's contemplation through a free use of mystery

---

[33] Cf. *Strom*. 4. 23. 148. 1; 5. 2. 14. 2 (referring to Plato, *Phaedrus*, 246–9), as also 7. 7. 40. 1–2; 6. 11. 86. 1.

[34] *Strom*. 5. 11. 67. 1–2. The reference is to Plato, *Phaedo*, 67d. Cf. *Strom*. 4. 3. 12. 5.

[35] *Strom*. 4. 1–14. For Clement's ideas on martyrdom, see W. H. C. Frend, *Martyrdom and Persecution in the Early Church* (Oxford, 1965), 355–8, who points out that Clement 'is the first Christian writer who placed the ascetic ideal on the same level as that of the martyr' (ibid. 356), and E. E. Malone, *The Monk and the Martyr* (Washington, 1950), 4–14.

[36] *Strom*. 6. 8. 68. 1, referring to 1 Cor. 2: 9.

[37] Cf. Alcinous, *Didaskalikos*, 10, for the ambivalent relation between the πρωτὸς θεός or πατήρ and his relation to the κόσμος νοητός.

[38] Cf. Camelot, *Foi et Gnose*, 97. This aspect seems to be completely overlooked by Lilla, for whom 'The higher knowledge which the γνωστικός possesses is nothing but a contemplation of the intelligible world' (*Clement of Alexandria*, 163).

terms such as ἐποπτεία,[39] and combines this term with more biblical expressions such as 'knowing' or 'seeing God' (γιγνώ-σκειν or ὁρᾶν τὸν θεόν).[40] Just as it was the incarnate Christ who taught the apostles how to interpret the Scriptures correctly, so it is Christ who makes known the knowledge of the Father.[41] The entry into the hidden mysteries is an 'illumination',[42] admitted into which the Gnostic desires to become 'wholly light', rather than luminous by participation.[43] Thus Clement describes man as reaching full contemplation of God, and rest in him, through the purification involved in *gnōsis* and as a result of the inner light:

Gnōsis is therefore quick in purifying, and fit for that acceptable transformation to the better. Whence also with ease it removes [the soul] to what is akin to the soul, divine and holy, and by its own light conveys man through the mystic stages of advancement, until it restores [him] to the crowning place of rest; teaching the pure in heart to contemplate God, face to face, with knowledge and comprehension. (*Strom.* 7. 10. 56. 7–57. 1)

The description of the final vision of God in *gnōsis*, the culmination of piety and the fulfilment of the promise granted in faith, as rest (ἀνάπαυσις) recurs throughout Clement's work.[44]

In the same way that the Gnostic's ascent from the material and sensible world is not limited to an ascent to the intellectual realm, but to a personal, 'face to face', vision of God, so too the abstraction involved is not simply intellectual. In *Stromata* 7 Clement portrays this ascent as consisting fundamentally of prayer. For Clement prayer is essentially 'converse with God'.[45] Whilst some (that is, simple believers) may pray at the set hours, Clement's Gnostic 'prays throughout his whole life, endeavouring by prayer to have fellowship with

---

[39] e.g. *Strom.* 7. 11. 68. 4. This term is also used in the baptismal context of the *Paedagogus*, e.g. 1. 6. 28. 1, 7. 54. 1. Cf. Plato, *Phaedrus*, 250c.

[40] e.g. *Strom.* 7. 7. 47. 3. For a complete listing of Clement's use of such terms, O. Stählin (ed.), *Clement Alexandrinus, Register*, GCS, 39 (Leipzig, 1936), is indispensable. Cf. Völker, *Der wahre Gnostiker*, 403–6.

[41] Cf. *Strom.* 1. 20. 97. 2; 4. 25. 156. 1; 5. 1. 12. 3; 7. 1. 2. 2–3, 3. 16. 6.

[42] *Strom.* 5. 10. 64. 4–5.

[43] *Strom.* 7. 12. 79. 5.

[44] e.g. *Paed.* 1. 6. 29. 3, 12. 102. 2; *Strom.* 6. 16. 138. 3; 7. 11. 68. 5.

[45] *Strom.* 7. 7. 39. 6; cf. Völker, *Der wahre Gnostiker*, 411.

God'.[46] It is essentially an interior prayer that Clement describes, speaking in silence yet crying inwardly.[47] Such prayer has a similar effect to the abstraction involved in the allegorical interpretation of Scripture and that effected by the disciplines of philosophy. Thus Clement writes:

So also we raise the head and lift the hands to heaven, and stand on tiptoe at the closing utterance of the prayer, following the eagerness of the spirit directed towards the intellectual essence; and endeavouring to detach the body from the earth, by lifting it upwards along with the uttered words, constraining the soul, winged with the desire of better things, to ascend into the holy place, magnanimously despising (καταμεγαλοφρονοῦντες) the fetters of the flesh. For we know well that the Gnostic willingly departs from the whole world, just as the Jews did from Egypt, showing clearly, above all, that he will be as near as possible to God. (*Strom.* 7. 7. 40. 1–2)[48]

The abstraction effected in prayer is not simply that of an intellectual ascent or purification, but an endeavour to loosen the body itself from the earth, 'magnanimously despising' the flesh and the world, in an attempt to be as close to God as possible. It is in this sense that Clement interprets the words of Christ, 'Unless you hate your father and mother and your own life . . .' (Luke 14: 26), to mean a 'hatred of the inordinate affections of the flesh, which possess the powerful spell of pleasure' and a 'magnanimous contempt for all that belongs to the creation and nutriment of the flesh'.[49]

This function of prayer, to abstract the soul from the world, and its consequent 'magnanimous contempt' for the flesh, is paralleled by the demand for a detached but none the less thankful use of the world. Prayer encompasses the whole life of man, making it into a continual 'festival', whilst the need for detachment is matched by a sober or noble enjoyment:

Holding festival, then, in our whole life, persuaded that God is altogether on every side present, we cultivate our fields praising; we sail the sea, hymning; in all the rest of our conversation we conduct ourselves according to the rule. The Gnostic is then very closely allied to God, being at once sober and cheerful in all things—sober, on

<hr />

[46] *Strom.* 7. 7. 40. 3; cf. *Strom.* 7. 12. 73. 1.
[47] *Strom.* 7. 7. 39. 6; cf. *Strom.* 7. 7. 36. 5.
[48] Referring to Plato, *Phaedrus*, 246bc.
[49] *Strom.* 7. 12. 79. 6.

account of the bent of his soul towards the Divinity, and cheerful on account of his consideration of the blessings of humanity which God has given us. (*Strom*. 7. 7. 35. 6–7)[50]

Clement stresses, throughout the *Stromateis*, that the Gnostic is characterized by his giving thanks to God for all things, for 'such (eucharistic) souls can never be separated from God'.[51] This cheerfulness is in fact the reverse side of the sober detachment of the Gnostic; it is his detachment from the gifts that enables the Gnostic to ascribe thanks to God in his use of them. Thus Clement combines these two descriptions, and writes that the Gnostic offers to God 'a sober enjoyment (τὴν σεμνὴν ἀπόλαυσιν) of all things . . . using the speech (λόγος) which was bestowed on him in acknowledging thanks for the gift and for the use of it'.[52] Ultimately, however, the 'magnanimous contempt', which Clement ascribes to the Gnostic, extends beyond the 'chains of the flesh' to typify his attitude to all the good things of the world.[53] His true pleasure does not consist in the 'sober enjoyment of all things', for *gnōsis* itself supplies 'harmless pleasures and exaltation' (ἡδονὰς ἀβλαβεῖς καὶ ἀγαλλίασιν), and as such *gnōsis* is worth pursuing for its own sake.[54]

Such *gnōsis* not only effects a detachment and a 'noble contempt', but its acquisition by instruction corresponds to an ethical effort, for from it 'right conduct can never be separated'.[55] Clement repeatedly stresses the two aspects or 'paths'—works (ἔργα) or *ascēsis* and instruction—which lead to the 'perfection of salvation'.[56] These two paths are not unrelated, for fundamentally *gnōsis* is also an activity, a 'purification

---

[50] Cf. *Strom*. 7. 7. 49. 3. For life as a continual festival see Epictetus, *Discourses*, 4. 1. 99–110.

[51] *Strom*. 6. 14. 113. 3. Thus the Gnostic martyr thankfully sheds blood (*Strom*. 4. 21. 130. 5); the body of the Gnostic, as one on a distant pilgrimage, gives thanks for its sojourn on its departure (*Strom*. 4. 24. 166. 1), for thanksgiving is not only for the soul but for the body (*Strom*. 5. 10. 61. 5; 6. 14. 113. 3). A similar emphasis on joy is found in the Stoics, but again the more direct influence is likely to be Philo; cf. Völker, *Der wahre Gnostiker*, 518.

[52] *Strom*. 7. 7. 36. 4.   [53] *Strom*. 7. 12. 78. 3.

[54] *Strom*. 6. 12. 99. 3.   [55] *Strom*. 2. 10. 47. 4.

[56] *Strom*. 4. 6. 39. 1. Cf. Völker, *Der wahre Gnostiker*, 254; Wytzes, 'Twofold Way'.

of the guiding principle (ἡγεμονικόν)'.[57] Their interrelation becomes more apparent in Clement's descriptions of the ideal state in which both *ascēsis* and instruction culminate. The intensification of *ascēsis*, which we considered earlier, corresponds to the surpassing of the aim of moderation (μετριο-πάθεια), demanded of the Christian in the *Paedagogus*, by the ideal of *apatheia* which dominates the *Stromateis*.[58] Clement is unambiguous that the cessation of all desire, rather than moderation, is required in order to reach perfection, and this is achieved through both *gnōsis* and *ascēsis* or training:

We must therefore raise the gnostic and perfect man from all passion of soul; for *gnōsis* produces training (συνάσκειν) and training habit or disposition, and such a state as this produces *apatheia*, not moderation. For complete eradication of desire (παντελῆς τῆς ἐπιθυμίας ἐκκοπή) reaps as its fruit *apatheia*. (*Strom.* 6. 9. 74. 1)

Here *gnōsis* is described as producing training, whilst, as we saw earlier, Clement also regards *gnōsis* as the perfection of *ascēsis*.[59] This ambivalence simply reinforces the fact that the two are interrelated, and lead to perfection in *apatheia*. It must be noted that, on one occasion, Clement categorically asserts that *ascēsis* will not of itself produce *apatheia*; for this is attained only by the addition of the power of God.[60] Following Clement's own intimation, most scholars have pointed to the Stoic provenance of the term *apatheia*, whilst disagreeing widely on the extent of the influence of this Stoic ideal on Clement's thought.[61] Clement sometimes suggests that the

---

[57] *Strom.* 4. 6. 39. 2.

[58] *Strom.* 6. 13. 105. 1.

[59] *Strom.* 2. 9. 45. 1, cited above; cf. *Strom.* 6. 8. 68. 3, 9. 78. 4. That Clement does not uniformly qualify the *ascēsis* resulting from *gnōsis* with the prefix σύν is shown by *Strom.* 7. 7. 48. 6, concerning the Olympic athlete and the Gnostic, where the συνάσκησιν depends upon him.

[60] *QDS* 21. 1, cited and discussed above.

[61] In *Strom.* 7. 14. 84. 2, Clement suggests that he could find many other more biblical testimonies for the *apatheia* of the Gnostic, but that, for brevity, he will leave the task for others. Similarly, at *Strom.* 7. 1. 1. 4, Clement acknowledges that his expressions may seem to differ from those of Scripture; but, he asserts, they have the same source and the same meaning. For E. de Faye, the identification between Clement's understanding of *apatheia* and that of the Stoics was absolute (*Clément d'Alexandrie: Étude sur les rapports du Christianisme et de la Philosophie grecque au IIe siècle*, 2nd edn. (Paris, 1906),

Gnostic remains subject to those 'passions' that are necessary for the maintenance of the body.[62] A little later, however, we are given as an example the apostles, who 'gnostically mastered' even those 'passible movements which seem to be good', such as courage, zeal, and joy.[63] Moreover, the Gnostic, Clement believes, will no longer need even such virtues as temperance (σωφροσύνη), as he will no longer need to control desire.[64]

The ambivalence in Clement's descriptions of *apatheia* points to the fact that *apatheia* is not to be equated simply with a deadened sensitivity. As we have seen, Clement thinks of passion as 'an excessive appetite, exceeding the measures of the Logos (τὸν λόγον) or an appetite unbridled and disobedient to reason (λόγῳ)'.[65] Thus *ascēsis* aims not so much at removing the natural movements of man, but at subjecting them to a strict obedience to the L/logos and dissociating them from pleasure (ἡδονή); the Gnostic who has intensified his *ascēsis*, and no longer has to struggle with the passions, the disobedient movements of the soul under the sway of pleasure, has attained *apatheia*, a state in which the body can function naturally without interfering with the Gnostic's true desires. For this reason, the Gnostic is in a state of immutability or peace.[66] For Clement the struggle for *apatheia* is, moreover, connected to the desire to perfect the image with the likeness, for just as God is impassible (ἀπαθής), so must man be if he is to be fully assimilated to God.[67] Separating himself from the passions, the Gnostic becomes 'already fleshless' (ἄσαρκος) and lives 'above the world'.[68]

295); so too P. Guilloux, 'L'Ascétisme de Clément d'Alexandrie', *RAM* 3 (1922), 296. Lilla suggests that the more direct influence was Neoplatonism and especially Philo (*Clement of Alexandria*, 103–6). On the other hand, Völker points to the integral position of *apatheia* within Clement's 'Christian asceticism', and claims to see 'eine Umdeutung der stoischen Konzeption der Apathie' (*Der wahre Gnostiker*, 530).

[62] *Strom.* 6. 9. 71. 1.
[63] *Strom.* 6. 9. 71. 3–4. On what feelings and movements are left to the Stoics in their state of *apatheia*, see Nussbaum, *Therapy of Desire*, 398–401.
[64] *Strom.* 6. 9. 76. 2.   [65] *Strom.* 2. 13. 59. 6.
[66] For Clement's connection between ἀπάθεια and ἀταραξία, see e.g. *Strom.* 4. 7. 55. 4; as ἄτρεπτος, esp. *Strom.* 2. 11. 51. 6–52. 3; for this passage, cf. Philo, *Post. Cain*, 9. 27; and for the connection to εἰρήνη, esp. *Strom.* 4. 6. 40. 3.
[67] Cf. *Strom.* 2. 18. 81. 1; 7. 3. 13. 3, 12. 72. 1.
[68] *Strom.* 7. 14. 86. 7; cf. *Strom.* 7. 3. 18. 2, 12. 79. 3.

As a consequence of divesting himself of the passions, the Gnostic also becomes sinless.[69] However, as we have noted, the most important characteristic of Clement's description of *apatheia* is that it is not simply a negative state; abstention from evil or sin is not enough.[70] Both *gnōsis* and *apatheia* culminate, and find their completion, in beneficence or doing good (εὐποιΐα). Thus Clement writes that, whilst the first purification, the perfection of the common believer, is abstention (ἀποχή) from evil things,

In the case of the Gnostic, after that which is reckoned perfection in others, his righteousness advances to activity in beneficence. And in whoever the intensification of righteousness advances to the doing of good, in his case perfection abides in the unchanging habit of beneficence after the likeness of God. (*Strom.* 6. 7. 60. 3)

The one who has passed from moderation to *apatheia* and is then perfected by beneficence becomes, according to Clement, 'equal to the angels', and radiates in his exercise of beneficence, hastening, by *gnōsis*, to the abode of the apostles.[71] Such people also become true presbyters and deacons of the Church, not by being ordained by men, but by being truly righteous.[72] The true Gnostic can never, according to Clement, be totally withdrawn from the world and from concern for others; rather, his perfection lies in beneficence, or, as he once terms it, 'lordly beneficence' (κυριακῇ εὐποιΐα).[73] In the same way, an essential aspect of the Gnostic's prayer is prayer for the salvation of others, and this makes the Gnostic, being thus assimilated to the Saviour, 'salvific' (σωτήριος).[74] Likewise, an important task of the Gnostic is the instruction of others, even if there is only one listener.[75] The characteristics of *apatheia*, beneficence, and assimilation are brought together by Clement in a striking passage:

---

[69] *Strom.* 7. 3. 14. 2; see also *Strom.* 7. 12. 80. 2.
[70] *Strom.* 4. 6. 29. 2; 6. 12. 103. 2–4.
[71] *Strom.* 6. 13. 105. 1. The idea of becoming ἰσάγγελος, taken from Luke 20: 36, is also found in *Paed.* 2. 9. 79. 2, 82. 3, 10. 100. 3; *Strom.* 7. 10. 57. 5, 14. 84. 2. Cf. Frank, *ΑΓΓΕΛΙΚΟΣ ΒΙΟΣ*, 130–5.
[72] *Strom.* 6. 13. 106. 1–2.
[73] *Strom.* 4. 6. 29. 2.
[74] *Strom.* 6. 9. 77. 5. On prayer for others, see *Strom.* 7. 7. 41. 6.
[75] Cf. *Strom.* 1. 10. 49. 1; 2. 10. 46. 1; 7. 1. 4. 2, 9. 52. 1.

This is the activity of the perfected Gnostic, to have converse with God through the great High Priest, being made like the Lord, as far as may be, by means of the whole service (θεραπεία) towards God, [a service] which tends to the salvation of men, through care of the goodness towards us, and on the other side, through liturgy, through teaching and through beneficence in deeds. Being assimilated to God, the Gnostic even forms and creates himself (ἑαυτὸν κτίζει καὶ δημι-ουργεῖ), and adorns those who hear him; assimilating, as far as possible, by an *ascēsis* which tends to *apatheia*, to him who is by nature impassible; and this is uninterrupted converse and communion with the Lord. (*Strom.* 7. 2. 13. 2–3)

Clement's strong language in this passage (the Gnostic, likened to God, 'forms and creates himself' and adorns others) is balanced by emphasis on the service of God, on prayer, on teaching, on the culmination of *ascēsis* in an *apatheia* character-ized by beneficence, all of which assimilate him to God.

Alongside these themes of *gnōsis*, *apatheia*, and beneficence, lies the dynamic of love (ἀγάπη). Although Clement describes love as the culmination of the process beginning with fear and progressing through faith,[76] in the life of the perfect Gnostic love functions as both cause and effect. Thus in describing the relation between love and *gnōsis*, Clement maintains both that *gnōsis* culminates in love[77] and that love is perfected by *gnōsis*.[78] This ambivalence again reinforces the fact that, for Clement, love and *gnōsis* can never be separated, and, ulti-mately, are one and the same.[79] Likewise, love is portrayed as 'blossoming into beneficence', while it is through love that the Gnostic does good, for love is the only true motive.[80] Simi-larly, 'the perfect one ought therefore to practise love, and thence to hasten to divine friendship, fulfilling the command-ments from love'.[81] Love, the cause and form of the Gnostic's life, renders him a son and friend of God.[82] Possessed by this love, the Gnostic no longer feels affection (φιλεῖ) for anyone

---

[76] *Strom.* 2. 12. 53. 3; cf. *Strom.* 4. 7. 53. 1.

[77] e.g. *Strom.* 7. 10. 57. 4; Camelot understands this περαιουμένη to imply a surpassing (*Foi et Gnose*, 125).

[78] e.g. *Strom.* 2. 9. 45. 1.

[79] Admirably demonstrated by Méhat, *Étude sur les 'Stromates'*, 476.

[80] Cf. *QDS* 28. 4; *Strom.* 4. 22. 135. 4.

[81] *Strom.* 4. 13. 93. 2.

[82] *Strom.* 7. 11. 68. 1.

with a common affection (κοινὴν φιλίαν), but loves (ἀγαπᾷ) the Creator through the creatures.[83] For Clement, such love for God is a reciprocating love (ἀνταγαπᾶν), just as the holiness and the benevolence of the Gnostic are a 'kind of corresponding movement of providence'.[84] Finally, by loving God to the utmost of one's abilities, one acquires incorruptibility; for the more one loves, the more one enters into God.[85]

There is a particularly striking feature of Clement's portrayal of the ideal Gnostic state that must be noted. Clement frequently utilizes the Aristotelian-Stoic term 'habit' or 'disposition' (ἕξις) to describe the Gnostic's *apatheia* or beneficence.[86] Again using Stoic terminology, Clement specifies that this 'habit' is unchangeable or unshakeable (ἀναπόβλητος, ἀμετάβολος, ἀμετάπτωτος): 'the Gnostic's perfection lies in the unchanging habit of beneficence, according to the likeness of the Lord'.[87] Christ set the pattern for man, when he assumed passible flesh, and trained it to a habit of *apatheia*.[88] It is, for Clement, through love and *gnōsis*, which perfects *ascēsis*, that the Gnostic's 'disposition' is rendered infallible. This is well expressed in the following passage:

As *gnōsis* is not born with men, but is acquired, and the learning of it in its elements demands application, training and growth; and then from incessant practice it passes into a habit; so, when perfected in the mystic habit, it abides, being made infallible through love. (*Strom.* 6. 9. 78. 4)

Clement even suggests that in the one who has acquired unshakeable virtue by 'gnostic *ascēsis*', habit 'becomes nature'.[89] It is from this position that we can understand

[83] *Strom.* 6. 9. 71. 5.

[84] *Paed.* 1. 3. 9. 1; *Strom.* 7. 7. 42. 3. The word ἀνταγαπᾶν had previously been used by Philo, *Migr. Abr.* 10. 50.

[85] *QDS* 27. 5.

[86] Cf. *Strom.* 4. 22. 138. 1 (but see *Strom.* 3. 10. 69. 3); 4. 12. 137. 1; 7. 7. 38. 4. For the background of the term ἕξις in Aristotle, see *Nicomachean Ethics*, 2. 5, 1105b19–1106a13; and for Chrysippus, *SVF* 3. 384, 93. 28. Cf. *SVF* 3. 272, 66. 40.

[87] *Strom.* 6. 7. 60. 3; cf. *Strom.* 6. 9. 73. 5; 7. 7. 46. 7, 9. For the Stoic doctrine of ἀρετή as ἀναπόβλητος, cf. *SVF* 1. 569, 129. 28; as ἀμετάπτωτος, *SVF* 1. 202, 50. 4.

[88] *Strom.* 7. 2. 7. 5.

[89] *Strom.* 7. 7. 46. 9; cf. *Strom.* 4. 22. 138. 3.

Clement's assertion that every action of the Gnostic is a 'right action' compared to the 'medium actions' of simple believers and the sinful activity of pagans.[90] It is not simply that each particular action of the Gnostic is good, but rather that all his activity stems from a good disposition.[91] In this disposition there is no conflict between the will, the judgement, and the corresponding activity.[92] So Clement can describe the Gnostic's imitation of God as achieved in 'performing good actions by the faculty of reason'.[93] More specifically, it is the Gnostic's disposition of beneficence that makes the energy exerted in every act 'good', so that the Gnostic passes his life as the 'image and likeness' of God.[94]

We have noted in passing how Clement associates each of the characteristics of the Gnostic with assimilation to God, perfecting the image by the likeness.[95] This theme runs throughout Clement's work, determining his asceticism.[96] For Clement this is ultimately a processes of deification. As those who devote themselves to Isomachus become farmers, and the disciples of Plato become philosophers, so those 'who listen to the Lord, and follow the prophecy given by him, will be formed perfectly in the image of the teacher, and made a god walking about in the flesh'.[97] This was the reason for the Incarnation itself, that God having become man, man might 'learn from man how to become god'.[98] The life of the Gnostic finds its completion in this goal, and therefore he 'studies to become god'.[99]

---

[90] *Strom.* 6. 14. 111. 3, cited and discussed above.

[91] Such an attitude is characteristic of Platonic philosophy in general. Cf. W. Jaeger: δικαιοσύνη for Plato 'does not lie in separate actions, but in the ἕξις, the permanent state of having a *good will*' (*Paideia: The Ideals of Greek Culture*, trans. G. Highet (Oxford, 1944–5), 2. 242).

[92] *Strom.* 2. 17. 77. 5.   [93] *Strom.* 6. 16. 136. 3.

[94] *Strom.* 4. 22. 137. 1.

[95] For assimilation through *apatheia*, see *Strom.* 7. 3. 13. 3; through worship, teaching, and beneficence, *Strom.* 7. 3. 13. 2; by *ascēsis* aimed at being ἀνεπιθύμητος, *Strom.* 7. 12. 72. 1; through doing good (ἀγαθοποιΐα), *Strom.* 4. 22. 137. 1; through beneficence, *Strom.* 6. 7. 60. 3; through love, *Strom.* 6. 9. 73. 6; through prayer for others, *Strom.* 6. 9. 77. 4–5. That the Gnostic is in both the image and in the likeness, see esp. *Strom.* 2. 19. 97. 1.

[96] Cf. Völker, *Der wahre Gnostiker*, 580; Mayer, *Das Gottesbild*, 19.

[97] *Strom.* 7. 16. 101. 4.   [98] *Prot.* 1. 8. 4.

[99] *Strom.* 6. 14. 113. 3.

Clement's vivid descriptions of the Gnostic as having achieved, through *ascēsis* and instruction, a permanent and unshakeable state of *apatheia* and beneficence perfected in love, have received varied evaluations by scholars. Some are tempted to see in them an attainable mystical condition,[100] whilst others, including Völker, consider it to be an idealized picture, which aims to surpass the Stoics' descriptions of their own sages.[101] Despite his more categorical claims, which we have considered above, there is nevertheless an ambivalence in Clement's thought. The infallible state of the Gnostic is one which must be maintained by prayer and co-operation: 'He will pray that he may never fall from virtue, co-operating (συνεργῶν) strenuously in order that he may continue infallible.'[102] The infallible disposition of the perfect Gnostic is therefore one which he has and simultaneously prays for: ἔχων ἅμα καὶ εὐχόμενος.[103] The life of the Gnostic can perhaps be described, in Völker's words, as 'eine Doppelstimmung'.[104]

However, this tension in the Gnostic's life is not simply one of maintaining an ideal state, of having and praying for its permanence, within the same horizon of the present. It is, rather, the eschatological tension of 'already but not yet', and it is this which produces the ambivalence in Clement's portrait of the perfect Gnostic. His bold assertions about the Gnostic's perfected state take their place within equally striking statements describing a vivid proleptic eschatology. For Clement one of the principle functions of *gnōsis* and love is to render the future already present. That this is so is because ultimately both *gnōsis* and love are eschatological realities.[105] Thus he writes that the Gnostic, 'being persuaded by *gnōsis* how each future thing shall be, possesses it'.[106] Similarly, 'through love

---

[100] So F. Buri, *Clemens Alexandrinus und der paulinische Freiheitsbegriff* (Zurich, 1939), 47.

[101] Cf. Völker, *Der wahre Gnostiker*, 455 n. 2; also T. Rüther, *Das sittliche Forderung der Apatheia*, 81, and Pohlenz, 'Klemens von Alexandrien', 167. Casey attempts to mediate between the two positions ('Clement of Alexandria', 63).

[102] *Strom*. 7. 7. 46. 5.

[103] *Strom*. 7. 7. 44. 5.

[104] Völker, *Der wahre Gnostiker*, 504.

[105] Cf. Méhat, *Étude sur les 'Stromates'*, 475.

[106] *Strom*. 7. 7. 47. 5.

the future is already present (ἐνεστὸς ἤδη τὸ μέλλον) for him'.[107]
This is possible because of the trustworthiness of the One in
whom he believes. Thus he continues:

For he has believed, through prophecy and the *parousia*, on God who
lies not. And what he believes he possesses, and he keeps hold of the
promise (for he who has promised is Truth). And through the
trustworthiness of him who has promised, he has firmly laid hold of
the end of the promise by knowledge. (*Strom.* 6. 9. 77. 1)

This anticipation is also effected through prayer,[108] and is
closely associated with the joy that makes the Gnostic's life a
continual 'holy festival': 'the Gnostic rejoices in things present
and is glad on account of those things promised as if they were
present', for he knows them by anticipation.[109] Finally, bringing *gnōsis* and love together, Clement specifically connects this
proleptic anticipation with the Gnostic's unchangeable state:

The one who by love is already in the midst of that which will be,
anticipating (προειληφὼς) hope by *gnōsis*, does not desire anything,
having as far as possible, the very thing desired. Accordingly, then, he
continues in the exercise of gnostic love in the one unvarying state.
(*Strom.* 6. 9. 73. 4–5)

It is in his anticipation of his true eschatological state that the
Gnostic remains, after a long ascent through *ascēsis* and instruction, in an unvarying state of love and *gnōsis*. The
Gnostic's true existence, his perfected state in love and
gnōsis, is therefore a proleptic realization of what *is already*
his final existence.

This dynamic proleptic tension in which the Gnostic lives
certainly parallels Clement's descriptions of the proleptic
existence of the neophyte which we considered earlier. However, it is of the utmost importance to note that this proleptic
existence of the Gnostic is not the result of baptism, but
the culmination of a long process of *ascēsis* and instruction,
the result of a thorough *paedeia*. Despite the fact that in the
Stromateis Clement very rarely refers to the sacramental life or
to the Church, Mayer and Völker are no doubt right when they

---

[107] *Strom.* 6. 9. 77. 1.
[108] Cf. *Strom.* 7. 7. 43. 1, 12. 79. 2.
[109] *Strom.* 7. 7. 47. 4.

claim that for Clement the ascent to gnostic perfection is dependent upon the grace bestowed in baptism.[110] This is true to the extent that Clement speaks of this gnostic perfection as being achieved only by Christians. But it is not correct to infer from this that it is the grace of baptism, and specifically the eschatological life bestowed proleptically therein, that determines the form of the Gnostic's perfection and the particular modality of his *ascēsis*. With regard to the Gnostic's form of anticipation (πρόληψις), Clement not only ascribes it to the effect of *ascēsis* rather than baptism, but, in distinction to baptism, characterizes it as a 'second saving change':

And, in my view, the first saving change is that from heathenism to faith, as I have said before; and the second, that from faith to *gnōsis*. And the latter culminating in love, here and now gives the loving to the loved, that which knows to that which is known. (*Strom.* 7. 10. 57. 4)

Clement likewise speaks of initiation into 'greater mysteries' after passing through the 'lesser mysteries'.[111] Clement also describes the initiation into these hidden mysteries as an 'illumination' (φωτισμός), transposing a term which was closely associated with the sacrament of baptism into the context of a mystical, gnostic initiation and the imparting of a 'spiritual grace'.[112] This is further demonstrated in the passage we have already considered, where Clement distinguishes between the salvation of the common believer and the 'fitting and becoming salvation' of the Gnostic.[113]

We have noted throughout this study the deeply ambivalent nature of Clement's synergism. The *ascēsis* that Clement demands from the Christian, and the intensification of this *ascēsis* for those who would achieve gnostic perfection, is within man's own capacity, and, at least on the lower ethical level, determined by his own ideas and ideals.[114] The Gnostic's

[110] Cf. Mayer, *Das Gottesbild*, 8, 47–9; Völker, *Der wahre Gnostiker*, 147, 601. Cf. Mees, 'Jetzt und Dann', 134.

[111] Cf. *Strom*. 1. 1. 15. 3; 4. 1. 3. 1; 5. 11. 71. 1. Cf. Marsh, 'Use of μυστήριον'.

[112] *Strom*. 5. 10. 64. 4–5, referring to Rom. 1: 11. Cf. Camelot, *Foi et Gnose*, 99. [113] *Strom*. 6. 14. 111. 3.

[114] It is an *ascēsis* that finds its limits, rather than its motivation, in Christ; see the discussion above in Ch. 5.

intensified *ascēsis* is perfected by the dynamic experience of anticipation, culminating in *apatheia* and beneficence permeated by *gnōsis* and love. But, coming at the end of the process of *ascēsis* and instruction, its form is already determined by that process. Thus, for example, as we have already noted when considering the place of marriage in the Gnostic's life, Clement specifies that this anticipation takes place once the married Christian Gnostics have already borne children and become as brother and sister, which they will be 'in reality after putting off the flesh'.[115] Similarly, we have noted Clement's ambivalent descriptions of the Gnostic's attitude to the good things of this world. Whilst the Gnostic will use everything thankfully, his attitude towards them is fundamentally one of 'magnanimous contempt', for his joys and 'harmless pleasures' lie elsewhere. And this 'magnanimous contempt' of the Gnostic is, for Clement, ultimately determined by the anticipation itself. Thus he writes:

For it is impossible that the one who has once been made perfect by love, and feasts eternally and insatiably on the boundless joys of contemplation should delight in small and grovelling things. For what rational cause remains any more to this one, who has gained 'the light inaccessible' [1 Tim. 6: 16], for reverting to the worldly goods? Although not yet according to time and place, but by that gnostic love through which the inheritance and perfect restitution follow, the Giver of the reward confirms through deeds what the Gnostic, by choosing gnostically, has anticipated beforehand by love. (*Strom.* 6. 9. 75. 1–2)

Clement's ambivalence regarding the status, for the Gnostic, the true Christian, of the good things of this world is thus grounded in the Gnostic's anticipation, which, in turn, is founded not on baptism, but on the intensified *ascēsis* demanded of those seeking perfection. It is because of the attraction of their own hope, as Clement asserts elsewhere, that the Gnostic 'magnanimously despises' all the good things of this world and life in it.[116]

The asceticism proposed by Clement produces a Christian who is characterized by 'composure, tranquillity, calmness and

---

[115] *Strom.* 6. 12. 100. 3.
[116] *Strom.* 7. 12. 78. 3.

peace'.[117] The asceticism required of newly converted Christians, who hope for salvation through moderation (μετριο-πάθεια), is dominated by the demand of living according to the L/logos and the suspicious abstention from pleasures. The intensified asceticism of the true Gnostic, who desires to be saved 'rightly and becomingly' and, beyond salvation itself, to be dignified with the highest honours, culminates in a state of *apatheia*. No longer subject to the disordered movements of the passions, the Gnostic exercises beneficence and works for the salvation of others. However, with the passible movements set in rational order, and dissociated from pleasure, the Gnostic has no need of even those movements which might seem to be good, such as courage, zeal, and joy. The Gnostic 'magnanimously despises' the good things of this world, whilst enjoying his own 'harmless pleasures and exaltation'.

On both levels, the proposed asceticism attempts to protect the rational dimension of the Christian, the intellect (νοῦς)—that which is distinctively human and in the image of God—in a secure self-sufficiency, against any possible threats that might arise both through pleasures, especially those of the body, even the God-given pleasures that accompany the body's natural functions, and from the uncertainty that is a corollary of dependency. The only pleasures to be enjoyed are those that are non-threatening. Other forms of joy—for instance, that experienced in the vulnerability of love—are too dangerous. Hence, the style of asceticism which Clement advocates leads to praise marriage in which there is no significance or value ascribed to its interpersonal dimensions, nor, consequently, to human sexuality beyond that of procreation. More fundamentally, the self-sufficiency created by this asceticism, which, it is claimed, imitates the self-sufficiency of God, does not even depend upon God. Although it is stated that man cannot achieve *apatheia* without the help of God, the asceticism by which he makes himself worthy to receive this gift is one which is within his own capacity, and one whose ideal, and every detail, is established by Clement himself, attempting to surpass the cultivated ideal of his day. In this style of asceticism there is no real engagement with man's bodily reality, as created by God—his concrete, societal

[117] *Paed.* 2. 7. 60. 5.

existence—nor, ultimately, with his dependence upon God. Clement directs his readers' attention inwards, to focus on what is most properly their own, under their own control.[118] Inwardly aspiring to their own ideals, Christians remain, for Clement, tiptoeing on the earth.

[118] Nussbaum's characterization of the changes involved in reaching the Stoic state of *apatheia* would also apply to Clement: 'It is the change from suspense and elation to solid self-absorption; from surprise and spontaneity to measured watchfulness; from wonder at the separate and external to security in that which is oneself and one's own. To follow Seneca's sexual metaphors, it is the change from passionate intercourse, giving birth, and child-rearing to parthenogenic conception, followed by the retention of the conceived child forever inside the womb' (*Therapy of Desire*, 401).

Conclusion

From a close reading, on their own terms, of the texts of Irenaeus of Lyons and Clement of Alexandria, this study has delineated two very different theologies of the existence and nature of the human being, two contrasting styles of asceticism and anthropology: for Irenaeus, asceticism is the expression of man living the life of God in all dimensions of the body—that which is most characteristically human and in the image of God; for Clement, it is man's attempt at a divine, godlike life, protecting the rational element—that which is peculiarly human and in the image of God—from any possible disturbance or threat from without, especially from or through the body, or from the vulnerability of dependency. These two perspectives have significant implications for their view of human sexuality: for Irenaeus, sexuality is a fundamental characteristic of human existence as a fleshly being, a permanent part of the framework within which men and women grow towards God; Clement, on the other hand, is led by the internal dynamics of his style of asceticism to limit human sexuality strictly by the finality of procreation, and thence to postulate its redundancy in the resurrection, and, proleptically, for all married Christians after having children.

Perhaps the most striking aspect of Irenaeus's theology is the intimate link between theology proper and anthropology: the truth of man is revealed in the Incarnation, which at the same time is the primary, if not the sole, revelation of God. Adam was created as the type of the One to come, and the manifestations of God in the Old Testament were always prophetic revelations of the incarnate Son. Adam was animated by the breath of life, which prefigured the future vivification of the sons of God by the Spirit: initially, of the incarnate Son, and subsequently, through the grace of baptism, of those adopted as sons in him. Christ revealed the full truth of what it is to be human, vivified by the Spirit; in the present, adopted sons possess a pledge, or 'part', of the Spirit, preparing them for their full vivification in the resurrection. Thus the life of the Christian still 'lies hidden with Christ in God' (Col. 3: 3): it is an eschatological reality, which is anticipated in Christian life here and now, and revealed most fully in the confession of martyrdom. Irenaeus does not 'spiritualize' the reality of martyrdom. The fact of death itself, in all its dimensions (pedagogical and remedial), is too important, as is the reality, and pedagogical value, of man's apostasy. Christians learn, and thereby become truly human, by experiencing both their own weakness and the power of God. Thus to become fully human demands their engagement with the concrete situations in which they find themselves in life: there is no room, as Berthouzoz put it, for 'l'ethique de l'abstention preventive'.[1]

The second striking aspect of Irenaeus's theology is that it emphasizes the body, fashioned in the image of God, almost to the extent of ignoring human interiority. In itself, the life of the soul is nothing; all the soul's activities depend upon the body with which it is inseparably bound. Whilst the importance of the body was a key feature in Irenaeus's anti-Gnostic polemic, that importance is derived from the whole matrix of Irenaeus's theology: it is that in which God has chosen to reveal both himself and the truth of man's being; so it may be considered the most essential characteristic of the human being. Without denying the reality of the Pauline notion of 'the flesh', man estranged from God in sin, Irenaeus sees the human body as primarily flesh. It is, furthermore, a flesh which is either male or female—that is, sexual—and this is the basis and framework for man's growth towards God.

A third important dimension of Irenaeus's theology is the emphasis on man's basic dependence on God, a dependence in which lies man's true freedom. The Spirit, bestowed on Adam and Eve according to their created state, as a breath of life, and bestowed on those adopted as sons in a manner befitting such dignity, as the Spirit from the Father, is an essential component of the human constitution. However, whilst being 'their Spirit', it is, nevertheless, not a 'part' of man, since the Spirit is

---

[1] Berthouzoz, *Liberté et grâce*, 236.

of God. Irenaeus elaborates this same interplay in terms of life: God is the source of life, and when he provides life, man lives. Freedom is never impaired by this dependence. Indeed, as we have seen, an increasing dependence or subjection is the mark of a greater measure of true freedom: an increased subjection implies a greater receptivity to the creative activity of God, enabling man to partake of the life of God, his only life, in an ever fuller measure.

It is the complex woven by these three dimensions that forms Irenaeus's characteristic understanding of asceticism and anthropology: human beings living the life of God in their flesh. It is the Spirit that absorbs the weakness of the flesh and manifests living human beings: living, because of the Spirit, 'their' Spirit; and human, because of the flesh. Christians do not so much develop and exercise virtues, as manifest the virtue of God in their bodies. In this asceticism, the relationship between God and man cannot strictly be called 'synergy'—not, at least, as Clement employs the term. Irenaeus himself variously attempts to explain this relationship in terms of participation or vision, which itself implies participation. Yet, while receiving life from God, it is nevertheless man who lives, and does so as the glory of God.

Finally, with his insistence on the reality of the flesh, and his articulation of asceticism in terms of the strength of the Spirit overcoming the weakness of the flesh, rather than as the development of virile virtues, Irenaeus is never tempted to suggest that both men and women become male in the exercise of such virtues, or that they outgrow or shed their sexual existence. Whilst procreation is proper to humans at the appropriate age, it does not exhaust the significance of their existence as male and female. Just as the truth of human nature still lies in the eschaton, when man will be fully vivified by the Spirit, so is the full significance of human sexuality is eschatological. For Irenaeus, Christ's words, 'He who made them from the beginning made them male and female, and said, "For this reason shall a man leave his father and mother and be joined to his wife, and the two shall be one flesh"' (Matt. 19: 4–6), expresses a truth about human existence which actual human beings, because of their weakness and incontinence, are still being prepared to attain by salvific concessions. However,

the fullness of the liberty of the sons of God is not characterized by such concessions, but, I have suggested, by Irenaeus's
portrayal of Adam and Eve 'kissing and embracing each other
in holiness' (*Dem.* 14), taken not as a mythical picture of
protological innocence, but as a description of true, eschatological, human existence.[2]

The asceticism and anthropology of Clement, on the other
hand, are governed by Clement's conviction that it is not the
body but the intellect which is in the image of God, and by the
scope and capability he ascribes to free will. He by no means
disparages the body; his polemic against the Gnostics would
not have permitted him to do so. In fact, he praises the body as
capable, when suitably purified, of being a shrine of the Spirit.
Clement also develops a very interesting analysis of the nature
of the baptized's new existence in terms of a proleptic eschatology: the anticipatory possession of the new eschatological
life, here and now, in which the baptized is already perfect,
sanctified, and illumined. Moreover, Clement is genuinely
concerned to maintain, at length, the dignity and the sanctity
of marriage, something which sets him apart from the more
usual patristic concern to defend the loftiness of virginity.

However, as we have seen, the manner in which Clement
develops a theology of asceticism makes the picture much more
problematic. The numerous precepts and ideals, advising a life
lived according to *logos*, which Clement borrowed from contemporary philosophy, were indeed transformed by being
placed within the context of *the Logos* incarnate. But the
example of the incarnate Logos actually curtails, rather than
inspires, Clement's ascetic tendencies. Clement clung to an
ideal of inner tranquillity and serenity which was to be attained
and maintained by buttressing the intellect, through the
exercise of virtue (understood in terms of self-control and
self-restraint), against anything which might disturb or ensnare

---

[2] There is an interesting similarity between Irenaeus's theology, so presented, and L. Irigaray's attempts to explain sexual difference within the
terms of a *parousia* of God who, rather than remaining in an inaccessible
transcendence, is present here and now, in and through the body. From this
perspective, the horizon of sexual difference offers the possibility of an
enduring transfiguration of the world, which she describes as the 'third era',
the 'time of the Spirit and the Bride'. Cf. *An Ethics of Sexual Difference*, trans.
C. Burke and G. C. Gill (London, 1993), esp. 147–50.

it, in particular the (God-given) pleasures which are associated with the body's natural needs. Thus, not only are Christians to limit their activity to whatever is strictly 'natural and necessary'; they are to dissociate themselves from whatever natural pleasures might accompany their actions. Clement's proposed asceticism is characterized by a suspicious abstention. Christians are to 'tiptoe on the earth', inwardly aspiring to higher things, rather than fully engaged in their bodily lives.

These tendencies are heightened when Clement describes his ideal for the higher Christian life of the true Gnostic. Such Gnostics 'form and create themselves', desiring not simply to be saved, but also to perfect their lives through an intensified asceticism and instruction, that they might be saved 'rightly and becomingly'. Achieving this state, the Gnostics attain to an angelic, fleshless condition, in which they live above the world, 'magnanimously despising' the good things of the world, enjoying instead their own 'harmless pleasures', while practising unceasing interior prayer and holding a continual festival. Although the infallible, mystical habit of *gnōsis*, *apatheia*, love, and beneficence is a proleptic anticipation, it is an anticipation based upon the Gnostic's intensified asceticism rather than on the grace of baptism. Indeed, Clement characterizes it as a 'second saving change' beyond that of baptism.

The influence of Clement's proposed style of asceticism upon his appreciation of human sexuality is immense. His attitude towards the dynamics of human sexuality is summed up in his advice, to men, that it is better not to look at women, because if they do so, they risk falling into desire: existence as male and female is a danger and a threat to his ideal of inner tranquillity, rather than a possible horizon for manifesting the life and love of God. Indeed, when discussing marriage, he very seldom speaks of love between the spouses. As sexual intercourse is natural, but necessary only to the extent that it enables the continuation of the race, Clement's overriding concern is that marriage should be governed by the finality of procreation, which Clement nevertheless praises as co-operation with the work of creation. As this is the only function he concedes to human sexuality, he is inevitably led to suggest that in the resurrection, when there is no longer marriage and procreation, the sexual character of human flesh will be shed.

This state is to be anticipated once married couples have ceased to have children, through the practice of continence understood as self-control. Again it is an anticipation brought about by a particular style of asceticism rather than through the grace bestowed in baptism.

It is especially interesting to note how Clement articulates his theology of asceticism in terms of 'synergy'. Within the context of an abstract definition of synergy, Clement asserts that a co-operative cause offers nothing of itself, but merely intensifies the activity of that which acts by itself. But, as we have also seen, Clement, in an equally formal context, specifies that a co-operative cause does contribute some power of its own. More importantly, however, when it comes to speaking of Christian asceticism, the style that Clement proposes is definitely one in which two agents work from themselves towards the same goal, a goal which is not so much that of salvation as the desire to maintain Clement's cultivated ideal, to be saved 'rightly and becomingly'. Christians are to acquire and practise the virtues by following the pedagogy of Christ, the practice of the commandments as expounded and expanded by Clement, and through this exercise be prepared for the reception of grace. The synergy which Clement proposes is merely external; it is the pedagogy of the commandments of Christ (or rather, of Clement's ascetic ideals), which Christians fulfil, thus achieving the desired goal of being saved in a 'right and becoming' fashion.

These two very different elaborations of asceticism and anthropology clearly correspond to two different narratives inscribing man.[3] The narrative for Irenaeus is the economy unfolded in Scripture—creation and animation by a breath, apostasy, preparation, adoption, and finally life through death—as the pattern for the whole human race and for each human being. With his emphasis on the fleshly existence of man, Irenaeus is committed to taking seriously man's contingent, particular, and limited existence, together with the risks and conflicts of life, and ultimately death, as intrinsic to the maturation of man and his growth towards God. It is this

---

[3] See R. Williams, *The Wound of Knowledge*, 2nd rev. edn. (London, 1990), 24–39, for an insightful analysis of the narratives unfolded by the Gnostics, Irenaeus, and Clement.

particularity and diversity of human life which is 'the theatre of God's saving work',[4] rather than the cosmic dramas of the Gnostic myths in which the particular man, with his own history, plays no role. Finally, to bring man to the perfection for which he was originally intended, God acts in history, no longer as an external Creator, but as a particular man. While the basic distinction between Creator and created (rather than spirit and matter) remains, a communion between the two is now effected. In his own life and death the Son realizes the image and likeness of God, yet does so *as man*, thereby enabling man, *as man*, also to manifest God's likeness.

For Clement, on the other hand, the narrative into which man is inscribed is a *paideia*, which, through progressive training and instruction, leads, beyond salvation, to the heights of Gnostic perfection. In this scheme, the activity of the Word of God is arranged according to the three stages of man's journey towards God: first, through exhortation; second, through the Pedagogue Jesus; and finally, through the teaching Word. This is the pattern of the spiritual life, of man's ascent to God. For Clement, the work of Christ is essentially instruction: whereas simple Christians remain at the fleshly letter, the Gnostic knows how to penetrate this veil to attain the spiritual truth. Aiming to transcend the flesh, the Gnostic is not concerned with its particulars, with their risks and dangers. He may use the good things of the world, but for him they have no value; his 'harmless pleasures' lie elsewhere.

By exploring the topics of asceticism and anthropology within the overall theological context of the writings of Irenaeus and Clement, these analyses have challenged many aspects of the traditional interpretations of their work, such as the role of the apostasy or of the Spirit for Irenaeus, and the proleptic dimension in Clement's analysis of baptismal life. But, beyond such particular details of interpretation, is the broader issue of the significance of such analyses, both for the historiographical task of understanding these and similar texts, and, subsequently, of sketching the larger history of Christian asceticism, and also for the task of attempting to understand ourselves as human.

For the historiographical issue of understanding early

[4] Ibid. 25, perhaps alluding to *AH* 4. 33. 7.

Christian texts, these analyses have shown the necessity of understanding what a particular writer has to say within the whole context in which that writer develops his thought. As E. A. Clark observed, in the concluding reflections to the International Conference on Asceticism, 'what vision of asceticism we come to advance depends greatly upon the context in which scholars put the evidence'.[5] Yet we can only put the evidence in a context other than its own, and so make it relevant for ourselves, once we have understood it as it is, within its own context. The evidence, at least in the case of such theological texts as have been discussed, does not exist simply as a store of facts from which we could pretend to write an objective history or, more subtly, to rewrite such history while openly stating our methodological presuppositions. The evidence is already in an interpreted state, embedded within a framework which may not be commensurable with our own. It is doubtful whether Foucault's horizontal analysis of different styles of subjectivity or Brown's socio-historical analysis in their projects of tracing the genealogy of the modern sexual subject can adequately comprehend the properly theological dimensions either of Irenaeus's asceticism and anthropology— man living, or incarnating, the life and strength of God in his body—or, to a lesser extent, of the proleptic dimension in Clement's analysis of baptismal life.

The objection might be raised, as it was against Foucault's work,[6] that the analyses presented here are not located in the 'real' social and political world. It is true that this study has limited itself to particular texts, and to the reflections elaborated within these texts themselves, considered within the context of their *explicit* polemic against Gnosticism. The analyses have little, if anything, to say about the daily life of Irenaeus's or Clement's married Christians or the actual existence of Clement's ideal Gnostic. For this, use must be made of many other types of evidence, such as economic, legal, or artistic, each requiring an appropriate hermeneutic. Such historiography would give a broader social and political context for

[5] E. A. Clark, 'The Ascetic Impulse in Religious Life', in Wimbush and Valantasis (eds.), *Asceticism*, 510.

[6] Cf. Lloyd, 'Mind on Sex', review of Foucault, *The Use of Pleasure*; see also the response to Lloyd by Cameron, 'Redrawing the Map', 267.

considering early Christian texts, but one, it must be remembered, which is not necessarily that of the text being studied. Neither can one assume that issues in the 'real world', typically meaning the world of our own concerns, are even addressed by any given text. Certainly all historical interpretation takes place, as is commonly recognized, within a hermeneutic circle that embraces the text itself, the tradition which has handed it down to us, and our own context. Yet the legitimate concern to locate such theological texts within the 'real' world of social, political, and economic circumstances must not become a selective filter for seeing only our own concerns and preoccupations, blinding us to the concerns of the texts themselves. Moreover, the hermeneutic circularity of historical interpretation entails that we allow ourselves to be challenged by our material, for our preconceptions to be revised, to think otherwise than we previously thought. One cannot bypass the task of attempting to understand such texts as they present themselves by focusing solely on the broader context read in terms of our own concerns. Patristic scholarship must be able to benefit from work done within other disciplines, to respond to the challenge of looking afresh and in new ways at history, yet must, nevertheless, remain faithful to its texts themselves.

With regard to the larger history of Christian asceticism, the analyses presented here, different as they are, must be taken as an attempt not to determine dogmatically what 'Christian asceticism' is or should be, but to investigate the forms that Christian asceticism, and its anthropology, took before the emergence of its classical form in monasticism. There is a striking similarity, at least in their outward aspect, between Clement's ideal of *apatheia*—tranquillity, detachment, and perpetual interior prayer—and much of what was to emerge later as the monastic ideal. Clement's works were certainly known in the desert,[7] and it is possible that Antony came from a background influenced by Alexandrian thought such as that of Clement,[8] but actual influences are, as ever, elusive. On the

---

[7] Palladius mentions that a certain female desert dweller, Collythus, possessed works of Clement; cf. *Lausiac History*, 60. Given the paucity of such information, this statement is significant.

[8] Cf. S. Rubenson, *The Letters of St. Antony: Monasticism and the Making of a Saint*, rev. edn. (Philadelphia, 1995); see also the critical response of

other hand, the state of Irenaeus's text indicates that his work
was primarily used by later heresiologists, rather than as the
inspiration for later patristic writers.[9] Irenaeus's emphasis on
the flesh and his teaching that the body was in the image of
God were soon marginalized by the pervasive influence of
Origen's theology, and were never retrieved thereafter.[10] Yet,
looking beyond the outward aspect to the style involved, it is
possible that Clement's ideals underwent a more significant
transformation in their monastic manifestation, perhaps along
Irenaean lines,[11] than the Stoic ideals had undergone at the
hands of Clement.

Besides the question of a possible influence of Clement's
works on early monasticism, his elaboration of a theology of
asceticism in terms of synergy, the internal coherence that
this has with the ideal of self-control, and the suggestion that
humans will shed their sexual characteristics in the resurrection, begs comparison with the later theorist of the ascetic
life, Gregory of Nyssa. The Greek fathers, outside the
parameters of the debate between Augustine and Pelagius,
have typically been represented as having taught a 'synergy'
between God and man. This is especially true of Gregory of

G. Gould to the 1st edn., 'Recent Work on Monastic Origins: A Consideration of the Questions Raised by Samuel Rubenson's *The Letters of St.
Antony*', *St. Patr.* 25 (Leuven, 1993), 405–16.

[9] For a full analysis, see Fantino, *L'Homme*, 188–90, and, for a more
optimistic assessment, O. Reimherr, 'Irenaeus Lugdunensis', 16–25.

[10] Florovsky argues that the so-called anthropomorphites retained the same
primitive theology as Irenaeus, but were persuaded otherwise by Origenist/
Evagrian monks, causing much distress. After being persuaded to read
Scripture 'mystically', rather than in an allegedly anthropomorphite
manner, Abba Serapion is reported to have said, while weeping and groaning
on the ground, 'They have taken my God from me, and I have now none to
behold, and whom to worship and address I know not' (John Cassian,
Conferences, 10. 3). Cf. G. Florovsky, 'The Anthropomorphites in the
Egyptian Desert', in *idem*, *Aspects of Church History* (Belmont, Mass.,
1976), 89–96.

[11] Cf. D. Burton-Christie, *The Word in the Desert* (Oxford, 1993), esp. ch. 7.
His description of Poemen's advice as 'that the single most important act for
surviving in the desert is the act of trust—to place oneself completely in the
hands of God' (p. 224), is reminiscent of Minns's characterization of
Irenaeus's position, that man 'needs to learn above all to relax in the hands
of God' (*Irenaeus*, 64); both are diametrically opposed to the self-control
shown by Clement's Gnostic in 'forming and creating himself'.

Nyssa.[12] Moreover, Gregory, it is held, taught the protological and eschatological sexless existence of human beings, elaborated through the idea of a double creation, in which sexuality was added in foresight of the Fall.[13] As such, sexuality, for Gregory, is basically remedial, permitting the increase of the human race to the number originally foreseen by God. Within this framework, marriage has an important role to play in increasing the human race to the foreordained number, but it is essentially secondary, an 'economic' state conditioned by the fallen world, to be transcended in the higher states of virtue, fully realized in virginity and celibacy, which re-establish man's original paradisal state in anticipation of the resurrection.[14] However, the question needs to be raised whether the style of the synergy proposed by Gregory is the same as that of the synergy developed by Clement.[15] If so, is there a necessary correlation between a synergetic asceticism, with the emphasis on self-control, and the exaltation of a sexless state of virginity or continence? Alternatively, should Gregory's 'synergy' be explained within the framework of participation, perhaps along the lines developed by Irenaeus?[16] If so, is there then room for a more positive appreciation of human sexuality in Gregory of Nyssa's writings, such as the reading of *De virginitate* proposed by M. D. Hart, who argues that for Gregory the highest

[12] Cf. E. Mühlenberg, 'Synergism in Gregory of Nyssa', *ZNTW* 68 (1977), 93–122; and, more recently, V. E. F. Harrison, *Grace and Human Freedom according to St. Gregory of Nyssa* (Lewiston, NY, 1993).

[13] Cf. esp. *On the Making of Man*, 16–17, 22.

[14] Elaborated, with much more nuance, by H. U. von Balthasar, *Présence et Pensée* (Paris, 1942), and J. Daniélou, *Platonisme et théologie mystique*, 2nd edn. (Paris, 1954). See also F. Floëri, 'Le Sens de la "division des sexes" chez Grégoire de Nysse', *RSR* 27 (1953), 105–11; P. Pisi, *Genesis e Phthorá: Le motivazioni protologiche della virginità in Gregorio di Nissa e nella tradizione dell'enkrateia* (Rome, 1981); V. E. F. Harrison, 'Male and Female in Cappadocian Theology', *JTS* ns 41. 2 (1990), 441–71.

[15] Jaeger suggests a sharp contrast between the two: Gregory speaks of the 'co-operation of the Spirit' (or of God or Christ), while Clement describes man as the one who co-operates; cf. *Two Rediscovered Works*, 103. My analysis of 'synergy' in Clement, however, has led to a different understanding: two agents, acting individually, towards the same goal.

[16] Cf. D. L. Balás, *ΜΕΤΟΥΣΙΑ ΘΕΟΥ: Man's Participation in God's Perfections according to Saint Gregory of Nyssa* (Rome, 1966), who notes, in passing (8–9; 94 n. 136; 95 n. 139), the similarity between Gregory's and Irenaeus's description of life in terms of participation.

embodiment of virtue is to be found in the life which combines *leitourgia* and contemplation either in marriage or in celibacy?[17]

Lastly, within the horizon of the task of understanding ourselves as human beings, the contrast drawn in this study between the position of Irenaeus, which demands that we live openly in dependence upon God, in the fullness of our created fleshly, sexual being, and that of Clement, which exhorts us to rise above the vulnerability of our fleshly being in a self-controlled self-sufficiency, has interesting parallels with the two conflicting tendencies discerned by Nussbaum in ancient Greek thought.[18] In her essay 'Transcending Humanity', Nussbaum presents these conflicting tendencies in terms of the choice that Odysseus had to make between staying with Calypso, to live the untroubled, immortal life of a god with a god, and so transcend his human nature, or returning to Penelope, to live as a human in human society, with all the vulnerability, tribulations, and certainty of death that this entails.

The life of a god is indeed a desirable and intelligible choice, for such a life is not subject to any of the constraints which make human life transitory, limited, precarious, and often miserable. And alongside such negative motivation is the positive attraction of transcendence itself. Following a philosophical tradition at least as old as Xenophanes, which held that the sole activity of a divine being was thinking, Plato and those who followed him maintained that the highest, and most proper, activity for human beings was philosophical contemplation. Although we might resemble the lower forms of life,

---

[17] Cf. M. D. Hart, 'Marriage, Celibacy and the Life of Virtue: An Interpretation of Gregory of Nyssa's *De Virginitate*' (Ph.D. diss., Boston College, 1987); *idem*, 'Reconciliation of Body and Soul'; *idem*, 'Gregory of Nyssa's Ironic Praise of the Celibate Life', *HJ* 33 (1992), 1–19. For a re-examination of Gregory's *On the Making of Man*, see my article, 'The Rational Animal: A Rereading of Gregory of Nyssa's *De hominis opificio*', *JECS* 7. 2 (1999), 219–47.

[18] Cf. M. C. Nussbaum, *The Fragility of Goodness: Luck and Ethics in Greek Tragedy and Philosophy* (Cambridge, 1986, repr. 1989); *idem*, 'Transcending Humanity', in *Love's Knowledge* (Oxford, 1990), 365–91; *idem*, *Therapy of Desire*. See also the various articles on Nussbaum's work, and her response, in R. V. Norman and C. H. Reynolds (eds.), *Symposium on* The Fragility of Goodness, *Soundings*, 72. 4 (1989).

and seem to live in subjection to nature and fate, there is part of us, Plato insisted, that is 'divine, immortal, intellectual, unitary, indissoluble, ever unchanging';[19] and it is this rational element that must govern the rest of our being, thereby securing us from the vicissitudes of fate and bodily life. Similarly, the later philosophical schools of the Hellenistic period, with the possible exception of Scepticism, offered various techniques, based on the domination of reason, for the formation and shaping of the self. Their claim to be *the* 'art of life' asserts that they can do more than any other source of *logos* in healing and governing the soul. In contrast to superstition and popular philosophy, where the outcome is always uncertain, true philosophy claims 'to remove that element of darkness and uncontrol from human life, making *tuchē* subordinate to an intelligent and intelligible *technē*',[20] thereby offering its adherents the possibility of a *'godlike* life'.[21]

However, Odysseus did not stay with Calypso, but rather chose to return to his mortal bride. To have remained with Calypso would have brought Odysseus's story to an end: he would no longer have had the opportunity to demonstrate those virtues and achievements which are characteristically human, or indeed be truly in love, for when even the gods fall in love, it is with mortal humans.[22] The Greek poets, according to Nussbaum, had understood the fact that 'part of the peculiar beauty of *human* excellence just *is* its vulnerability'.[23] Human beings are not gods, neither the transcendently anthropomorphized Olympians nor the purely intellectual divinity of the philosophical tradition. Accordingly, the truly good life for human beings is not the immortal life of the Olympians, nor one of contemplation (an acceptable activity when subordinated to other specifically human ends), but one which recognizes and accepts the full range of human values. Nussbaum finds such a position elaborated most comprehensively and

[19] Plato, *Phaedo*, 80b.
[20] Nussbaum, *Therapy of Desire*, 50.
[21] Ibid. 497.
[22] Note, however, C. Osborne's criticism of Nussbaum's analysis of the role of love in Hellenistic philosophy, in 'Love's Bitter Fruits: Martha C. Nussbaum *The Therapy of Desire: Theory and Practice in Hellenistic Ethics*', *Philosophical Investigations*, 19. 4 (1996), 318–28.
[23] Nussbaum, *Fragility of Goodness*, 2.

consistently in Aristotle. Philosophizing within the confines of the 'appearances' of things, Aristotle acknowledged that central human values, such as courage, moderation, generosity, and friendship, can be found only in a life which is subject to risk, need, and limitation. As Nussbaum puts it, 'Their nature *and* their goodness are constituted by the fragile nature of human life.'[24]

There is an evident similarity between the tendency discerned by Nussbaum in Greek philosophy, to attempt to live a godlike life through the hegemonic exercise of reason, and the position of Clement, as analysed in this study. This is perhaps not surprising given Clement's philosophical background and orientation. What is particularly interesting, however, is the similarity between the other tendency delineated by Nussbaum, which emphasizes the fragility and dependence of human nature, and the position of Irenaeus as presented here. It is possible that this is in part due to a similar methodology. According to Nussbaum, for Aristotle the 'philosophical method is committed to and limited by' the *phaino-mena*, the way things appear, so that the order which philosophy discerns is 'the order that is *in* our language and the world around us as we see and experience it'.[25] Likewise, Irenaeus insists that we must found our theology upon what actually exists, so that we might never wander from the true comprehension of things as they are, regarding both God and ourselves.[26]

What is unique to Irenaeus and the Christian tradition he represents, however, is the affirmation that this life is also the life of God. Although her work is not concerned with Christian theology, this is a point which is recognized, in passing, by Nussbaum:

[24] Nussbaum, *Fragility of Goodness*, 341.

[25] Ibid. 240, 262. One must note, however, that this aspect of Nussbaum's interpretation of Aristotle has been subjected to severe criticism; see e.g. J. M. Cooper's review of *Fragility of Goodness* in *Philosophical Review*, 97. 4 (1988), 543–64.

[26] Cf. *AH* 2. 25. 1; 5. 2. 3; *Dem.* 3. As von Balthasar puts it, for Irenaeus, 'Theology begins by seeing what is . . . It is either realistic or it is not theology at all. . . . The primary aim is not to think, to impose Platonic intellectual or even mythical categories on things, but simply to *see* what *is*' (*Glory of the Lord*, 2. 45).

For Christianity seems to grant that in order to imagine a god who is truly superior, truly worthy of worship, truly and fully just, we must imagine a god who is human as well as divine, a god who has actually lived out the non transcendent life and understands it in the only way that it can be understood, by suffering and death.[27]

The life and death of Christ within this world not only endorse the value of the human situation, but refocus and hold our attention on the world in which we live. What is involved here is more than, in Nussbaum's words, the 'thought experiment' which concluded that 'a perfect being would perform intellectual contemplation'.[28] What is only imagined by Nussbaum is a key conviction for Irenaeus, that through a death witnessing to Christ, Christians attain to the full status of human beings as sons of God in the crucified and risen Son of God.

Finally, if the style of asceticism as self-control, ultimately culminating in the exaltation of abstinence and virginity, is indeed a more universal phenomenon, as the work of Foucault and Nussbaum suggests, either as the stylization of one's life as an *œuvre* or as the attempt to protect the dignity of reason against the vicissitudes of fate and nature, or, more generally, as the human attempt at a divine, godlike life, can this be given a theological explanation in terms of Irenaeus's interpretation of the fig-leaves used by Adam? According to Irenaeus, Adam's response to his fallen situation was to impose upon himself, and Eve, a state of continence, which 'gnaws and frets the body'. It was a confused, adolescent reaction to his new, fallen situation, in which he felt unworthy to approach God. It is as if Adam wanted to make amends, to cover up the mistake he had made, and to conform himself, by his self-imposed continence, to what he considered to be divine. Although Adam expressed repentance through this action, this style of continence, as with any self-imposed state or attitude, limits human openness towards God, thereby perpetuating the Fall and the failure to be truly human, 'the glory of God'.

Such, then, are some of the issues arising from this work. The extent to which they are real issues for us, as we attempt to understand our own history and our own selves, as human

---

[27] Nussbaum, 'Transcending Humanity', 375.
[28] Ibid. 383.

beings, depends greatly upon the degree to which we allow ourselves to be challenged by voices from the past. To do this requires an openness, together with its own *ascēsis*, a disciplined reading. But this is not an option: 'Only when we turn thoughtfully toward what has already been thought, will we be turned to use for what must still be thought.'[29]

[29] M. Heidegger, *Identity and Difference*, trans. J. Stambaugh (New York, 1969), 41.

BIBLIOGRAPHY

PRIMARY WORKS

Clement of Alexandria

Texts

Clemens Alexandrinus I: Protrepticus, Paedagogus, ed. O. Stählin, 3rd edn. rev. U. Treu, GCS 12 (Berlin: Akademie Verlag, 1972).

Clemens Alexandrinus II: Stromata I–VI, ed. O. Stählin, 3rd edn. rev. L. Früchtel, GCS 52 (Berlin: Akademie Verlag, 1960).

Clemens Alexandrinus III: Stromata VII, VIII, Excerpta ex Theodoto, Eclogae Propheticae, Quis Dives Salvetur, Fragmente, ed. O. Stählin, 2nd edn. rev. L. Früchtel and U. Treu, GCS 17 (Berlin: Akademie Verlag, 1970).

Protreptique, ed. C. Mondésert, rev. A. Plassart, SC 2, 4th edn. (Paris: Cerf, 1976).

Le Pédagogue, I, ed. H. I. Marrou, trans. M. Harl, SC 70 (Paris: Cerf, 1960).

Le Pédagogue, II, trans. C. Mondésert, notes by H. I. Marrou, SC 108 (Paris: Cerf, 1965).

Le Pédagogue, III, ed. C. Mondésert and C. Matray, notes by H. I. Marrou, SC 158 (Paris: Cerf, 1970).

Les Stromates, I, ed. C. Mondésert, trans. C. Caster, SC 30 (Paris: Cerf, 1951).

Les Stromates, II, ed. C. Mondésert, notes by P. T. Camelot, SC 38 (Paris: Cerf, 1954).

Les Stromates, V, ed. A. Le Boulluec, trans. P. Voulet, SC 278–9 (Paris: Cerf, 1981).

Translations

Ferguson, J., *Clement of Alexandria: Stromateis, Books One to Three*, FC 85 (Washington: Catholic University of America, 1991).

Oulton, J. E. L., and H. Chadwick, *Alexandrian Christianity*, The Library of Christian Classics, 2 (London: SCM, 1954) [contains *Strom*. 3 and 7].

Roberts, A., and J. Donaldson (eds.), ANF 2 (1887; repr. Grand Rapids, Mich.: Eerdmans, 1989) [*Paed*. 2. 10 and *Strom*. 3 trans. into Latin].

Wood, S. P., *Clement of Alexandria: Christ the Educator*, FC 23 (New York: Fathers of the Church, 1954).

Reference works

Stählin, O. (ed.), *Clemens Alexandrinus, Register*, GCS 39 (Leipzig: Hinrich, 1936).
—— *Clemens Alexandrinus, Register: Zitatenregister, Testimonienregister, Initienregister für die Fragmente, Eigennamenregister*, GCS 39. 1 (Berlin: Akademie Verlag, 1980).

Irenaeus of Lyons

Texts

Against the Heresies

Erasmus, D. (ed.), *Opus eruditissimum divi Irenaei episcopi Lugdunensis in quinque libros digestum* . . . (Basel, 1526).
Harvey, W. W. (ed.), *Sancti Irenaei episcopi Lugdunensis libros quinque adversus haereses*, 2 vols. (Cambridge, 1857).
Massuet, E. (ed.), *Sancti Irenaei episcopi Lugdunensis et martyris detectionis et eversionis falso cognominatae agnitionis libri quinque* (Paris, 1710); repr. PG 7 (Paris, 1857).
Rousseau, A., and L. Doutreleau (eds.), *Contre les Hérésies, Livre I*, SC 263–4 (Paris: Cerf, 1979).
—— *Contre les Hérésies, Livre II*, SC 293–4 (Paris: Cerf, 1982).
—— *Contre les Hérésies, Livre III*, SC 210–11 (Paris: Cerf, 1974).
Rousseau, A., B. Hemmerdinger, L. Doutreleau, and C. Mercier (eds.), *Contre les Hérésies, Livre IV*, SC 100 (Paris: Cerf, 1965).
Rousseau, A., L. Doutreleau, and C. Mercier (eds.), *Contre les Hérésies, Livre V*, SC 152–3 (Paris: Cerf, 1969).
Ter-Mekerttschian, K., and E. Ter-Minassiantz (eds.), *Irenäus, Gegen die Häretiker.* Ἔλεγχος καὶ ἀνατροπὴ τῆς ψευδωνύμου γνώσεως, *Buch IV u. V in armenischer Version*, TU 35. 2 (Leipzig: Hinrich, 1910).

Demonstration of the Apostolic Preaching

Ter-Mekerttschian, K., and E. Ter-Minassiantz (eds. and trans.), *Des heiligen Irenäus Schrift zum Erweise der apostolischen Verkündigung . . . in armenischer Version entdeckt und in Deutsche übersetzt . . . mit einem nachwort und Anmerkungen von A. Harnack*, TU 31. 1 (Leipzig: Hinrich, 1907).
Ter-Mekerttschian, K., and S. G. Wilson, with Prince Maxe of Saxony (eds. and Eng. trans.; French trans. J. Barthoulot), *Εἰς ἐπίδειξιν τοῦ ἀποστολικοῦ κηρύγματος. The Proof of the Apostolic*

Preaching, with Seven Fragments, PO 12. 5 (1917; repr. Turnhout: Brepols, 1989).

Fragments

Holl, K. (ed.), *Fragmente vornicänischer Kirchenväter aus den Sacra Parallela*, TU 20. 2 (Leipzig: Hinrich, 1899).
Jordan, H. (ed.), *Armenische Irenaeusfragmente*, TU 36. 3 (Leipzig: Hinrich, 1913).
Renoux, C. (ed.), *Nouveaux fragments armeniens de l'"Adversus Haereses" et de l'"Epideixis"*, PO 39. 1 (Turnhout: Brepols, 1978).

Translations

Against the Heresies

Grant, R. M., *Irenaeus of Lyons* (New York: Routledge, 1997) [extracts].
Keble, J., *Five Books of S. Irenaeus, Against the Heresies* (London: James Parker, 1872).
Roberts, A., and J. Donaldson (eds.), ANF 1 (1887; repr. Grand Rapids, Mich.: Eerdmans, 1987).
Unger, D. J., rev. J. J. Dillon, *St Irenaeus of Lyons Against the Heresies, Book 1*, ACW 55 (New York: Paulist Press, 1992).

Demonstration of the Apostolic Preaching

Behr, J., *The Apostolic Preaching* (New York: Saint Vladimir's Seminary Press, 1997).
Froidevaux, L. M., *Irénée de Lyon: Démonstration de la Prédication Apostolique*, SC 62 (Paris: Cerf, 1959).
Rousseau, A., *Démonstration de la Prédication Apostolique*, SC 406 (Paris: Cerf, 1995).
Smith, J. P., *St Irenaeus: Proof of the Apostolic Preaching*, ACW 16 (New York: Newman, 1952).
Weber, S., *Des Heiligen Irenäus Schrift zum Erweis der apostolischen Verkündigen*, BKV (Kempton and Munich: Kösel, 1912), 1–68 (583–650).

Reference works

Reynders, B. (ed.), *Lexique comparé du texte grec et des versions latine, arménienne et syriaque de l'"Adversus Haereses" de saint Irénée*, CSCO 141–2, subsidia 5–6 (Louvain: Peeters, 1954).
—— *Vocabulaire de la "Démonstration" et des fragments de S. Irénée* (Louvain: Éditions de Chevetogne, 1958).
Sanday W., and C. H. Turner (eds.), *Novum Testamentum Sancti Irenaei* (Oxford: Clarendon Press, 1923).

Other Texts

Alcinous, *Didaskalikos. Enseignement des doctrines de Platon*, ed.
J. Whittaker (Paris: Belles Lettres, 1990); trans. J. Dillon, *The
Handbook of Platonism* (Oxford: Clarendon Press, 1993).
Aristotle, *Nicomachean Ethics*, ed. and trans. H. Rackham, LCL
Aristotle, 19 (Cambridge, Mass.: Harvard University Press, 1990).
——*Posterior Analytics*, ed. and trans. H. Tredennick, LCL Aris-
totle, 15 (Cambridge, Mass.: Harvard University Press, 1976).
Athenagoras, *Legatio* and *On the Resurrection*, ed. and trans. W. R.
Schoedel, OECT (Oxford: Clarendon Press, 1972).
Augustine, *Answer to Julian*, in *Answer to the Pelagians*, II, trans. R. J.
Teske, in *The Works of Saint Augustine*, I/24, ed. J. Rotelle (New
York: New City Press, 1998).
Barnabas, *The Epistle of Barnabas*, ed. and trans. K. Lake, LCL
Apostolic Fathers, 1 (Cambridge, Mass.: Harvard University Press,
1985).
Basil of Caesarea, *On the Holy Spirit. Sur le Saint-Esprit*, ed. and
French trans. B. Pruche, SC 17 bis (Paris: Cerf, 1968); English trans.
D. Anderson (New York: Saint Vladimir's Seminary Press, 1980).
Cabasilas, Nicholas, *A Commentary on the Divine Liturgy*, trans. J. M.
Hussey and P. A. McNulty (London: SPCK, 1960).
Cassian, John, *Conferences. Iohannis Cassiani Opera*, 1, *Collationes*,
ed. M. Petschenig, CSEL 13 (Vienna, 1886); trans. B. Ramsey,
ACW 57 (New York: Paulist Press, 1997).
Didascalia Apostolorum. The Didascalia Apostolorum in Syriac, ed.
and trans. A. Vööbus, CSCO 402, 408; Scriptores Syri 176, 180
(Louvain: Peeters, 1979).
Epictetus, *Discourses*, ed. and trans. W. A. Oldfather, LCL (Cam-
bridge, Mass.: Harvard University Press, 1989).
Epicurus, *Epicurea*, ed. H. Usener (Leipzig: Teubner, 1887).
The Epistle to Diognetus, ed. and trans. K. Lake, LCL Apostolic
Fathers, 1 (Cambridge, Mass.: Harvard University Press, 1985).
Eusebius, *Ecclesiastical History*, ed. and trans. K. Lake, LCL (Cam-
bridge, Mass: Harvard University Press, 1980).
Galen, *Galeni compendium Timaei Platonis aliorumque dialogorum
synopsis quae extant fragmenta*, ed. P. Kraus and R. Walzer, Plato
Arabus, 1, ed. R. Walzer (London: Warburg Institute, 1951).
Gregory of Nyssa, *Catechetical Oration*, ed. J. H. Srawley (Cam-
bridge: Cambridge University Press, 1903); trans. NPNF, ser. 2, 5
(Grand Rapids, Mich.: Eerdmans, 1979), 473–509.
——*On the Making of Man. De hominis opificio*, PG 44. 125–256;
trans. P. Schaff and H. Wace (eds.), NPNF, ser. 2, 5 (Grand
Rapids, Mich.: Eerdmans, 1979), 387–427.

——*On Perfection. De perfectione*, ed. W. Jaeger, in *Gregorii Nysseni Opera*, 8. 1 (Leiden: Brill, 1986); trans. V. W. Callahan, in *St Gregory of Nyssa: Ascetical Works*, FC 58 (Washington: Catholic University of America, 1967), 95–122.

Hermas, *The Shepherd*, ed. and trans. K. Lake, LCL Apostolic Fathers, 2 (Cambridge, Mass.: Harvard University Press, 1976).

Ignatius of Antioch, *Letters*, ed. and trans. K. Lake, LCL Apostolic Fathers, 1 (Cambridge, Mass: Harvard University Press, 1976).

Jerome, *Letters. St Jérôme: Lettres*, ed. and French trans. J. Labourt (Paris: Belle Lettres, 1953).

Justin Martyr, *Dialogue with Trypho. Iustini martyris dialogus cum Tryphone*, ed. M. Marcovich, PTS 47 (Berlin and New York: De Gruyter, 1997); trans. in ANF 1 (1887; repr. Grand Rapids, Mich.: Eerdmans, 1987), 194–270.

——*Apologies. Iustini martyris apologiae pro christianis*, ed. M. Marcovich, PTS 38 (Berlin and New York: De Gruyter, 1994); trans. L. W. Barnard, *St Justin Martyr: The First and Second Apologies*, ACW 56 (New York: Paulist Press, 1997).

Leontius ('of Byzantium'), *De Sectis*, PG 86. 1193–1268.

Maximus the Confessor, *Quaestiones ad Thalassium*, PG 90. 243–786.

Musonius Rufus, *C. Musonii Rufi Reliquiae*, ed. O. Hense (Leipzig: Teubner, 1905).

——'Musonius Rufus: The Roman Socrates', ed. and trans. C. E. Lutz, *Yale Classical Studies*, 10 (1947), 3–151; repr. (New Haven: Yale University Press, 1947.

Origen, *On First Principles. Traité des Principes*, ed. and French trans. H. Crouzel and M. Simonetti, SC 252, 268 (Paris: Cerf, 1978, 1980); English trans. G. W. Butterworth (Gloucester, Mass.: Peter Smith, 1973).

——*Homilies on Genesis. Homélies sur la Genèse*, ed. and French trans. H. de Lubac and L. Doutreleau, SC 7, 3rd edn. (Paris: Cerf, 1966); English trans. R. E. Heine, *Origen: Homilies on Genesis and Exodus*, FC 71 (Washington: Catholic University of America, 1982).

Palladius, *Lausiac History*, ed. C. Butler, Text and Studies, 6. 2 (1898; repr. Hildesheim: G. Olms, 1967); trans. R. T. Meyer, ACW 34 (Westminster: Newman, 1965).

Philo, *Allegorical Interpretation* (*Leg. Alleg.*), ed. and trans. F. H. Colson and G. H. Whitaker, LCL Philo, 1 (Cambridge, Mass.: Harvard University Press, 1991).

——*On Abraham* (*Abr.*), ed. and trans. F. H. Colson, LCL Philo, 6 (Cambridge, Mass.: Harvard University Press, 1935).

——*On the Account of the World's Creation given by Moses* (*Opif.*), ed.

and trans. F. H. Colson and G. H. Whitaker, LCL Philo, 1 (Cambridge, Mass.: Harvard University Press, 1991).

Philo, *On Dreams, that they are God-sent* (*Somn.*), ed. and trans. F. H. Colson and G. H. Whitaker, LCL Philo, 5 (Cambridge, Mass.: Harvard University Press, 1939).

——*On Drunkenness* (*Ebr.*), ed. and trans. F. H. Colson and G. H. Whitaker, LCL Philo, 3 (Cambridge, Mass.: Harvard University Press, 1930).

——*On the Migration of Abraham* (*Migr. Abr.*), ed. and trans. F. H. Colson and G. H. Whitaker, LCL Philo, 4 (Cambridge, Mass.: Harvard University Press, 1932).

——*On the Posterity of Cain and his Exile* (*Post. Cain*), ed. and trans. F. H. Colson and G. H. Whitaker, LCL Philo, 2 (Cambridge, Mass.: Harvard University Press, 1929).

——*Who is the Heir of Divine Things* (*Quis rer. div. her.*), ed. and trans. F. H. Colson and G. H. Whitaker, LCL Philo, 4 (Cambridge, Mass.: Harvard University Press, 1932).

Plato, *Laws*, ed. and trans. R. G. Bury, LCL Plato, 10–11 (Cambridge, Mass.: Harvard University Press, 1961).

——*Phaedo*, ed. and trans. H. N. Fowler, LCL Plato, 1 (Cambridge, Mass.: Harvard University Press, 1990).

——*Phaedrus*, ed. and trans. H. N. Fowler, LCL Plato, 1 (Cambridge, Mass.: Harvard University Press, 1990).

——*Republic*, ed. and trans. P. Shorey, LCL Plato, 5–6 (Cambridge, Mass.: Harvard University Press, 1963).

——*Symposium*, ed. and trans. W. R. H. Lamb, LCL Plato, 3 (Cambridge, Mass.: Harvard University Press, 1983).

——*Timaeus*, ed. and trans. R. G. Bury, LCL Plato, 9 (Cambridge, Mass.: Harvard University Press, 1981).

The Martyrdom of Polycarp, ed. and trans. K. Lake, LCL Apostolic Fathers, 2 (Cambridge, Mass: Harvard University Press, 1976).

Soranus, *Gynaecia*, ed. I. Ilberg, Corpus Medicorum Graecorum, 4 (Leipzig: Teubner, 1927); trans. O. Temkin, *Gynecology* (1953; Baltimore: Johns Hopkins University Press, 1991).

Stoicorum Veterum Fragmenta, ed. J. von Arnim (Leipzig: Teubner, 1903–24).

Tatian, *Oration to the Greeks*, ed. and trans. M. Whittaker, OECT (Oxford: Clarendon Press, 1982).

Tertullian, *On the Resurrection*, ed. and trans. E. Evans (London: SPCK, 1960).

——*Against the Valentinians. Contre les Valentiniens*, ed. and French trans. J. C. Fredouille, SC 280–1 (Paris: Cerf, 1980, 1981); English

trans. ANF 3 (1887; repr. Grand Rapids, Mich.: Eerdmans, 1989), 503–20.
Theophilus of Antioch, *To Autolycus*, ed. and trans. R. M. Grant, OECT (Oxford: Clarendon Press, 1970).
The Gospel according to Thomas, ed. and trans. A. Guillaumont [*et al.*] (Leiden: Brill, 1959).

Reference works

Lampe, G. W. H. (ed.), *A Patristic Greek Lexicon* (Oxford: Clarendon Press, 1961, repr. 1989).
Liddell, H. G., and R. Scott (eds.), *A Greek–English Lexicon*, 9th edn., rev. H. S. Jones and R. McKenzie (Oxford: Clarendon Press, 1996).
Աւետիքեան, Գ., Սիւրմէլեան, Խ., and Աւգերեան, Մ. (eds.), *Նոր Բառգիրք Հայկազեան Լեզուի* (Venice: San Lazzaro Press, 1836–7; repr. Erevan: State University Press, 1979–81).

SECONDARY WORKS

Aland, B., 'Fides und subiectio: Zur Anthropologie des Irenäus', in A. M. Ritter (ed.), *Kerygma und Logos: Beiträge zu den geistesgeschichtlichen Beziehungen zwischen Antike und Christentum. Festschrift für Carl Andresen zum 70. Geburtstag* (Göttingen: Vandenhoeck and Ruprecht, 1979), 9–28.
Aldama, J. A. de, 'Adam, typus futuri', *Sacris Erudiri*, 13 (1962), 266–80.
Alès, A. d', 'La Doctrine de la récapitulation en S. Irénée', *RSR* 6 (1916), 185–211.
—— 'La Doctrine de l'Esprit en saint Irénée', *RSR* 14 (1924), 497–538.
Alexandre, M., 'Early Christian Women', in G. Duby and M. Perrot (eds.), *A History of Women in the West*, 1: *From Ancient Goddesses to Christian Saints*, ed. P. Schmitt Pantel, trans. A. Goldhammer (Cambridge, Mass.: Harvard University Press, 1992), 409–44.
Altermath, F., 'The Purpose of the Incarnation according to Irenaeus', *St. Patr.* 13, TU 116 (Berlin: Akademie Verlag, 1975), 63–8.
—— *Du corps psychique au corps spirituel: Interprétation de 1 Cor. 15.35–49 par les auteurs chrétiens de quatre premiers siècles*, Beiträge zur Geschichte der biblische Exegese, 18 (Tübingen: Mohr, 1977).
Anderson, G., 'Celibacy or Consummation in the Garden? Reflections

on Early Jewish and Christian Interpretations of the Garden of Eden', *HTR* 82. 2 (1989), 121–48.

Andia, Y. de, 'La Résurrection de la chair selon les Valentiniens et Irénée de Lyon', *Les Quatre Fleuves*, 15–16 (1982), 59–70.

——*Homo vivens: Incorruptibilité et divinisation de l'homme selon Irénée de Lyon* (Paris: Études Augustiniennes, 1986).

—— 'Modèles de l'unité des testaments selon Irénée de Lyon', *St. Patr.* 21 (Leuven: Peeters, 1989), 49–59.

Arbesmann, R., 'Fasting and Prophecy in Pagan and Christian Antiquity', *Traditio*, 7 (1949–51), 1–71.

Ariès, P. and Béjin, A. (eds.), *Western Sexuality: Practice and Precept in Past and Present Times* (Oxford: Blackwell, 1985).

Aspegren, K., *The Male Woman: A Feminine Ideal in the Early Church* (Uppsala: Academia Upsaliensis, 1990).

Aubineau, M., 'Incorruptibilité et divinisation selon S. Irénée', *RSR* 44 (1956), 25–52.

Aune, D. E., *The Cultic Setting of Realized Eschatology in Early Christianity*, supplement to *Novum Testamentum*, 28 (Leiden: Brill, 1977).

Bacq, P., *De l'ancienne à la nouvelle alliance selon S. Irénée: Unité du livre IV de l'Adversus Haereses* (Paris: Éditions Lethielleux, Presses Universitaires de Namur, 1978).

Balás, D. L., *ΜΕΤΟΥΣΙΑ ΘΕΟΥ: Man's Participation in God's Perfections according to Saint Gregory of Nyssa*, Studia Anselmiana, 55 (Rome: Pontificum Institutum S. Anselmi, 1966).

—— 'The Use and Interpretation of Paul in Irenaeus' Five Books Adversus Haereses', *Second Century*, 9. 1 (1992), 27–39.

Balthasar, H. U. von, *Présence et pensée: Essai sur la philosophie religieuse de Grégoire de Nysse* (Paris: Beauchesne, 1942).

—— *The Glory of the Lord: A Theological Aesthetics*, 2, trans. A. Louth, F. McDonagh, and B. McNeil, ed. J. Riches (1962; Edinburgh: T. and T. Clark, 1984).

Bauer, W., *Orthodoxy and Heresy in Earliest Christianity* (London: SCM, 1972).

Beard, M., 'The Sexual Status of Vestal Virgins', *JRS* 70 (1980), 12–27.

Behr, J., 'Irenaeus *AH* 3. 23. 5 and the Ascetic Ideal', *SVTQ* 37. 4 (1993), 305–13.

—— 'The Rational Animal: A Rereading of Gregory of Nyssa's *De hominis opificio*', *JECS* 7. 2 (1999), 219–47.

—— 'Shifting Sands: Foucault, Brown and the Framework of Christian Asceticism', *HJ* 34. 1 (1993), 1–21.

Bengsch, A., *Heilsgeschichte und Heilswissen: Eine Untersuchung zur*

Struktur und Entfaltung des theologischen Denkens im Werk "Adversus Haereses" des hl. Irenäus von Lyon (Leipzig: St Benno, 1957).

Benoît, A., *Le Baptême chrétien au second siècle: La théologie des Pères* (Paris: Presses Universitaires de France, 1953).

——*Saint Irénée: Introduction à l'étude de sa théologie*, Études d'Histoire et de Philosophie Religieuses, 52 (Paris: Presses Universitaires de France, 1960).

Bentivegna, G., *Economia di salvezza e creazione nel pensiero di S. Ireneo* (Rome: Herder, 1973).

Bentivegna, J., 'A Christianity without Christ by Theophilus of Antioch', *St. Patr.* 13, TU 116 (Berlin: Akademie Verlag, 1971), 107–31.

Berrouard, M. F., 'Servitude de la Loi et liberté de l'Evangile selon S. Irénée', *LV* 61 (1963), 41–60.

Berthouzoz, R., *Liberté et grâce suivant la théologie d'Irénée de Lyon* (Fribourg en Suisse: Éditions Universitaires; Paris: Cerf, 1980).

Bigg, C., *The Christian Platonists of Alexandria* (Oxford: Clarendon Press, 1886).

Black, M., 'The Tradition of Hasidean–Essene Asceticism: Its Origins and Influence', in M. Simon (ed.), *Aspects du Judéo-Christianisme: Colloque de Strasbourg 23–25 Avril 1964* (Paris: Presses Universitaires de France, 1965), 19–32.

Blanchard, Y. M., *Aux Sources du Canon: Le témoignage d'Irénée* (Paris: Cerf, 1993).

Bolgiani, F., 'La tradizione eresiologica sull'Encratismo. I: Le notizie di Ireneo', in Accademia delle Scienze di Torino, *Atti*, ii: *Classe di Scienze Morali, Storiche e Filologiche*, 91 (1956), 343–419.

——'La tradizione eresiologica sull'encratismo. II: La confutazione di Clemente di Alessandria (parte prima)', in Accademia delle Scienze di Torino, *Atti*, ii: *Classe di Scienze Morali, Storiche e Filologiche*, 96 (1961–2), 537–664.

——'La polemica di Clemente Alessandrino contro gli Gnostici Libertini del III libro degli "Stromati"', *Studi e Materiali di Storia delle Religioni*, 38 (1967), *Studi in Onore di Alberto Pincherle*, i. 86–136.

Boman, T., *Hebrew Thought Compared with Greek* (New York: Norton, 1970).

Bonner, G., 'Martyrdom: Its Place in the Church', *Sobornost*, 5. 2 (1983), 6–21.

Bonwetsch, N., *Die Theologie des Irenäus*, Beiträge zur Förderung christlicher Theologie, 2. 9 (Gütersloh, 1925).

Bousset, W., *Jüdisch-christlicher Schulbetrieb in Alexandria und Rom: Literarische Untersuchungen zu Philo und Clemens von Alexandria,*

Justin und Irenäus, Forschung zur Religion und Literatur der Alten und Neuen Testaments, NF 6 (Göttingen, 1915).

Bousset, W., *Kyrios Christos: Geschichte des Christusglaubens von den Anfängen des Christentums bis Irenaeus*, 2nd edn. (Göttingen: Vandenhoeck and Ruprecht, 1921); trans. J. E. Steely, *Kyrios Christos: A History of Belief in Christ from the Beginnings of Christianity to Irenaeus* (New York and Nashville, Tenn.: Abingdon Press, 1970).

Boyarin, D., 'Body Politic among the Brides of Christ: Paul and the Origins of Christian Sexual Renunciation', in V. L. Wimbush and R. Valantasis (eds.), *Asceticism* (Oxford: Oxford University Press, 1995), 459–78.

Brakke, D., 'The Problem of Nocturnal Emissions in Early Christian Syria, Egypt, and Gaul', *JECS* 3. 4 (1995), 419–60.

Broudéhoux, Jean-Paul, *Mariage et Famille chez Clément d'Alexandrie*, Théologie Historique, 11 (Paris: Beauchesne, 1970).

Brown, P., 'The Rise and Function of the Holy Man in Late Antiquity', *JRS* 61 (1971), 80–101.

——*The Making of Late Antiquity* (Cambridge, Mass.: Harvard University Press, 1978).

——'Late Antiquity', in P. Ariès and G. Duby (eds.), *A History of the Private Life*, 1: *From Pagan Rome to Byzantium*, ed. P. Veyne, trans. A. Goldhammer (Cambridge, Mass.: Belknap Press, 1987), 237–311.

——*The Body and Society: Men, Women and Sexual Renunciation in Early Christianity* (New York: Columbia University Press, 1988; London: Faber, 1989).

——'The Notion of Virginity in the Early Church', in B. McGinn, J. Meyendorff, and J. Leclercq (eds.), *Christian Spirituality: Origins to the Twelfth Century* (London: SCM, 1989), 427–44.

——'Bodies and Minds: Sexuality and Renunciation in Early Christianity', in D. M. Halperin, J. J. Winkler, and F. I. Zeitlin (eds.), *Before Sexuality: The Construction of Erotic Experience in the Ancient Greek World* (Princeton: Princeton University Press, 1990), 479–93.

Brown, R. F., 'On the Necessary Imperfection of Creation: Irenaeus *Adversus Haereses* IV. 38', *SJT* 28. 1 (1975), 17–25.

Buri, F., *Clemens Alexandrinus und der paulinische Freiheitsbegriff* (Zurich: M. Niehans, 1939).

Burrus, V., *Chastity as Autonomy: Women in the Stories of Apocryphal Acts*, Studies in Women and Religion, 23 (Lewiston, NY: Edwin Mellen, 1987).

—— 'Hierarchalization and Genderization of Leadership in the Writings of Irenaeus', *St. Patr.* 21 (Leuven: Peeters, 1989), 42–8.

Burton-Christie, D., *The Word in the Desert: Scripture and the Quest for Holiness in Early Christian Monasticism* (Oxford: Oxford University Press, 1993).

Butterworth, G. W., 'The Deification of Man in Clement of Alexandria', *JTS* 17 (1916), 157–69.

Camelot, T., *Foi et Gnose: Introduction a l'étude de la connaissance mystique chez Clément d'Alexandrie* (Paris: Vrin, 1945).

Cameron, A., 'Redrawing the Map: Early Christian Territory after Foucault', *JRS* 76 (1986), 266–71.

—— 'Virginity as Metaphor: Women and the Rhetoric of Early Christianity', in A. Cameron (ed.), *History as Text: The Writing of Ancient History* (London: Duckworth, 1989), 181–205.

—— 'Ascetic Closure and the End of Antiquity', in V. L. Wimbush and R. Valantasis (eds.), *Asceticism* (Oxford: Oxford University Press, 1995), 147–61.

Casey, R. P., 'Clement of Alexandria and the Beginnings of Christian Platonism', *HTR* 18 (1925), 39–101.

Castelli, E. A., 'Asceticism—Audience and Resistance', in V. L. Wimbush and R. Valantasis (eds.), *Asceticism* (Oxford: Oxford University Press, 1995), 178–87.

Chadwick, H., 'Enkrateia', in *Reallexikon für Antike und Christentum* (Stuttgart: A. Hiersemann, 1960), 5. 343–65.

—— 'Clement of Alexandria', in A. H. Armstrong (ed.), *The Cambridge History of Later Greek and Early Christian Philosophy* (Cambridge: Cambridge University Press, 1967), 168–81.

—— *Early Christian Thought and the Classical Tradition* (Oxford: Clarendon Press, 1987).

Clark, E. A., *Clement's Use of Aristotle: The Aristotelian Contribution to Clement of Alexandria's Refutation of Gnosticism* (Lewiston, NY: Edwin Mellen, 1977).

—— 'Ascetic Renunciation and Feminine Advancement: A Paradox of Late Ancient Christianity', *Anglican Theological Review*, 63 (1981), 240–57; repr. in Clark, *Ascetic Piety and Women's Faith*, 175–208.

—— 'The State and Future of Historical Theology: Patristic Studies', *Union Papers*, 2 (New York: Union Theological Seminary, 1982), 46–56; repr. in Clark, *Ascetic Piety and Women's Faith*, 3–19.

—— *Ascetic Piety and Women's Faith: Essays on Late Ancient Christianity*, Studies in Women and Religion, 20 (Lewiston, NY: Edwin Mellen, 1986).

—— 'Devil's Gateway and Bride of Christ: Women in the Early

Christian World', in E. A. Clark, *Ascetic Piety and Women's Faith*, 23–60.

Clark, E. A., 'Adam's Only Companion: Augustine and the Early Christian Debate on Marriage', *Recherches Augustiniennes*, 21 (1986), 139–62.

—— 'Foucault, the Fathers and Sex', *JAAR* 56. 4 (1988), 619–41.

—— 'The Ascetic Impulse in Religious Life: A General Response', in V. L. Wimbush and R. Valantasis (eds.), *Asceticism* (Oxford: Oxford University Press, 1995), 505–10.

Clément, O., 'Life in the Body', *Ecumenical Review*, 33 (1981), 128–46.

Constantelos, D. J., 'Irenaeos of Lyons and his Central Views on Human Nature', *SVTQ* 33. 4 (1989), 351–65.

Coolidge, J. S., *The Pauline Basis of the Concept of Scriptural Form in Irenaeus*, in W. Wuellner (ed.), *Protocol of the Eighth Colloquy: 4 November 1973*, The Center for Hermeneutical Studies in Hellenistic and Modern Culture (Berkeley: University of California Press, 1974).

Cooper, J. M., review of M. C. Nussbaum, *The Fragility of Goodness* (Cambridge, 1986), *Philosophical Review* 97. 4 (1988), 543–64.

Crouzel, H., 'Le "Vrai Gnostique" de Clément d'Alexandrie d'apres W. Völker', *RAM* 31 (1955), 77–83.

Cullman, O., *Christ and Time*, trans. F. V. Filson (London: SCM, 1951).

Czesz, B., 'La continua presenza dello Spirito Santo nei tempi del Vecchio e del Nuovo Testamento secondo S. Ireneo (*Adv. haer.* IV,13,15)', *Augustinianum*, 20. 3 (1980), 581–5.

Daley, B. E., *The Hope of the Early Church: A Handbook of Patristic Eschatology* (Cambridge: Cambridge University Press, 1991).

Daniélou, J., 'S. Irénée et les origines de la théologie de l'histoire', *RSR* 34 (1947), 227–31.

—— *Platonisme et théologie mystique: Doctrine spirituelle de saint Grégoire de Nysse*, 2nd edn. (Paris: Aubier, 1954).

—— *The Development of Christian Doctrine before the Council of Nicaea*, 1: *The Theology of Jewish Christianity*, trans. J. A. Baker (London: Darton, Longman and Todd, 1964).

—— *The Development of Christian Doctrine before the Council of Nicaea*, 2: *The Gospel Message and Hellenistic Culture*, trans. J. A. Baker (London: Darton, Longman and Todd, 1973).

—— *L'Être et le temps chez Grégoire de Nysse* (Leiden: Brill, 1970).

Derrett, J. D. M., 'Primitive Christianity as an Ascetic Movement', in V. L. Wimbush and R. Valantasis (eds.), *Asceticism* (Oxford: Oxford University Press, 1995), 88–107.

Dodds, E. R., *Pagan and Christian in an Age of Anxiety: Some Aspects of Religious Experience from Marcus Aurelius to Constantine* (Cambridge: Cambridge University Press, 1965; repr. 1990).

Donovan, M. A., 'Irenaeus in Recent Scholarship', *Second Century*, 4. 4 (1984), 219–41.

—— 'Alive to the Glory of God', *TS* 49. 2 (1988), 283–97.

—— 'Irenaeus: At the Heart of Life, Glory', in A. Callahan (ed.), *Spiritualities of the Heart* (New York: Paulist Press, 1989), 11–22.

Douglas, M., *Purity and Danger: An Analysis of Concepts of Pollution and Taboo* (London: Routledge and Kegan Paul, 1969).

Edwards, M. J., 'Gnostics and Valentinians in the Church Fathers', *JTS* ns 40. 1 (1989), 26–47.

Eijk, T. H. J. van, 'Marriage and Virginity, Death and Immortality', in J. Fontaine and C. Kannengiesser (eds.), *EPEKTASIS: Mélanges offerts au Cardinal J. Daniélou* (Paris: Beauchesne, 1972), 209–35.

Elm, S., *'Virgins of God': The Making of Asceticism in Late Antiquity* (Oxford: Oxford University Press, 1994).

Evdokimov, P., *La Femme et le salut de monde: Étude d'anthropologie chrétienne sur les charismes de la femme* (Tournai: Casterman, 1958).

—— *Sacrement de l'amour* (Paris: Éditions de l'Epi, 1962).

Évieux, P., 'La Théologie de l'accoutumance chez saint Irénée', *RSR* 55 (1967), 5–54.

Fantino, J., *L'Homme, image de Dieu chez saint Irénée de Lyon* (Paris: Cerf, 1984).

—— 'La Création *ex nihilo* chez saint Irénée: Étude historique et théologique', *RSPhTh* 76. 3 (1992), 421–42.

—— *La Théologie d'Irénée: Lecture des Écritures en réponse à l'exégèse gnostique: Une approche trinitaire* (Paris: Cerf, 1994).

Farkasfalvy, D., 'Theology of Scripture in St Irenaeus', *RB* 78 (1968), 319–33.

Faye, E. de, *Clément d'Alexandrie: Étude sur les rapports du Christianisme et de la Philosophie grecque au IIe siècle*, 2nd edn. (Paris: E. Leroux, 1906).

Ferguson, J., *Clement of Alexandria* (New York: Twayne, 1974).

Flesseman-van Leer, E., *Tradition and Scripture in the Early Church*, Van Gorcum's Theologische Bibliotheek, 26 (Assen: Van Gorcum, 1954).

Floëri, F., 'Le Sens de la "division des sexes" chez Grégoire de Nysse', *RSR* 27 (1953), 105–11.

Florovsky, G., *Creation and Redemption* (Belmont, Mass.: Nordland, 1976).

—— 'Creation and Creaturehood', in *Creation and Redemption*, 43–78.

Florovsky, G., 'The "*Immortality*" of the Soul', in *Creation and Redemption*, 213–40.

—— *Aspects of Church History* (Vaduz: Büchervertriebsanstalt, 1987).

—— 'The Patristic Age and Eschatology', in *Aspects of Church History*, 63–78.

—— 'The Anthropomorphites in the Egyptian Desert', in *Aspects of Church History*, 89–96.

Floyd, W. E. G., *Clement of Alexandria's Treatment of the Problem of Evil* (Oxford: Oxford University Press, 1971).

Fontaine, J., and C. Kannengiesser (eds.), *EPEKTASIS: Mélanges patristiques offerts au Cardinal J. Daniélou* (Paris: Beauchesne, 1972).

Foucault, M., *Histoire de la sexualité*, 1: *La Volonté de savoir* (Paris: Gallimard, 1976); trans. R. Hurley, *History of Sexuality, An Introduction* (Harmondsworth: Penguin, 1990).

—— 'Le Combat de la chasteté', *Communications*, 35 (1982), 15–25; trans. in P. Ariès and A. Béjin (eds.), *Western Sexuality* (Oxford: Blackwell, 1985), 14–25; rev. trans. in Rabinow (ed.), *Michel Foucault*, 185–97.

—— *Histoire de la sexualité*, 2: *L'Usage des plaisirs* (Paris: Gallimard, 1984); trans. R. Hurley, *The Use of Pleasures* (Harmondsworth: Penguin, 1987).

—— *Histoire de la sexualité*, 3: *Le Souci de soi* (Paris: Gallimard, 1984); trans. R. Hurley, *The Care of the Self* (Harmondsworth: Penguin, 1990).

—— 'The Ethic of Care for the Self as a Practice of Freedom, an Interview with Foucault on Jan. 20, 1984', in J. Bernauer and D. Rasmussen (eds.), *The Final Foucault* (Cambridge, Mass.: MIT Press, 1988), 1–20.

—— 'The Concern for Truth', *Littéraire*, 207 (May 1984), 18–23; trans. A. Sheridan, in Kritzman (ed.), *Michel Foucault*, 255–67.

—— 'The Return of Morality', *Les Nouvelles* (28 June 1984); trans. T. Levin and I. Lorenz, in Kritzman (ed.), *Michel Foucault*, 242–54.

—— 'An Aesthetics of Existence', *Le Monde* (15–16 July 1984); trans. A. Sheridan, in Kritzman (ed.), *Michel Foucault*, 47–53.

—— 'Technologies of the Self', in L. H. Martin, H. Gutman, and P. H. Hutton (eds.), *Technologies of the Self: A Seminar with Michel Foucault* (London: Tavistock, 1988), 16–49.

—— 'Sexuality and Solitude', in Rabinow (ed.), *Michel Foucault*, 175–84.

—— 'Self Writing', in Rabinow (ed.), *Michel Foucault*, 207–22.

—— 'On the Genealogy of Ethics: An Overview of Work in Progress', in Rabinow (ed.), *Michel Foucault*, 253–80.

Fox, R. L., *Pagans and Christians* (New York: Viking, 1987).

Fraade, S. D., 'Ascetical Aspects of Ancient Judaism', in A. Green (ed.), *Jewish Spirituality: From the Bible through the Middle Ages* (London: Routledge and Kegan Paul, 1986), 253–88.

Francis, J. A., *Subversive Virtue: Asceticism and Authority in the Second-Century Pagan World* (University Park, Pa.: Pennsylvania State University Press, 1995).

Frank, [K.] S., *ΑΓΓΕΛΙΚΟΣ ΒΙΟΣ: Begriffsanalytische und begriffs- geschichtliche Untersuchung zum 'engelgleichen Leben' im fruhen Mönchtum* (Münster: Aschendorff, 1964).

Frend, W. H. C., *Martyrdom and Persecution in the Early Church: A Study of a Conflict from the Maccabees to Donatus* (Oxford: Black- well, 1965).

Friesen, J., 'A Study of the Influence of Confessional Bias on the Interpretations in the Modern Era of Irenaeus of Lyons' (Ph.D. diss., Northwestern University, Evanston, Ill., 1977).

Funck, F., 'Klemens von Alexandrien über Familie und Eigentum', *Theologische Quartalschrift*, 53 (1871), 427–49.

Gächter, P., 'Unsere Einheit mit Christus nach dem hl. Irenäus', *ZKT* 58 (1939), 503–32.

Gadamer, H. G., *Wahrheit und Methode*, 5th edn. (Tübingen: Mohr, 1986), trans. J. Weinsheimer and D. G. Marshall (New York: Continuum, 1997).

Gleason, M. W., 'The Semiotics of Gender: Physiognomy and Self- Fashioning in the Second Century C. E.', in D. M. Halperin, J. J. Winkler, and F. I. Zeitlin (eds.), *Before Sexuality: The Construction of Erotic Experience in the Ancient Greek World* (Princeton: Prince- ton University Press, 1990), 389–415.

Gonzalez Faus, J. I., *Creación y progreso en la teología de San Ireneo* (Barcelona, 1968).

—— *Carne de Dios: Significado salvador de la Encarnación en la teología de San Ireneo* (Barcelona, 1969).

Gould, G., 'Recent Work on Monastic Origins: A Consideration of the Questions Raised by Samuel Rubenson's *The Letters of St Antony*', *St. Patr.* 25 (Leuven: Peeters, 1993), 405–16.

Grant, R. M., 'Irenaeus and Hellenistic Culture', *HTR* 42 (1949), 41– 51; repr. in R. M. Grant, *After the New Testament* (Philadelphia, 1967), 158–69.

—— 'Aristotle and the Conversion of Justin', *JTS* ns 7 (1956), 246–8.

—— 'The Social Setting of Second-Century Christianity', in E. P. Sanders (ed.), *Jewish and Christian Self-Definition*, 1: *The Shaping of Christianity in the Second and Third Centuries* (Philadelphia: Fortress, 1980), 16–29.

Grant, R. M., *Christian Beginnings: Apocalypse to History* (London: Variorum Reprints, 1983).

—— *Greek Apologists of the Second Century* (London: SCM, 1988).

Guilloux, P., 'L'Ascétisme de Clément d'Alexandria', *RAM* 3 (1922), 282–300.

Hadot, P., *Exercices spirituels et philosophie antique*, 3rd rev. edn. (Paris: Études Augustiniennes, 1993).

Halperin, D. M., J. J. Winkler, and F. I. Zeitlin (eds.), *Before Sexuality: The Construction of Erotic Experience in the Ancient Greek World* (Princeton: Princeton University Press, 1990).

Hardman, O., *The Ideals of Asceticism: An Essay in the Comparative Study of Religion* (London: SPCK, 1924).

Harnack, A., *History of Dogma*, trans. of 3rd German edn. (London, 1896).

—— 'Der Presbyter-Prediger des Irenäus (IV,27,1–32,1): Bruchstücke und Nachklänger der ältesten exegetisch-polemischen Homilien', in *Philotesia: Paul Kleinert zum LXX Geburtstag* (Berlin: Trowitzsch, 1907), 1–37.

Harpham, G. C., *The Ascetic Imperative in Culture and Criticism* (Chicago: University of Chicago Press, 1987).

—— 'Old Water in New Bottles: The Contemporary Prospects for the Study of Asceticism', *Semeia*, 58 (1992), 135–48.

Harrison, V. E. F., 'Male and Female in Cappadocian Theology', *JTS* ns 41. 2 (1990), 441–71.

—— *Grace and Human Freedom according to St Gregory of Nyssa*, Studies in the Bible and Early Christianity, 30 (Lewiston, NY: Edwin Mellen, 1993).

Hart, M. D., 'Marriage, Celibacy and the Life of Virtue: An Interpretation of Gregory of Nyssa's *De virginitate*' (Ph.D. diss., Boston College, 1987).

—— 'Reconciliation of Body and Soul: Gregory of Nyssa's Deeper Theology of Marriage', *TS* 51 (1990), 450–78.

—— 'Gregory of Nyssa's Ironic Praise of the Celibate Life', *HJ* 33 (1992), 1–19.

Hauschild, W. D., *Gottes Geist und der Mensch: Studien zur frühchristlichen Pneumatologie* (Munich: C. Kaiser, 1972).

Heidegger, M., *Identity and Difference*, trans. J. Stambaugh (New York: Harper, 1969).

Heine, S., *Frauen der frühen Christenheit* (Göttingen: Vandenhoeck and Ruprecht, 1986); trans. J. Bowden, *Women and Early Christianity: Are the Feminist Scholars Right?* (London: SCM, 1987).

Hemmerdinger, B., 'Les "Notices et extraits" des bibliothèques grecques de Bagdad par Photius', *REG* 69 (1956), 101–3.

—— 'Observations critiques sur Irénée, IV (*Sources chrétiennes* 100), ou les mesaventures d'un philologue', *JTS* ns 18. 2 (1966), 308–22.

Héring, J., *Étude sur la doctrine de la chute et de la préexistence des âmes chez Clément d'Alexandrie*, Bibliothèque de l'École des Hautes Études, Sciences Religieuses, 38 (Paris: E. Leroux, 1923).

Hitchcock, F. R. M., *Clement of Alexandria* (London: SPCK, 1899).

—— *Irenaeus of Lugdunum: A Study of his Teaching* (Cambridge: Cambridge University Press, 1914).

—— 'Loofs' Theory of Theophilus of Antioch as a Source of Irenaeus', *JTS* 38 (1937), 130–9, 255–66.

—— 'Loof's Asiatic Source (IQA) and the Pseudo-Justin *De resurrectione*', *ZNTW* 36 (1937), 35–60.

Hoeck, A. van den, *Clement of Alexandria and his Use of Philo in the Stromateis: An Early Christian Reshaping of a Jewish Model* (Leiden: Brill, 1988).

Hoffman, D. L., *The Status of Women and Gnosticism in Irenaeus and Tertullian* (Lewiston, NY: Edwin Mellen, 1995).

Houssiau, A., *La Christologie de saint Irénée* (Louvain: Publicationes Universitaires, 1955).

—— 'Le Baptême selon Irénée de Lyon', *ETL* 60 (1984), 45–59.

Hunter, D. G., 'The Language of Desire: Clement of Alexandria's Transformation of Ascetic Discourse', *Semeia*, 57 (1992), 95–111.

Irigaray, L., *An Ethics of Sexual Difference*, trans. C. Burke and G. G. Gill (London: Athlone, 1993).

Jaeger, W., *Paideia: The Ideals of Greek Culture*, trans. from 2nd German edn. by G. Highet, 3 vols. (Oxford: Blackwell, 1944–5).

—— *Two Rediscovered Works of Ancient Christian Literature: Gregory of Nyssa and Macarius* (Leiden: Brill, 1954).

—— *Early Christianity and Greek Paideia* (Cambridge, Mass.: Belknap Press, 1961).

Jaschke, H. J., 'Pneuma und Moral: Der Grund christlicher Sittlichkeit aus der Sicht des Irenäus von Lyon', *SM* 14 (1976), 239–81.

—— *Der Heilige Geist im Bekenntnis der Kirche: Ein Studie zur Pneumatologie des Irenäus von Lyon im Ausgang vom altchristlichen Glaubensbekenntnis*, Münsterische Beiträge zur Theologie, 40 (Münster: Aschendorff, 1976).

Javelet, R., 'Marie, La femme médiatrice', *RSR* 58 (1984), 162–71.

Jenkins, D. E., 'The Make-up of Man according to St Irenaeus', *St. Patr.* 6, TU 81 (Leipzig: Hinrich, 1962), 91–5.

Jonas, H., *The Gnostic Religion: The Message of the Alien God and the*

Beginnings of Christianity, 2nd rev. edn. (1958, London: Routledge, 1992).

Joppich, G., *Salus Carnis: Eine Untersuchung in der Theologie des hl. Irenäus von Lyon*, Münsterschwarzacher Studien, 1 (Münsterschwarzach: Vier-Türme, 1965).

Jouassard, G., 'Amorces chez saint Irénée pour la doctrine de la maternité spirituelle de la Sainte Vierge', *Nouvelle Revue Mariale*, 7 (1955), 217–32.

—— 'Le "Signe de Jonas" dans le livre IIIe de l'*Adversus haereses* de saint Irénée', in *L'Homme devant Dieu: Mélanges offerts au Père Henri de Lubac*, 1: *Exégèse et patristique* (Paris: Aubier, 1963), 235–46.

Kereszty, R., 'The Unity of the Church in the Theology of Irenaeus', *Second Century*, 4. 4 (1984), 202–18.

Kinder, D., 'Clement of Alexandria: Conflicting Views on Women', *Second Century*, 7. 4 (1990), 213–20.

Klebba, E., *Die Anthropologie des hl. Irenaeus*, Kirchengeschichtliche Studien, 2. 3 (Münster, 1894).

Koch, H., 'Zur Lehre von Urstand und von der Erlösung bei Irenäus', *TSK* 96–7 (1925), 183–214.

Kritzman, L. D. (ed.), *Michel Foucault: Politics, Philosophy, Culture: Interviews and Other Writings 1977–84* (London: Routledge, 1988).

Ladaria, L. F., *El Espíritu en Clemente Alejandrino: Estudio teológico-antropológico* (Madrid: UPCM, 1980).

Lampe, G. W. H., 'Early Patristic Eschatology', in *Eschatology*, Scottish Journal of Theology Occasional Papers, 2 (Edinburgh and London: Oliver and Boyd, n.d.), 17–35.

Lanne, D. E., 'La Vision de Dieu dans l'oeuvre de saint Irénée', *Irénikon*, 33 (1966), 311–20.

Lassiat, H., *Pour une théologie de l'homme. Création . . . Liberté . . . Incorruptibilité: Insertion du thème anthropologique de la jeune tradition romaine dans l'œuvre d'Irénée* (Lille: Service de reproduction des thèse, Univ. de Lille, 1972).

—— *Promotion de l'homme en Jésus-Christ d'après Irénée de Lyon* (Tours: Mame, 1974).

—— 'L'Anthropologie d'Irénée', *NRT* 100 (1978), 399–417.

Lattey, C., 'The Deification of Man in Clement of Alexandria: Some Further Notes', *JTS* 17 (1916), 257–62.

Lawson, J., *The Biblical Theology of St Ireneaus* (London: Epworth Press, 1948).

Lebeau, P., 'KOINONIA: La signification du salut selon S. Irénée', in J. Fontaine and C. Kannengiesser (eds.), *EPEKTASIS: Mélanges offerts au Cardinal J. Daniélou* (Paris: Beauchesne, 1972), 121–7.

Leduc, C., 'Marriage in Ancient Greece', in G. Duby and M. Perrot (eds.), *A History of Women in the West*, 1: *From Ancient Goddesses to Christian Saints*, ed. P. Schmitt Pantel, trans. A. Goldhammer (Cambridge, Mass.: Harvard University Press, 1992), 235–94.

Leyerle, B., 'Clement of Alexandria on the Importance of Table Etiquette', *JECS* 3 (1995), 123–41.

Lilla, S. R. C., 'Middle-Platonism, Neo-Platonism and Jewish Alexandrine Philosophy in the Terminology of Clement of Alexandria's Ethics', *Archivo Italiano per la Storia della Pietà*, 3 (1962), 3–36.

——*Clement of Alexandria: A Study in Christian Platonism and Gnosticism* (Oxford: Oxford University Press, 1971).

Lloyd, G. E. R., 'The Mind on Sex', review of M. Foucault, *The Use of Pleasure*, *New York Review of Books*, 33. 4 (13 March 1986), 24–8.

Long, A. A., and D. N. Sedley (eds.), *The Hellenistic Philosophers* (Cambridge: Cambridge University Press, 1987).

Loofs, F., *Theophilus von Antiochien Adversus Marcionem und die anderen theologischen Quellen bei Irenäus*, TU 46. 2 (Leipzig: Hinrich, 1930).

Louth, A., *The Origins of the Christian Mystical Tradition: From Plato to Denys* (Oxford: Clarendon Press, 1981).

——*Discerning the Mystery: An Essay on the Nature of Theology* (Oxford: Clarendon Press, 1989).

——Review of P. Brown, *The Body and Society* (New York, 1988), *JTS* ns 41 (1990), 231–5.

Lündstrom, S., *Studien zur lateinischen Irenäusübersetzung* (Lund: Gleerup, 1943).

——*Neue Studien zur lateinischen Irenäusübersetzung*, Lunds Universitets Årsskrift, NF Aud. 1, Bd. 44, n. 8 (Lund: Gleerup, 1948).

——*Übersetzungstechnische Untersuchungen auf dem Gebiete der christlichen Latinität*, Lunds Universitets Årsskrift, NF Aud. 1, Bd. 55, n. 3 (Lund: Gleerup, 1955).

McGinn, B., J. Meyendorff, and J. Leclercq (eds.), *Christian Spirituality: Origins to the Twelfth Century* (London: SCM, 1989).

MacIntyre, A., *After Virtue: A Study in Moral Theory*, 2nd edn. (Notre Dame, Ind.: Notre Dame University Press, 1984).

McNamara, J. A., *A New Song: Celibate Women in the First Three Christian Centuries* (Binghampton, NY: Harrington Park Press, 1985).

MacRae, G. W., 'Why the Church Rejected Gnosticism', in E. P. Sanders (ed.), *Jewish and Christian Self-Definition*, i: *The Shaping of Christianity in the Second and Third Centuries* (Philadelphia: Fortress, 1980), 126–33.

Maier, H. O., 'Clement of Alexandria and the Care of the Self', *JAAR* 62. 3 (1994), 719–45.

Malina, B. J., 'Pain, Power and Personhood: Ascetic Behaviour in the Ancient Mediterranean', in V. L. Wimbush and R. Valantasis (eds.), *Asceticism* (Oxford: Oxford University Press, 1995), 162–77.

Malone, E. E., *The Monk and the Martyr* (Washington: Catholic University of America, 1950).

Markus, R. A., 'Pleroma and Fulfillment: The Significance of History in St Irenaeus' Opposition to Gnosticism', *VC* 8 (1954), 193–224.

—— 'The Problem of Self-Definition: From Sect to Church', in E. P. Sanders (ed.), *Jewish and Christian Self-Definition, 1: The Shaping of Christianity in the Second and Third Centuries* (Philadelphia: Fortress, 1980), 1–15.

Marrou, H. I., 'Virginity as an Ideal, and the Position of Women in Ancient Civilization', in *Chastity*, trans. L. C. Sheppard, Religious Life, 5 (London: Blackfriars, 1955), 28–38.

—— 'Humanisme et christianisme chez Clément d'Alexandrie d'apres le *Pédagogue*', *Fondation Hardt, Entretiens sur l'Antiquite Classique*, 3 (1955), 183–200.

—— 'Morale et spiritualité chrétiennes dans le *Pédagogue* de Clément d'Alexandrie', *St. Patr.* 2, TU 64 (Berlin: Akademie Verlag, 1957), 538–46.

—— Review of A. Benoît, *Saint Irénée: Introduction à l'étude de sa théologie* (Paris, 1960), *REA* 65 (1963), 452–6.

—— *Histoire de l'éducation dans l'antiquité*, 6th edn. (Paris: Seuil, 1965).

Marsh, H. G., 'The Use of μυστήριον in the Writings of Clement of Alexandria with Special Reference to his Sacramental Doctrine', *JTS* 37 (1936), 64–80.

May, G., *Creation Ex Nihilo: The Doctrine of 'Creation out of Nothing' in Early Christian Thought*, trans. A. S. Worrall (Edinburgh: T. and T. Clark, 1994).

Mayer, A., *Das Gottesbild im Menschen nach Clemens von Alexandrien*, Studia Anselmiana, 15 (Rome: Herder, 1942).

Meeks, W. A., 'The Image of the Androgyne: Some Uses of a Symbol in Earliest Christianity', *History of Religions*, 13 (1974), 165–208.

—— *The Origins of Christian Morality: The First Two Centuries* (New Haven: Yale University Press, 1993).

Mees, M., 'Clemens von Alexandrien über Ehe und Familie', *Augustinianum*, 17 (1977), 113–31.

—— 'Jetzt und Dann in der Eschatologie Klemens von Alexandrien', *Augustinianum*, 18 (1978), 127–37.

Méhat, A., *Étude sur les 'Stromates' de Clément d'Alexandrie*, Patristica Sorbonensia, 7 (Paris: Seuil, 1966).

—— 'Saint Irénée et les Charisms', *St. Patr.* 17 (Oxford: Pergamon Press, 1982), 719–24.

Meijering, E. P., 'Ireneaus' Relation to Philosophy in the Light of his Concept of Free Will', in W. den Boer [*et al.*] (eds.), *Romanitas et christianitis: Studia Iano Henrico Waszink oblata* (Amsterdam, London: North Hollons, 1973), 221–32.

Meredith, A., 'Asceticism, Christian and Greek', *JTS* ns 27 (1976), 313–32.

Merki, H., Ὁμοίωσις θεῷ: *Von der platonischen Angleichung an Gott zur Gottähnlichkeit bei Gregor von Nyssa* (Fribourg: Paulusdruck, 1952).

Miles, M. R., *The Fullness of Life: Historical Foundations for a New Asceticism* (Philadelphia: Westminster, 1981).

Minns, D., *Irenaeus* (London: Geoffrey Chapman, 1994).

Mondesert, C., 'Vocabulaire de Clément d'Alexandrie: le mot λογικός', *RSR* 42 (1954), 258–65.

Mortley, R., *Connaissance religieuse et hérmeneutique chez Clément d'Alexandrie* (Leiden: Brill, 1973).

—— 'The Past in Clement of Alexandria: A Study of an Attempt to Define Christianity in Socio-cultural Terms', in E. P. Sanders (ed.), *Jewish and Christian Self-Definition*, 1: *The Shaping of Christianity in the Second and Third Centuries* (Philadelphia: Fortress, 1980), 186–200.

Mühlenberg, E., 'Synergism in Gregory of Nyssa', *ZNTW* 68 (1977), 93–122.

Müller, M., 'Freiheit: Über Autonomie und Gnade von Paulus bis Clemens von Alexandrien', *ZNTW* 25 (1926), 177–236.

Murray, A., 'Peter Brown and the Shadow of Constantine', *JRS* 73 (1983), 191–203.

Musurillo, H., 'The Problem of Ascetical Fasting in the Greek Patristic Writers', *Traditio*, 12 (1956), 1–64.

Nagel, P., *Die Motivierung der Askese in der alten Kirche und der Ursprung des Mönchtums*, TU 95 (Berlin: Akademie Verlag, 1966).

Nagey, M., 'Translocation of Parental Images in Fourth-Century Ascetic Texts: Motifs and Techniques of Identity', *Semeia*, 58 (1992), 3–23.

Nautin, P., *Lettres et écrivains chrétiens des IIe et IIIe siècles* (Paris: Cerf, 1961).

Nellas, P., *Deification in Christ: Orthodox Perspectives on the Nature of the Human Person*, trans. N. Russell (New York: St Vladimir Seminary Press, 1987).

Newsom, C. A., 'The Case of the Blinking I: Discourse of the Self at Qumran', *Semeia*, 57 (1992), 13–23.

Nielsen, J. T., *Adam and Christ in the Theology of Irenaeus of Lyons: An Examination of the Function of the Adam–Christ Typology in the Adversus Haereses of Irenaeus, against the Background of the Gnosticism of his Time*, Van Gorcum's Theologische Bibliothek, 40 (Assen: Van Gorcum, 1968).

Noormann, R., *Irenäus als Paulusinterpret: Zur Rezeption und Wirkung der paulinischen und deuteropaulinischen Briefe im Werke des Irenäus von Lyon*, Wissenschaftliche Untersuchungen zum Neuen Testament, 2. 66 (Tübingen: Mohr, 1994).

Norman, R. V., and C. H. Reynolds (eds.), *Symposium on* The Fragility of Goodness, *Soundings*, 72. 4 (1989).

Norris, R. A., *God and the World in Early Christian Theology: A Study on Justin Martyr, Irenaeus, Tertullian and Origen* (London: Adam and Charles Black, 1966).

—— 'Irenaeus' Use of Paul in His Polemic Against the Gnostics', in W. S. Babcock (ed.), *Paul and the Legacies of Paul* (Dallas: Southern Methodist University Press, 1990), 79–98.

Nussbaum, M. C., *The Fragility of Goodness: Luck and Ethics in Greek Tragedy and Philosophy* (Cambridge: Cambridge University Press, 1986; repr. 1989).

—— 'Transcending Humanity', in M. C. Nussbaum, *Love's Knowledge: Essays on Philosophy and Literature* (Oxford: Oxford University Press, 1990), 365–91.

—— *The Therapy of Desire: Theory and Practice in Hellenistic Ethics* (Princeton: Princeton University Press, 1994).

Nygren, A., *Agape and Eros*, trans. P. S. Watson (London: SPCK, 1982).

Ochagavía, J., *Visibile Patris Filius: A Study of Irenaeus' Teaching on Revelation and Tradition*, Orientalia Christiana Analecta, 171 (Rome: Pontificium Institutum Orientalium Studiorum, 1964).

Olson, M. J., *Irenaeus, the Valentinian Gnostics and the Kingdom of God (AH Book V): The Debate about 1 Corinthians 15.50* (Lewiston, NY: Edwin Mellin, 1992).

O'Neill, J. C., 'The Origins of Monasticism', in R. Williams (ed.), *The Making of Orthodoxy: Essays in Honour of H. Chadwick* (Cambridge: Cambridge University Press, 1989), 270–87.

Orbe, A., *Estudios Valentinianos, 1: Hacia la primera teología de la procesión del Verbo*, Analecta Gregoriana, 99–100 (Rome: Gregorian, 1958).

—— 'El hombre ideal en la teología de s. Ireneo', *Greg.* 43 (1962), 449–91.

—— 'El pecado de Eva, signo de division', *OCP* 29 (1963), 305–30.

—— 'El pecado original y el matrimonio en la teología del s. II', *Greg.* 45 (1964), 449–500.

—— 'Homo nuper factus: En torno a S. Ireneo, *adv. haer.* IV. 38. 1', *Greg.* 46 (1965), 481–544.

—— 'El sueño y el Paraíso: Iren., *Epid.* 13', *Greg.* 48 (1967), 346–9.

—— 'La definición del hombre en la teología del siglo IIe', *Greg.* 48 (1967), 522–76.

—— 'La atonia del espiritu en los Padres y teólogos del s.II', *La Ciudad de Dios*, 181 (1968), 484–528.

—— *Antropología de San Ireneo* (Madrid: Biblioteca des Autores Cristianos, 1969).

—— *Parábolas evangélicas en San Ireneo*, 2 vols. (Madrid: Biblioteca des Autores Cristianos, 1972).

—— 'Supergrediens angelos: AH V.36.1', *Greg.* 54 (1973), 5–69.

—— 'Los Valentinianos y el matrimonio espiritual: Hacia los orígenes de la mística nupcial', *Greg.* 58. 1 (1977), 5–53.

—— 'San Ireneo y la creación de la materia', *Greg.* 59. 1 (1978), 71–127.

—— 'Adversarios anónimos de la *salus carnis* (Iren. *adv. haer.* V.2. 2s)', *Greg.* 60. 1 (1979), 9–53.

—— 'San Ireneo y la doctrine de la reconciliación', *Greg.* 61. 1 (1980), 5–50.

—— 'Cinco exegesis ireneanas de Gn. 2.17b: *adv. haer.* V,23,1–2', *Greg.* 62 (1981), 75–113.

—— 'La virgen María abrogada de la virgen Eva: En torno a s. Ireneo, *adv. haer.* V.19.1', *Greg.* 63. 3 (1982), 453–506.

—— 'Visión del Padre e incorruptela según san Ireneo', *Greg.* 64. 2 (1983), 199–241.

—— '¿San Ireneo adopcionista? En torno a *adv. haer.* III.19.1', *Greg.* 65. 1 (1984), 5–52.

—— *Teología de San Ireneo: Comentario al libro V del Adversus Haereses*, 3 vols. (Madrid: Biblioteca des Autores Cristianos, 1985, 1987, 1988).

—— 'Deus facit, homo fit: Un axioma de san Ireneo', *Greg.* 69. 4 (1988), 629–61.

—— 'Gloria Dei vivens homo: Análisis de Ireneo, *adv. haer.* IV.20.1–7', *Greg.* 73. 2 (1992), 205–68.

Osborn, E. F., *The Philosophy of Clement of Alexandria*, Text and Studies, ns 3 (Cambridge: Cambridge University Press, 1954).

—— *Ethical Patterns in Early Christian Thought* (Cambridge: Cambridge University Press, 1976).

Osborn, E. F., 'Clement of Alexandria: A Review of Research, 1958–1982', *Second Century*, 3 (1983), 219–44.

Osborne, C., 'Love's Bitter Fruits: Martha C. Nussbaum *The Therapy of Desire: Theory and Practice in Hellenistic Ethics*', *Philosophical Investigations*, 19. 4 (1996), 318–28.

Pagels, E., *The Gnostic Gospels* (Harmondsworth: Penguin, 1980).

——*Adam, Eve and the Serpent* (London: Weidenfeld and Nicolson, 1988).

Palashkovsky, V., 'La Théologie eucharistique de S. Irénée, évêque de Lyon', *St. Patr.* 2, TU 64 (Berlin: Akademie Verlag, 1957), 277–81.

Patrick, J., *Clement of Alexandria* (Edinburgh and London: William Blackwood, 1914).

Pauley, W. C. de, 'Man: The Image of God. A Study of Clement of Alexandria', *Church Quarterly*, 100 (1925), 96–121.

Pearson, B. A., 'Jewish Elements in Gnosticism and the Development of Gnostic Self-Definition', in E. P. Sanders (ed.), *Jewish and Christian Self-Definition*, 1: *The Shaping of Christianity in the Second and Third Centuries* (Philadelphia: Fortress, 1980), 151–60.

Pétrement, S., *Le Dieu séparé: Les origines du gnosticisme* (Paris: Cerf, 1984); trans. C. Harrison, *A Separate God: The Origins and Teachings of Gnosticism* (San Francisco: Harper, 1990).

Pisi, P., *Genesi e Phthorá: Le motivazioni protologiche della virginità in Gregorio di Nissa e nella tradizione dell'enkrateia* (Rome: Ateneo, 1981).

Pohlenz, M., 'Klemens von Alexandrien und sein hellenisches Christentum', *NAWG*, Phil.-Hist. Klasse, Fachgr. 5, NF, 1. 5 (1943), 103–80.

Price, R. M., 'The Distinctiveness of Early Christian Ethics', *HJ* 31 (1990), 257–76.

Prümm, K., 'Göttliche Planung und menschliche Entwicklung nach Irenäus *Adversus Haereses*', *Scholastik*, 13 (1938), 206–24, 342–66.

——'Zur Terminologie und zum Wesen der christliche Neuheit bei Irenäus', in T. Klauser and A. Rucker (eds.), *Pisciculi: Studien zur Religion und Kultur des Altertums, Franz Joseph Dölger zum sechzigsten Geburtstag dageboten von Freunden, Verehrern und Schülern* (Münster: Aschendorff, 1939), 192–219.

Prunet, O., *La Morale de Clément d'Alexandrie et le Nouveau Testament*, Études d'Histoire et de Philosophie Religieuse, 61 (Paris: Presses Universitaires de France, 1966).

Quasten, J., *Patrology*, 1 (Utrecht: Spectrum, 1950).

Quatember, F., *Die christliche Lebenshaltung des Klemens von Alexandrinus nach seinem Pädagogus* (Vienna: Herder, 1946).

Rabbow, P., *Seelenführung: Methodik der Exerzitien in der Antike* (Munich: Kosel Verlag, 1954).

Rabinow, P. (ed.), *Michel Foucault: Ethics, Subjectivity and Truth* (New York: New Press, 1997).

Radford Reuther, R., 'Misogynism and Virginal Feminism in the Fathers of the Church', in R. Radford Reuther (ed.), *Religion and Sexism: Images of Woman in the Jewish and Christian Tradition* (New York: Simon and Schuster, 1974), 150–83.

Ramos-Lissón, D., 'Le Rôle de la femme dans la théologie de saint Irénée', *St. Patr.* 21 (Leuven: Peeters, 1989), 163–74.

Ranke-Heinemann, U., *Eunuchs for the Kingdom of Heaven: The Catholic Church and Sexuality*, trans. P. Heinegg (Harmondsworth: Penguin, 1991).

Reimherr, O., 'Irenaeus Lugdunensis', in V. Brown (ed.), *Catalogus translationum et commentariorum: Mediaeval and Renaissance Latin Translations and Commentaries, Annotated Lists and Guide*, 7 (Washington: Catholic University of America, 1992), 14–54.

Reumann, J., 'Οἰκονομία as "Ethical Accommodation" in the Fathers, and its Pagan Background', *St. Patr.* 3. 1, TU 78 (Berlin: Akademie Verlag, 1961), 370–9.

Richardson, W., 'The Basis of Ethics: Chryssipus and Clement of Alexandria', *St. Patr.* 9. 3, TU 94 (Berlin: Akademie Verlag, 1966), 87–97.

Ritter, A. M., 'Christentum und Eigentum bei Klemens von Alexandrien auf dem Hintergrund der frühchristlichen "Armenfrömmigkeit" und der Ethik der Kaiserzeitlichen Stoa', *ZKG* 86 (1975), 1–25.

Roberts, C. H., *Manuscript, Society and Belief in Early Christian Egypt* (London: Oxford University Press, 1979).

Robinson, H. W., *The Christian Doctrine of Man* (Edinburgh: T. and T. Clark, 1920).

Robinson, J. A., 'Notes on the Armenian Version of *Adv. Haereses* IV, V', *JTS* 32 (1930–1), 153–66, 370–93.

Rordorf, W., 'Marriage in the New Testament and in the Early Church', *JEH* 20 (1969), 193–210.

Rousseau, A., 'Le verbe "imprimé en forme de croix dans l'univers": A propos de deux passages de saint Irénée', in *Armeniaca: Mélanges d'études arméniennes* (Venice: S. Lazarus, 1969), 67–82.

—— 'La doctrine de saint Irénée sur la préexistence du Fils de Dieu dans Dém. 43', *Muséon*, 89 (1971), 5–42.

—— 'L'Éternité des peines de l'enfer et l'immortalité naturelle de l'âme selon saint Irénée', *NRT* 99 (1977), 834–64.

Rousselle, A., *Porneia: De la maîtrise du corps à la privation sensorielle*

(Paris: Presses Universitaires de France, 1983); trans. F. Pheasant, *Porneia: On Desire and the Body in Antiquity* (Oxford: Blackwell, 1988).

Rousselle, A., 'Jeunesse de l'antiquité tardive: Les leçons de lecture de Peter Brown', *Annales E.S.C.*, 40 (1985), 521–8.

——'Body Politics in Ancient Rome', in G. Duby and M. Perrot (eds.), *A History of Women in the West*, 1: *From Ancient Goddesses to Christian Saints*, ed. P. Schmitt Pantel, trans. A. Goldhammer (Cambridge, Mass.: Harvard University Press, 1992), 296–336.

Rubenson, S., *The Letters of St Antony: Monasticism and the Making of a Saint*, rev. edn. (Philadelphia: Fortress, 1995).

Rudolph, K., *Gnosis: The Nature and History of an Ancient Religion*, trans. R. McL. Wilson (Edinburgh: T. and T. Clark, 1983).

Rüther, T., *Die Lehre von der Erbsunde bei Klemens von Alexandrien* (Freiburg im Breisgau: Herder, 1922).

——*Die sittliche Forderung der Apatheia in den beiden ersten christlichen Jahrhunderten und bei Klemens von Alexandrien: Ein Beitrag zur Geschichte der christlichen Volkommenheitsbegriffes* (Freiburg im Breisgau: Herder, 1949).

Sagnard, F. M. M., *La Gnose valentinienne et le témoignage de saint Irénée* (Paris: Vrin, 1947).

Sanders, E. P. (ed.), *Jewish and Christian Self-Definition*, 1: *The Shaping of Christianity in the Second and Third Centuries* (Philadelphia: Fortress, 1980).

Scharl, E., 'Der Rekapitulationsbegriff des heiligen Irenäus', *OCP* 6 (1940), 376–416.

Schmöle, K., *Läuterung nach dem Tode und pneumatische Auferstehung bei Klemens von Alexandrien* (Münster: Aschendorff, 1974).

Schoedel, W. R., 'Theological Method in Irenaeus (*Adversus Haereses* 2.25–28)', *JTS* ns 35 (1984), 31–49.

Schutz, D. R., 'The Origin of Sin in Ireneaus and Jewish Pseudoepigraphical Literature', *VC* 32. 3 (1978), 161–90.

Schwanz, P., *Imago Dei als christologisch-anthropologisches Problem in der Geschichte der alten Kirch von Paulus bis Clemens von Alexandrien* (Halle: M. Niemeyer, 1970).

Seeberg, R., *Lehrbuch der Dogmengeschichte*, 3rd rev. edn. vols. 1–2 (Leipzig: Deichertsche, 1920).

Sfameni Gasparro, G., *Enkrateia e Antropologie: Le motivazioni protologiche della continenza e della verginità nel cristianesimo dei primi secoli e nello gnosticismo* (Rome: Institutum Patristicum Augustinianum, 1984).

——'Asceticism and Anthropology: *Enkrateia* and "Double Creation" in Early Christianity', in V. L. Wimbush and R. Valantasis (eds.), *Asceticism* (Oxford: Oxford University Press, 1995), 127–46.

Sherrard, P., *Christianity and Eros: Essays on the Theme of Sexual Love* (London: SPCK, 1976).

Simonin, H. D., 'A propos d'un texte eucharistique de S. Irénée: AH. IV.xviii.5', *RSPhTh* 23 (1934), 281–92.

Simpson, R. L., 'Grace and Free Will: A Study in the Theology of St Irenaeus', in R. L. Simpson (ed.), *One Faith: Its Biblical, Historical, and Ecumenical Dimensions: A Series of Essays in Honour of Stephen J. England* (Enid, Okla.: Phillips University Press, 1966), 59–72.

Sissa, G., 'Une Virginité sans hymen: Le Corps feminin en Grece ancienne', *Annales E.S.C.*, 39 (1984), 1119–39.

—— *Le Corps Virginal* (Paris: Vrin, 1987); trans. A. Goldhammer, *Greek Virginity* (Cambridge, Mass.: Harvard University Press, 1990).

—— 'Maidenhood without Maidenhead: The Female Body in Ancient Greece', in D. M. Halperin, J. J. Winkler, and F. I. Zeitlin (eds.), *Before Sexuality: The Construction of Erotic Experience in the Ancient Greek World* (Princeton: Princeton University Press, 1990), 339–64.

—— 'The Sexual Philosophies of Plato and Aristotle', in G. Duby and M. Perrot (eds.), *A History of Women in the West*, 1: *From Ancient Goddesses to Christian Saints*, ed. P. Schmitt Pantel, trans. A. Goldhammer, (Cambridge, Mass.: Harvard University Press, 1992), 46–81.

Smith, J. P., 'Hebrew Christian Midrash in Irenaeus Epid. 43', *Biblica*, 38 (1957), 24–34.

Smith, J. Z., 'The Garments of Shame', in J. Z. Smith (ed.), *Map is not Territory* (Leiden: Brill, 1978), 1–23.

Smith, M., *Clement of Alexandria and a Secret Gospel of Mark* (Cambridge, Mass.: Harvard University Press, 1973).

Spanneut, M., *Le Stoïcisme et les Pères de l'Église de Clément de Rome à Clément d'Alexandrie*, Patristica Sorbenensia, 1 (Paris: Seuil, 1957).

Stolz, A., *L'Ascèse chrétienne* (Chevetogne: D'Amay, 1948).

Stroumsa, G. G., *Another Seed: Studies in Gnostic Mythology* (Leiden: Brill, 1984).

—— '*Caro salutis cardo*: Shaping the Person in Early Christian Thought', *History of Religion*, 30. 1 (1990), 25–50.

Taylor, C., *Sources of the Self: The Making of the Modern Identity* (Cambridge, Mass.: Harvard University Press, 1989).

Thornton, L. S., 'St Irenaeus and Contemporary Theology', *St. Patr.* 2, TU 64 (Berlin: Akademie Verlag, 1957), 317–27.

Thunberg, L., 'The Human Person as Image of God: Eastern Christianity', in B. McGinn, J. Meyendorff, and J. Leclercq (eds.), *Christian Spirituality: Origins to the Twelfth Century* (London: SCM, 1989), 291–312.

Tiessen, T. L., *Irenaeus on the Salvation of the Unevangelized* (Metuchen, NJ, and London: Scarecrow Press, 1993).

Timothy, H., *The Early Christian Apologists and Greek Philosophy Exemplified by Irenaeus, Tertullian and Clement of Alexandria* (Assen: Van Gorcum, 1973).

Tollinton, R. B., *Clement of Alexandria: A Study in Christian Liberalism* (London: Williams and Norgate, 1914).

Torrance, T. F., 'Kerygmatic Proclamation of the Gospel: The *Demonstration of Apostolic Preaching* of Irenaios of Lyon', *GOTR* 37. 1–2 (1992), 105–21; repr. in T. F. Torrance, *Divine Meaning: Studies in Patristic Hermeneutics* (Edinburgh: T. and T. Clark, 1995), 56–74.

Tortorelli, K., 'Some Notes on the Interpretation of St Irenaeus in the Works of Hans Urs von Balthasar', *St. Patr.* 23 (Leuven: Peeters, 1989), 284–8.

Treadgold, W., 'Imaginary Early Christianity' [review article of A. Cameron, *Christianity and the Rhetoric of Empire* (Berkeley: University of California Press, 1992) and P. Brown, *Power and Persuasion in Late Antiquity* (Madison: University of Wisconsin Press, 1992)], *International History Review*, 15. 3 (1993), 535–45.

Tremblay, R., *La Manifestation et la vision de Dieu selon saint Irénée de Lyon*, Münsterische Beiträge zur Theologie, 41 (Münster: Aschendorff, 1978).

——'Le Martyre selon saint Irénée de Lyon', *SM* 16 (1978), 167–89.

Unger, D. J., 'The Divine and Eternal Sonship of the Word according to St Irenaeus of Lyons', *Laurentianum*, 14 (1973), 357–408.

Unnik, W. C. van, 'An Interesting Document of Second Century Theological Discussion (Irenaeus, Adv. Haer. 1. 10. 3)', *VC* 31 (1977), 196–228.

Vallée, G., 'Theological and Non-Theological Motives in Irenaeus' Refutation of the Gnostics', in E. P. Sanders (ed.), *Jewish and Christian Self-Definition*, 1: *The Shaping of Christianity in the Second and Third Centuries* (Philadelphia: Fortress, 1980), 174–85.

Veyne, P., 'The Roman Empire', in P. Ariès and G. Duby (eds.), *A History of the Private Life*, 1: *From Pagan Rome to Byzantium*, ed.

P. Veyne, trans. A. Goldhammer (Cambridge, Mass.: Belknap Press, 1987), 5–233.

Viller, M., and K. Rahner, *Aszese und Mystik in der Väterzeit* (Freiburg-im-Breisgau: Herder, 1939).

Völker, W., 'Die Vollkommenheitslehre des Clemens Alexandrinus in ihren geschichtlichen Zusammenhängen', *TZ* 3 (1947), 15–40.

—— *Der wahre Gnostiker nach Clemens Alexandrinus*, TU 57 (Berlin: Akademie Verlag, 1952).

Wagner, W., *Der Christ und die Welt nach Clemens von Alexandrien: Ein noch unveraltetes Problem in altchristlicher Beleuchtung* (Göttingen: Vandenhoeck und Ruprecht, 1903).

Wagner, W. H., *After the Apostles: Christianity in the Second Century* (Minneapolis: Fortress, 1994).

Walzer, R., *Galen on Jews and Christians* (Oxford: Oxford University Press, 1949).

Ware, K., 'The Monk and the Married Christian: Some Comparisons in Early Monastic Sources', *ECR* 6. 1 (1974), 72–83.

—— 'What is a Martyr?', *Sobornost*, 5. 1 (1983), 7–18.

—— 'The Way of the Ascetics: Negative or Positive?', in V. L. Wimbush and R. Valantasis (eds.), *Asceticism* (Oxford: Oxford University Press, 1995), 3–15.

Wendland, P., *Quaestiones Musonianae: De Musonio Stoico Clementis Alexandrini aliorumque auctore* (Berlin: Mayer and Mueller, 1886).

Werner, J., *Der Paulinismus des Irenaeus: Eine Kirchen- und Dogmengeschichtliche Untersuchung über das Verhältnis des Irenaeus zu der Paulinischen Briefsammlung und Theologie* (Leipzig: Hinrich, 1889).

Widmen, M., 'Irenäus und seine theologischen Väter', *ZTK* 54 (1957), 156–73.

Williams, M. A., *Rethinking "Gnosticism": An Argument for Dismantling a Dubious Category* (Princeton: Princeton University Press, 1996).

Williams, R., *The Wound of Knowledge*, 2nd edn. (London: Darton, Longman and Todd, 1990).

Wilson, R. M., 'The Early History of the Exegesis of Gen.1.26', *St. Patr.* 1, TU 63 (Berlin: Akademie Verlag, 1957), 420–37.

Wimbush, V. L., 'Rhetorics of Restraint: Discursive Strategies, Ascetic Piety and the Interpretation of Religious Literature', *Semeia*, 57 (1992), 1–9.

—— 'The Ascetic Impulse in Early Christianity: Some Methodological Challenges', *St. Patr.* 15 (Leuven: Peeters, 1993), 462–78.

—— (ed.), *Discursive Formations: Ascetic Piety and the Interpretation of Early Christian Literature*, *Semeia*, 57–8 (1992).

Wimbush, V. L., and R. Valantasis (eds.), *Asceticism* (Oxford: Oxford University Press, 1995).

Winden, J. C. M. van, *An Early Christian Philosopher: Justin Martyr's Dialogue with Trypho, Chapters One to Nine: Introduction, Text and Commentary* (Leiden: Brill, 1971).

Wingren, G., *Människan och Inkarnationen enligt Irenäus* (Lund: Cleerup, 1947); trans. R. Mackenzie, *Man and the Incarnation: A Study in the Biblical Theology of Irenaeus* (London: Oliver and Boyd, 1959).

Winkler, J. J., *The Constraints of Desire: The Anthropology of Sex and Gender in Ancient Greece* (New York: Routledge, 1990).

Winling, R., 'Une façon de dire le salut: La formule "être avec Dieu être avec Jésus Christ" dans les écrits de saint Irénée', *RSR* 58 (1984), 105–35.

Wood, A. S., 'The Eschatology of Irenaeus', *Evangelical Quarterly*, 41 (1969), 30–41.

Wyrwa, Dietmar, *Die christliche Platonaneignung in den Stromateis des Clemens von Alexandrien* (Berlin and New York: W. de Gruyter, 1983).

Wyschogrod, E., 'The Howl of Oedipus, the Cry of Héloïse: From Asceticism to Postmodern Ethics', in V. L. Wimbush and R. Valantasis (eds.), *Asceticism* (Oxford: Oxford University Press, 1995), 16–30.

Wytzes, J., 'The Twofold Way: Platonic Influences in the Work of Clement of Alexandria', *VC* 11 (1957), 226–48; 14 (1960), 129–53.

INDEX OF CITATIONS

Only the passages from Clement and Irenaeus which have been discussed are indexed.

GENERAL INDEX

Scholars' names are indexed only where there is a discussion of their works